A Translation Manual for the Caribbean (English–Spanish)

Un Manual de Traducción para el Caribe (Inglés–Español)

A Translation Manual for the Caribbean (English–Spanish)

Un Manual de Traducción para el Caribe (Inglés–Español)

Ian Craig and Jairo Sánchez

University of the West Indies Press
Jamaica • Barbados • Trinidad and Tobago
www.uwipress.com

University of the West Indies Press
7A Gibraltar Hall Road   Mona
Kingston 7   Jamaica
www.uwipress.com

© 2007 by Ian Craig and Jairo Sánchez
All rights reserved. Published 2007
www.caribbeantranslationmanual.com

11 10 09 08 07   5 4 3 2 1

Craig, Ian.
A translation manual for the Caribbean (English–Spanish) = Un manual de traducción para el
Caribe (Inglés–Español) / Ian Craig and Jairo Sánchez.

p. cm.

Includes bibliographical references.

ISBN: 978-976-640-196-2

1. Translating and interpreting. 2. English language – Translating into Spanish. 3. Spanish
language – Translating into English. I. Sánchez, Jairo. II. Title: A translation manual for
the Caribbean (English–Spanish). III. Title : Un manual de traducción para el Caribe
(Inglés–Español).

P306.C83 2007 428.0261

Book design by Roy Barnhill.
Cover design by Robert Kwak.

Printed in Canada

Para María y Michelle

CONTENTS

ACKNOWLEDGEMENTS / *AGRADECIMIENTOS*

The authors gratefully acknowledge the following persons and institutions for their kind contributions to this work / *Los autores desean agradecer a las siguientes personas e instituciones por su colaboración en este proyecto*: Jeannete Allsopp, Richard Allsopp, Robert Antoni, Melza Archibald, Pauline Bailey, the Campus Research Fund of the Office of Graduate Studies and Research (University of the West Indies, Cave Hill), the Caribbean Institute of Languages and International Business (Trinidad and Tobago), Annick Chapdelaine, Stacy Denny, Escuela Superior de Traductores e Intérpretes (Cuba), Martha Fernández, John Gilmore, Charles Hollingsworth, Sherma Henry, Tashena Hinds, Martha Isaac, Christiane Mayer, Evelyn O'Callaghan, María Teresa Ortega, Nieves Pueyo, Humberto Rueda Vecino, Angélica Sáenz, Sergio Bolaños, Mercedes Silva, Victor Simpson, Romel Springer, students of SPAN3504 Spanish Translation (Cave Hill campus), Tierramérica.

ABBREVIATIONS

DCEU *Dictionary of Caribbean English Usage*
OED   *Oxford English Dictionary*
SL   Source Language
ST   Source Text (formerly often called "the original text")
TL   Target Language
TT   Target Text (formerly often called "the translation" or "the translated text")

ABREVIATURAS

LM   Lengua Meta
LO   Lengua Origen
TM   Texto Meta (anteriormente designado con frecuencia como "la traducción" o "el texto traducido")
TO   Texto Origen (anteriormente designado con frecuencia como "el texto original", también en algunas corrientes se llama "texto fuente")

Since the basic unit of this manual is the chapter, it is always a good idea to read the chapter introductions (which are offered consecutively in English, then in Spanish) in order to contextualize the subsequent material. After the introduction, all chapters are divided into two sections, the first focusing on the translation into English of texts in Spanish, the second concentrating on the inverse procedure. Each of these sections presents between one and three source texts and their corresponding target texts (or translations), presented adjacently on the page, and followed by a commentary describing relevant features. Commentary is in the target language of each section (that is, if the translation discussed is into English, the commentary is in English, and likewise for Spanish). These are essentially reference materials designed to familiarize students or aspiring translators from both language backgrounds with aspects of translation in the specific area of discourse addressed by the given chapter. They can be critiqued together in class on an unseen basis or studied outside the classroom for subsequent discussion.

After these sections of commented, pre-translated material, a section of exercises provides material for practice and for reinforcing the concepts acquired in the chapter. Some exercises, inevitably, consist of translating similar texts to those analysed in the commented sections. The authors have made every attempt, nonetheless, to propose other types of exercise not necessarily involving the standard translation of passages, in response to the impression that many students find translation class monotonous because of its apparently exclusive focus on a single process – that of actually rendering a text in another language. Since this is in fact only the visible middle section of what is ideally a considerably longer process – involving analysis of the ST, consultation of similar material in the same area of discourse (particularly in the TL) and of appropriate reference works, the translation process itself, and proofreading (if possible by both the translator and by expert third parties) – it makes sense to include exercises that foreground activities other than the act of purely generating translations. Many deficiencies in translations are traceable to inadequate preparation before starting or lax quality-control mechanisms after drafting the target text. Since this and other constraints on the translation process are not understood by many non-specialists, particularly if they are monolingual, submission dates for professional translations often simply do not allow for adequate pre- and post-production phases of this kind. Good practice at the training stage, however, develops awareness of the importance of these phases, which in turn allows translators at least to aspire to high quality, to negotiate realistic deadlines when they are able, and to know when and how their translations are susceptible to improvement.

All chapters have a section of notes at the end of the printed volume giving references for the texts used and any other relevant information.

Bold text is used for two specialized purposes in this manual: where it highlights specific terms in sections of commentary and discussions, it indicates a technical term for which a definition appears in the glossary at the end of the printed manual or on the web site; in target texts (the right-hand column of the parallel texts in each chapter), bold text preceded by a superscript letter indicates a section of text which is specifically discussed in the commentary below, where the same text will appear alongside the same letter for ease of reference.

In the commentaries, italics are used to highlight words or phrases in a different language from that of the commentary (that is, in the great majority of instances, words or phrases appearing in Spanish in the commentary in English, and words or phrases appearing in English in the commentary in Spanish). Where such words or phrases are also direct quotations from the target text above, they are also enclosed in quotation marks to indicate this.

With regard to the web site (http://www.caribbeantranslationmanual.com), it is frequently used simply as a device to separate a ST in the manual from a TT that appears only on the web site, so that users of the printed text can produce their own TTs without undue influence from existing versions (this of course means resisting the temptation to peek at the web site before attempting your own version). Where the specific web page includes a translation of a text that readers are invited to attempt first in the printed text, a warning to this effect will initially appear in place of the translation in order to avoid "contamination by accidental exposure" to a pre-existing version. The site also contains, however, supplementary exercises and other materials that do not correspond to any direct reference from the printed text. The site content is largely divided according to the chapter headings and other sections of the printed text, while other supplementary materials are self-explanatory.

Dado que la unidad básica de este manual es el capítulo, siempre es una buena idea leer las introducciones (que se ofrecen primero en inglés y luego en español) para contextualizar el material que las sigue. Después de su introducción, los capítulos se dividen en dos secciones: la primera se centra en la traducción al inglés de textos en español, la segunda en el proceso inverso. Cada una de estas secciones presenta entre uno y tres textos de partida y sus correspondientes textos meta (o traducciones), presentados de forma adyacente en la página y seguidos de comentarios sobre sus características más relevantes. Los comentarios aparecen en la lengua meta de cada sección (es decir que en la traducción al inglés el comentario estará en inglés, y lo mismo sucederá con el español). Estos son básicamente materiales de referencia diseñados para familiarizar a los estudiantes, o a las personas que aspiran a ser traductores, de las dos procedencias lingüísticas con aspectos de la traducción en el área específica del discurso tratada en un capítulo dado. Se pueden analizar en grupo en la clase sin haber sido estudiados o pueden estudiarse antes de la clase para su discusión durante la sesión.

Después de estas secciones de comentarios y material previamente traducido, viene una sección de ejercicios que presenta material para practicar y reforzar los conceptos estudiados en el capítulo. Es inevitable que algunos ejercicios consistan en traducir textos similares a los analizados en las secciones comentadas. No obstante, los autores hemos hecho lo posible para proponer otro tipo de ejercicios que no necesariamente requieran la típica traducción de extractos, como respuesta a la impresión generalizada de que muchos estudiantes piensan que la clase de traducción es monótona porque aparentemente se enfoca en un sólo proceso – el trasvasar un texto a otra lengua. Ya que de hecho esto representa sólo el punto medio de lo que es idealmente un proceso mucho más largo – que requiere el análisis del TO, consultar material similar en la misma área del discurso (especialmente en la lengua meta) y en obras de referencia relevantes, el proceso de traducción en sí mismo, la corrección de pruebas (de ser posible por parte del traductor y de expertos en la materia) – parece lógico incluir ejercicios que promuevan actividades que no se limiten a la producción de traducciones. Muchas de las deficiencias en una traducción se pueden encontrar en una preparación previa inadecuada o en mecanismos laxos de control de calidad después de esbozar el texto meta. Debido a que muchas personas que no son especialistas en traducción, en particular si son monolingües, no entienden éstas y otras limitaciones en el proceso de la traducción, las fechas de entrega para las traducciones profesionales muchas veces simplemente no dejan tiempo para que estas fases de pre y post producción se lleven a cabo de manera apropiada. Sin embargo, la práctica adecuada en la etapa de capacitación desarrolla la conciencia de la importancia de estas fases, lo que a la vez les permite a los traductores al menos aspirar a producir textos de alta calidad, negociar fechas límite realistas cuando puedan, y saber cuándo y cómo sus traducciones pueden mejorar.

Todos los capítulos tienen una sección de notas al final de la versión impresa del manual en donde se dan las referencias a los textos utilizados y otra información relevante.

El texto en negrita tiene dos usos especializados en este manual: cuando destaca términos específicos en las secciones de los comentarios o discusiones indica el uso de un término técnico del que se da la definición en el glosario al final de la versión impresa del manual o en la página web; en el texto meta (la columna derecha de los textos paralelos presentados en cada capítulo), el texto en negrita precedido por una letra en superíndice indica una sección del texto que se discute en la sección de comentarios subsiguiente, en donde aparecerá el mismo texto con la misma letra para facilitar la referencia.

En los comentarios, las cursiva o bastardillas se usan para señalar una palabra o frase en otra lengua que la de los comentarios (es decir, en la gran mayoría de los casos, palabras o frases que aparecen en español en los comentarios en inglés, y palabras o frases que aparecen en inglés en los comentarios en español). Cuando estas palabras o frases también son citas directas del TM que aparece anteriormente, esto se señala colocándolas entre comillas.

En cuanto a la página web (http://www.caribbeantranslationmanual.com), se utiliza con frecuencia como un simple mecanismo para separar un TO en el manual de un TM que sólo aparece en la página web, para que los usuarios del texto impreso puedan producir su propio TM sin la interferencia de las versiones existentes (esto por supuesto implica resistir la tentación de mirar la página web antes de intentar producir una versión propia). Cuando la página web específica incluye una traducción de un texto que los lectores deberían intentar crear primero a partir del texto impreso, aparecerá un mensaje de advertencia en lugar de la traducción, para evitar la "contaminación por exposición accidental" a una versión existente. Sin embargo, el sitio también contiene ejercicios adicionales y otros materiales que no tienen una correspondencia directa con el texto impreso. El contenido del sitio se divide de acuerdo a los encabezados de los capítulos y otras secciones del libro. Habrá otros materiales adicionales cuyos títulos indicarán de manera clara sus contenidos.

Introduction: Translation in the Caribbean

THE REASONS FOR THIS MANUAL

The initial motive for writing this manual was strictly practical: as teachers of translation between English and Spanish in the Caribbean, the authors were convinced of the need for a sourcebook containing translated material, analyses, exercises and information with regional relevance. No such work existed, obliging the region's translation teachers and students either to consult works with predominantly North American or European content, or to find their own translated material in piecemeal fashion and analyse it for themselves. This conviction initially arose, then, not from any particular urge to high-light the distinctiveness of the variants of English and Spanish spoken in the Caribbean, but rather from the simple observation that translation students tended to show greater motivation when working with contexts that were relatively familiar to them.

While relevance of content may initially have been the primary concern, the question of Caribbean usage in English and Spanish is and should be to the fore in any translation classroom – or in any translator's mind – in the region. The unparalleled efficacy of translation as an instrument of textual analysis, requiring minute attention to the function and internal dynamics of the source text, inevitably also serves to point up differences between regional variants of a given language. In thoroughgoing vernacular contexts, these differences may be very obvious, as demonstrated in the chapters on literature and cinema in this volume. Other differences in the respective standard forms may be more subtle and lead to confusion or even conflict. Thus the word "several" – often synony-mous in British English with "a few; a small number", but in Caribbean English with "very many; a large number of" – became a bone of contention that caused some Caribbean students to doubt the competence in his native tongue of the English co-author of this text.[1] Equally heated debate was generated by the word "quite" in contexts such as "the film was quite good", which all Eastern Caribbean students clearly identified as meaning "better than just good", but which in British usage generally means "a little less than good". On the Spanish side, the Colombian co-author of this work caused perplex-ity in a bar in Spain with the simple request *¿me regalas una cerveza, por favor?*, which in his home country is a normal way of ordering a beer, but elsewhere very strongly suggests that the speaker is begging for a beer for which he has no intention of paying.

Another advantage of using regional source materials in the translation classroom is the acquisition of cultural knowledge through exposure to texts emanating from the "other side" of the linguistic divide that obstinately persists in the Caribbean. The pervasive tendency of the inhabitants of the region only to identify with those that speak the same language lives on long after other vestiges of the colonial past have been cast off and as others are being actively combated, suggesting that it is barely acknowledged on a conscious level by many Caribbean people. It is perhaps most obviously reflected at the level of nomenclature: a "Spanish" person in the anglophone Caribbean is thus anyone who speaks Spanish, though users of this misnomer agree that they would object to being designated as "English" merely on the basis of their mother tongue. Equally, the term "the Caribbean", at the level of casual speech, still often excludes non-English-speaking territories, while Belize and Guyana are sometimes misleadingly referred to as "islands" in order to include them in the fold. On the other hand, the presence of the continent of Latin America on the doorstep of the region – or perhaps vice versa – frequently causes the Caribbean to be subsumed as a sub-region or appendage in the Hispanic consciousness, as evidenced by the titles of events and institutions that include the formula *Latinoamérica y el Caribe* and in allusions by insular territories to *nuestro continente*. Even in Cuba, with its avowedly universalistic outlook, the term *Caribe* can sometimes be used to mean the *non-Hispanic* Caribbean, revealing that nation's own underlying affiliation to Latin America.

Other issues of naming tend to reveal the same constraining colonial divisions of knowledge: on the eve of the new millennium, a tiny minority of students in a Barbadian Spanish-language class could put a name to the face when shown Korda's famous shot of Ernesto *Che* Guevara, regarded as one of the most iconic photographic images ever produced (though the fact that fewer had difficulty identifying the Spanish actor Antonio Banderas suggests this may be attributable to a general lack of historical, rather than specifically regional, awareness). Only one or two out of twenty could supply the name of Nicaragua's capital city (Managua), a few more that of Costa Rica (San José), while none knew that of Honduras (Tegucigalpa). All knew the capital of France, Spain, Jamaica, and Trinidad and Tobago.

The West Indies, the French West Indies, the Dutch West Indies . . . "the Hispanic West Indies"? The awkwardness and rarity of this formula (though it is sometimes used, mainly in academic contexts, along with "Spanish West Indies") illustrate the gulf in self-definition, created largely by divergent processes of colonization and decolonialization and by the presence of Latin America, between the Hispanic Caribbean territories and its neighbours. A logical consequence of these multiple self-definitions is that the term "Caribbean" itself is of course a matter of perpetual dispute. Suffice to say here that the definition the authors had in mind when writing this book was as broad as possible and slightly expands that of former Association of Caribbean States' Secretary General Norman Girvan: "the entire Basin: all of the islands including the Bahamas and the entire littoral including Mexico, the whole of Central America, Panama, Colombia, Venezuela, Guyana, Suriname and French Guiana".[2] Though it may seem controversial to some, we follow Hillmann and D'Agostino in including the southern tip of Florida and Miami in our concept of the Caribbean, since the focus here is linguistic and, specifically, the flow of streams of translation activity.[3] We should add that while this manual aims to celebrate the diversity and multiplicity of the region, we inevitably sometimes refer to the Caribbean in a way that may seem to homogenize a reality that is irreducibly variegated, nuanced, complex . . . We hope any such simplifications will be accepted as inevitable sacrifices in the service of economy of expression.

   A TRANSLATION MANUAL FOR THE CARIBBEAN (ENGLISH–SPANISH)
UN MANUAL DE TRADUCCIÓN PARA EL CARIBE (INGLÉS–ESPAÑOL)

In short, although this manual is obviously intended as a practical tool for acquiring skills in translation, it also aspires to be a modest contribution towards greater mutual knowledge and understanding between the anglophone and Hispanic Caribbean territories by encouraging comparison and contrast in the areas covered in subsequent chapters.

INTER-TRAFFIC BETWEEN THE ANGLOPHONE AND HISPANIC CARIBBEAN REGION
Despite the obstinacy of the colonial schemes of division within the region, there are ever-spreading areas of affinity between the Hispanic and anglophone Caribbean territories that might be seen to favour more meaningful exchange and cooperation in future. Unlike the French or Dutch West Indies, the majority of both the Hispanic and anglophone Caribbean territories are classified as independent states. The common desire to assert and protect this independence in the face of attempts at control by the United States, principally, has led to a perceptible rapprochement between Cuba, particularly, and some anglophone Caribbean states since the years of suspicion resulting from the Socialist nation's use of Barbados to airlift troops to Angola in 1975, its sinking of a Bahamian gunboat in 1980, and its involvement in Jamaica under Michael Manley and in Grenada under Maurice Bishop. Hundreds of anglophone Caribbean students now routinely head to Cuba to study each year. Exchange programmes for students involving Mexico, Colombia, Venezuela and Costa Rica, particularly, have also prospered in recent years.

Equally, the desire to shore up Caribbean economic growth and security, particularly in the face of initiatives such as the Free Trade Area of the Americas, has led to the creation of bodies that cut across the linguistic divide, such as CARIFORUM, which links Haiti and the Dominican Republic to CARICOM, and the Association of Caribbean States, which links Caribbean and Central American countries with Mexico, Colombia and Venezuela. Strategic commercial alliances between the anglophone Caribbean and Latin American nations are seen by some as the only safeguard against overwhelming North American hegemony in a context of increasingly liberalized trade. Such alliances will generate potentially vast quantities of translation activity, as bilingual or multilingual documentation will be required initially to cement their legality and subsequently to sustain commercial activity between specific corporations. It is this drive towards increased trade across the language barriers that will generate the majority of professional opportunities for trained translators in the coming years.

In the area of tourism, anglophone Caribbean visitors to predominantly Spanish-speaking territories (Isla Margarita, Puerto Rico, Miami) are still often principally motivated by consumerism: the primary goal is to make up the cost of the trip by acquiring sufficient quantities of goods that are more expensive in the home territory. The hegemonic status of English means that the flow of translation in this context, as usual, favours English speakers, who in many instances can expect to find both printed information in English and knowledge of English on the part of the locals to facilitate their experience.

Hispanic visitors to the anglophone Caribbean still represent only a small minority of overall arrivals. Nonetheless, to the outsider it may be striking that a country like Barbados offers very little tourist information in Spanish, which after all is the official second language of the nation and of CARICOM, and has by far the highest number of speakers in the region (64 per cent of the "core" Caribbean population – the Greater and Lesser Antilles, plus the Guyanas, Surinam and Belize – are citizens of Cuba, the Dominican Republic and Puerto Rico).[4] This again reflects the persistence of a mental scheme of the Caribbean divided according to language, but it is also of course a consequence of the global dominance of the English language. While it is true that a majority of Hispanics who might visit the anglophone territories are likely to know enough English to get by – most would correctly predict that their visit would be onerous without such knowledge – it is well known that visitors are persuaded to return by positive "affect" in the tourist experience: the feeling that they were made personally welcome and that the destination welcomes "people like us". Improving knowledge of Spanish in the anglophone hospitality industry is one way of raising this affect rating, together with the increased presence of Spanish (and other languages) on web sites and in local documentation.

It is the area of migrant labour, not tourism, however, that is responsible for the most numerically significant incursion of Spanish speakers into the anglophone Caribbean. The citizens of the Dominican Republic who have settled, principally, in Antigua and St Kitts and Nevis now number in the thousands, a proportionately significant phenomenon in a low-population context. The effect of large numbers of Spanish speakers and the subsequent "Hispanicization" (or more accurately "Dominicanization") of some areas of these territories, with the establishment of shops and other enterprises functioning partly or principally in Spanish, is yet to be studied, but one thing is certain: it generates acts of translation on a daily basis, as the immigrants strive to integrate into their new medium and the existing anglophone population seeks to understand and accommodate the new arrivals. Indeed, the unobstructed flow of communication through a filter of translation that is both rigorous and sensitive is a necessity in such circumstances, if friction and social upheaval are to be avoided. Equally, the role of translation in mediating the relations between the large number of Cuban doctors and their patients in the anglophone region can hardly be underestimated.

TRANSLATION PEDAGOGY IN THE CARIBBEAN
In the anglophone Caribbean, as elsewhere in the world, the prioritization of the communicative approach to language learning has caused written translation to be relegated in importance or eliminated outright in secondary-school foreign language learning in recent years. By way of example, the 2002 Secondary Foreign Languages Curriculum for Barbados states that, "since the new Foreign Language Curriculum is primarily intended to develop oral competence, the types of evaluation recommended will be aimed at testing the skills of listening, speaking and reading, with lesser emphasis placed on writing"; and later, more explicitly, "it is not expected that direct translation into the target language will be required of the students". The pre-eminence of oral competence, understandably seen as the key to facilitating regional integration through foreign language pedagogy, thus tends to push activities such as written translation towards the periphery. This prioritization of oral skills also accords with a majority of anglophone Caribbean students' own aspirations in language learning, since a significant majority tend to identify oral mastery and fluency of the foreign language as their primary goal.

Also in common with other contexts outside the region, however, there are signs that tertiary education in the Caribbean is moving written translation back towards the centre of foreign language pedagogy, or at least ensuring that a pathway exists for those who

A TRANSLATION MANUAL FOR THE CARIBBEAN (ENGLISH–SPANISH)
UN MANUAL DE TRADUCCIÓN PARA EL CARIBE (INGLÉS-ESPAÑOL)

wish to develop specialized skills in the area. This manual, emanating from the Cave Hill campus of the University of the West Indies (UWI) in Barbados, is a small contribution towards that movement. At the UWI Mona campus in Jamaica, an undergraduate specialization in translation has been introduced, allowing students to take a translation-focused course at all three levels of the foreign language degree. This would provide preferential access to their existing masters degree in translation studies.

These initiatives aimed at developing competence in translation, while laudable, do not stand comparison with Hispanic Caribbean systems for training translators. This is logical, first because of the widespread assumption that native competence in English either places the burden of translation on the non-anglophone party, or obviates the need for it altogether. Second, the relative antiquity of Hispanic universities in the region has allowed them more time to cultivate effective systems. Thus the postgraduate programme in translation studies at the University of Puerto Rico, comprising a Master of Arts in translation and a post-master's Certificate of Specialization, has been training professional practitioners since 1970, and is able to reabsorb its own graduates as lecturers.

In the case of Cuba, however, it is not only the longevity of its programmes that has facilitated the development of translation as a discipline in tertiary education, but also the focus of its foreign language pedagogy overall: *all* Cuban foreign language students at the university level train primarily to be professional translators and interpreters. That is, it is assumed that the principal goal of anyone studying an English degree is to be able to translate and interpret into and out of the English language. Thus the objectives of the five-year undergraduate English programme at the University of Havana (founded 1728) are as follows:

> The Graduate in English Language should be able to function professionally in that language, and in another foreign language. [. . .] The language professional should be competent in:
>
> The translation process
> The interpreting process
> Linguistic research
> The process of foreign language teaching[5]

On the other hand, economic and political constraints have meant that the high level of formal training afforded by universities and other official institutions in Cuba is often not matched by immersion opportunities in the foreign language that would undoubtedly improve the quality of its practitioners still further, deepening their cultural knowledge and cultivating fluency. One way of mitigating this relative dearth of native-speaker exposure would be to facilitate the regular incorporation of anglophone Caribbean translation students into a phase of the Cuban (or indeed other Hispanic) programmes, a possibility that the University of the West Indies will be exploring in future.

TRANSLATION PRACTICE IN THE CARIBBEAN

Translation practice in the Caribbean cannot help but be as diverse as the region itself. It is inevitable that translation activity and services in Curacao, where many people can function with equal ease in Papiamento, Dutch, Spanish or English as the situation requires, will be organized differently than in a Creole-with-Standard English context such as

Jamaica. A meaningful account of translation practice in the region, therefore, would occupy a volume of its own and could only result from commissioned country studies and mutual consultation between their compilers. To exemplify this diversity of practices, we provide here a sketch of translation in Trinidad and Tobago, first, and in Cuba.

In the case of the former country, there is some evidence that suggests the volume of translated material and awareness of the importance of translation are both higher than in other anglophone Caribbean territories because of its extreme proximity to Venezuela. Its strategic position has led a number of multilingual organizations to base their operations there, such as the Association of Caribbean States (ACS), which generates a considerable daily demand for translations. Sadly, as with most institutions and companies in the region, the ACS does not employ in-house translators. Documents are prepared in English, French or Spanish, depending on the personnel working on a given project, and the translation is then commissioned from a freelance practitioner. However, similar types of text are offered to the same translators repeatedly – as long as previous work has proved to be of high quality – giving them some degree of stability and a regular affiliation with the organization. The volume of translation is on the increase as new associations and companies seek out a market in both the Caribbean and Latin America. Trinidad is responding to this increase by providing both public and private training centres. In the private sector, for example, CILCO (Caribbean Institute of Languages and International Business) offers both translation services and training for future translators in the form of an associate diploma in foreign languages (English <> Spanish translation), together with the option of obtaining a qualification from the British Institute of Linguists or the American Translators' Association (thus far, there is no equivalent Caribbean-wide accreditation). In the public sector, an institution such as COSTAATT (College of Science, Technology and Applied Arts of Trinidad and Tobago) offers professional translation services, though again using freelance translators. There is also a grouping known as the Translators and Interpreters Association of Trinidad and Tobago (TIATT), which seeks to act as an intermediary between translators and interpreters and their clients. Though this represents an attempt to bring together translation professionals, it must be said that many of these latter do not belong to it. The authors' research in Trinidad suggested that while many translators were interested in the idea of being members of an organization of this kind, they did not see it as especially important and thus continue to market themselves and make contacts on an individual basis.

With regard to the types of text most commonly translated, legal documents head the list, followed by commercial material. Legal texts form the foundation of the activities of the organizations mentioned above, explaining their relative prevalence. The abundance of commercial material is in turn attributable to Trinidad's status as perhaps the most industrialized of the Caribbean islands. An increasing quantity of consumer goods are manufactured there, particularly North American items seeking a niche in both the Caribbean and Latin American markets, so that labelling and documentation has to be in both Spanish and English.

Finally, court translating and interpreting is another specific area of professional activity for translators in Trinidad and Tobago.

In the case of Cuba, translation and interpreting activity is considerable because of the Revolution's consciously internationalist approach to culture and intellectual endeavour. Cuba is thus an important centre for international conferences, symposiums and fairs for participants in a variety of trades and professional activities, all serviced by officially provided interpreters and translators. The Havana-based Prensa Latina news agency, founded in 1959, offers another example of this scrupulous attention to translation: though primarily concerned with Latin America, the agency's web site can be accessed in Spanish, Italian, Portuguese or English.

In general, the considerable degree of organization in the field of translation reflects both the relatively high status afforded to translation/interpreting as a career path, and the broader Cuban tendency towards centralized supervision and absorption of professionals by official institutions in all areas. Almost all Cuban translators and interpreters thus develop through the university system and serve an apprenticeship administered by the Advanced School for Translators and Interpreters (Escuela Superior de Traductores e Intérpretes, ESTI), a national body that provides liaison between professionals and clients requiring their services, as well as integrated training programs and materials such as specialized glossaries and databases for its in-house personnel. The vast majority of professional practitioners are members of the Cuban Association of Translators and Interpreters (Asociación Cubana de Traductores e Intérpretes, ACTI).

Literary translators, who even in larger and more economically developed countries often do not formally associate with their fellow practitioners, can also seek honorary membership of a specialized guild affiliated with the Cuban National Union of Writers and Artists (Unión Nacional de Escritores y Artistas Cubanos, UNEAC).

TRANSLATION STUDIES AND THE CARIBBEAN

The field of "translation studies" has progressed very quickly since it was first defined as such in the 1970s, with the last ten to fifteen years generating a particularly rapid growth in new approaches and linkages with other disciplines. Before the 1970s, there was a very strong tendency to view translation exclusively from the point of view of linguistics, with theorists attempting to classify "shifts" that tended to occur in the process of translating from one language to another, or to establish various types of "**equivalence**" that translations might strive for or manifest. In the 1970s and 1980s, translation theorists sought to broaden the focus of the discipline by positing "functional" theories that explained translation praxis and processes in terms of the *purpose* of the translation. Since the 1990s, translation theories have sought to contextualize the process of producing and evaluating translations still further by examining the power relations that lead to the commissioning of translations of certain texts and not others, and by interpreting the strategies adopted by translators in terms of these power relations. Latterly, this preoccupation with the effect of power relations on the production of translations and the manner in which they are produced has extended to examinations of translation practice as it relates to specific vectors of power inequality, such as those obtaining in colonial and post-colonial societies, or in relation to gender.

Throughout this evolution, the tendency has been to move away from prescriptive approaches that presupposed a "right" way to translate a given source text, towards descriptive enquiries into why and how translations are produced and the spectrum of possible options open to the translator depending on the function of the translation, the pressures brought to bear on the process by various power brokers (such as authors, agents, publishers, literary critics, the academy, large corporations or other commissioners of translations), and the ideology of the translator (among other factors). In the context of this manual, all of this might seem to leave open the overriding, pragmatic question of interest to the trainee translator: how should I translate if I want my work to be professionally acceptable? The answer supplied by the theoretical background adumbrated above is that a translator should be as aware as possible of all the conditioning factors bearing on the process of actually producing a given target text from a given source text. Therefore, while the commentaries on specific translations given in this manual classify types of translation procedure according to linguistic terminology coined in the late 1950s (though still widely used today), every effort has been made to pay due attention to the context in which the translation has been produced, and to the ideological implications of both that context and the resulting target text itself.[6] This does not preclude an approach that is predominantly pragmatic and vocational when necessary: where prescriptive notions may seem to be inferable, this is generally because the prevailing *expectation* in the world of commercial translation dictates that a given approach or solution should probably be used. For example, in the chapter on film we assert that the expert film subtitler "must avoid carrying a subtitle across a cut to a different camera angle, for example, or prematurely revealing information that is first introduced visually in the original version". It is obvious that both these rules are sometimes consciously broken by good subtitlers on occasion because other more pressing constraints so demand it: the individual practitioner is of course free to transgress, to translate "against the grain", if he or she feels moved to do so; the aim here is simply to cultivate maximum awareness of how and when we are being transgressive.

This manual is emphatically not, however, intended systematically to advance knowledge of any theoretical approach to translation by applying it to the Caribbean context. Given the coexistence in the region of both colonial and postcolonial societies and its resultant linguistic, politico-social and ideological complexity, an application of recent approaches to translation such as the "polysystem" or postcolonial translation theories would undoubtedly enrich both these theories, on the one hand, and contemporary understanding of the Caribbean, more generally, on the other. Until the moment when such a work can be contemplated, the rather humbler aim of this manual is to contribute to ongoing efforts to "draw the map" of a Caribbean translation studies corpus that will incorporate both practical and theoretical studies from throughout the region.

TRANSLATION CONCEPTS AND STRATEGIES USED IN THIS MANUAL

Throughout this manual, bold type is used to indicate terms with a specific meaning in the field of translation, some of which are borrowed from related disciplines. In fact, translation is now often referred to as an "interdiscipline", making use of elements from the comparative study of languages, comparative stylistics, textlinguistics, sociolinguistics, terminology, general linguistics and cultural studies, among others, while at the same time returning new echoes to these fields. While all the boldface terms are explained in the glossary at the end of the book for occasional reference, here we discuss the most relevant of these so that the reader may be equipped with a theoretical framework for the translation process. Though the spatial limitations of this manual naturally prevent us from offering a fully comprehensive account of relevant terms, the interested reader will find further useful references to the matters addressed here in the bibliography or on the web page.

When a text is received for translation, the first step normally taken by the translator is to read it in its entirety, since the text itself, however long, can be viewed as the unit of translation. On reading it, accompanied by relevant information supplied by the client, the translator establishes the text type, such as scientific or journalistic, contract or advertisement. In this regard, it should not be forgotten that text types are not mutually exclusive: a journalistic article might be about a scientific discovery, for example. Particular turns of phrase, words and structures help us to determine what kind of source text is before us. We also assess the **coherence** of the text, meaning how its different components relate to each other conceptually, and its **cohesion**, meaning how given sections of text are linked to others (using cohesive markers such as "moreover", "however", "this", and so on). We also analyse the **information density** or **concision** of the text, meaning the ratio of information given to number of words used. We also consider whether the text makes direct or indirect reference to other texts (**intertextuality**). These and other concepts have been adapted from textlinguistics. Once the text has been read and analysed in this fashion, we look for similar texts in our own language (**textual immersion**). A contrastive analysis allows us to familiarize ourselves with the often divergent terminology and overall structure of similar text types in two different languages.

All texts are produced in a given context and with a specific goal in mind. Translation takes this into account: through a sociolinguistic and functional (**skopos**) analysis of the text, the translator establishes who produced the text, in what context and with what purpose. Here we might pay attention to markers that reveal the text's **social register** or **sociolect**, determining also whether the text belongs to a particular **dialect**, whether it contains elements that give it high prestige (**acrolectal**) or markers that show an awareness of gender. This process may also allow us to identify the text with the discourse of a specialized group (a **technolect** or **argot**, for example). The client generally supplies clues as to the function of the translation, which in turn helps the translator to decide how to deal with these sociolinguistic elements.

Once this preparatory phase is completed, we are in a position to undertake the translation itself. Some translation theorists have tried to describe and classify the procedures used by translators to arrive at their versions. Perhaps the best known such account is that of the French authors Jean-Paul Vinay and Jean Darbelnet, who established seven translation procedures. The authors divided these into two groups: direct and oblique translation procedures.

The direct procedures are **borrowing, calque** and **literal translation. Borrowing** means that the translator has taken an expression from the SL and reproduced it without modification in the TT. This procedure is generally used when an equivalent expression has not yet come into existence in the TL or when it makes reference to customs or objects that are exclusive to the source culture. Some examples of words that are commonly borrowed between English and Spanish are whisky (despite the Academy's insistence on *güisqui*), happening, roti, tango, piñata or fiesta latina.

The next procedure is **calque**, which means reproducing the form of the expression but replacing the elements with equivalents in the TL. Thus "Governor General" **calques** *Gobernador General*, as *balompié* does "football". As this last example shows, the two elements of the word are translated by equivalent terms in Spanish, but the form of the word is maintained even though it is much more natural in the SL than in the TL. Some authors distinguish between **calque** and naturalized **borrowing**. This latter procedure involves conservation of the sound patterns of the SL: thus *fútbol* is a naturalized **borrowing** of "football".

The final direct translation procedure is **literal translation**. Though some theorists distinguish between literal translation and word-for-word translation, they are treated as identical here. While **literal translation** is one of the most commonly used procedures, it is not always possible to use it because the structures and semantics of languages differ. Thus "three men came running" can be translated literally without difficulty as *tres hombres vinieron corriendo*. But "the Caribbean is seen as a safer choice than Europe", for example, translates word for word as *el Caribe es visto como una más segura elección que Europa*. The content of this translation is comprehensible, but it leaves much to be desired stylistically. First, the natural position of adjectives differs between English and Spanish ("safer choice" versus *elección más segura*); second, "choice" in this context may well translate better as *destino* (reminding us that the meaning of words is very strongly determined by their context). Finally, Spanish prefers the *se* construction to the true passive (*es visto* versus *se ve*). A less literal version would be *el Caribe se considera un destino más seguro que Europa*. As we can see, it is necessary to make a series of shifts on various levels (lexical, syntactic, grammatical, semantic, pragmatic, etc.) in order to arrive at a version that can be considered natural while remaining stylistically and pragmatically equivalent to the ST.

When literal translation cannot achieve these objectives, the translator may call upon oblique translation strategies, which Vinay and Darbelnet identify as **transposition, modulation, equivalence** and **adaptation**.

Transposition consists of replacing a part of the discourse (a grammatical category) with another, while preserving the overall semantic content of the expression. The authors distinguish between optional and obligatory **transposition**. The obligatory type is used when it is not possible to translate literally because an identical structure does not exist in both SL and TL, as in the case of singular to plural transposition: "furniture" > *muebles*; "it" as empty pronoun in phases such as "it was raining" > *llovía*; or with neutral adjective as subject: *lo importante del acuerdo . . .* > "What is important about the agreement . . . / The important thing about the agreement . . . ". Optional **transposition** occurs when the transposed version is stylistically preferable to the literal version, even though this latter is admissible, as in the case of the position of some adjectives: "three little houses" > *tres pequeñas casas / tres casas pequeñas*. Note here that the position of the adjectives in the two TT versions varies stylistically. With other adjectives the translator has no option: "The White House" > *La Casa Blanca*. Some Caribbean **dialects** use an adjective structure that varies from the standard: "She white car" = "Her white car".

Modulation is defined as a change of viewpoint, meaning that the same reality is expressed from a different perspective. While **transposition** means a shift of grammatical category, **modulation** implies a conceptual shift. A typical example of **modulation** is the shift from a negative expression to its positive equivalent: "it's not difficult to get lost" > *es fácil perderse*, or vice versa. It should be noted that the overall meaning is preserved, even though the manner of expressing it is shifted. Other types of **modulation** include shifting from an abstract to a concrete noun, the part for the whole, specific to general ("lion" > *felino*), from function to process, animate to inanimate, metaphor to non-metaphor, and so on.

The next translation procedure is **equivalence**. This can be defined as the use of an expression that has a similar effect in the TT, without necessarily having any word-for-word correspondence. The most common example of this procedure is in the translation of popular sayings, proverbs, onomatopoeias and clichés: "Birds of a feather (flock together)" > *Dios los hace y ellos se juntan.*

The final procedure offered by the authors is **adaptation**. Sometimes elements of the source culture are not accepted, shared or sometimes even known to the target culture, so that including them in the translation can impede the act of reading the text (the reader may find it incomprehensible), or may give rise to misunderstandings. Faced with **culture-bound** elements, translators may opt to translate such elements in such a way that the reader is brought to the target culture (**foreignizing translation**), or they may adapt such elements in such a way that the text is brought to the reader (**domesticating translation**). In Latin America, for example, football or soccer is the number one sport, while in the anglophone Caribbean cricket still occupies that role. We might imagine a situation in which in order to convey the idea of a fan who rejoices at seeing his team win, we might replace one sport with another in our text.

Other authors have extended the list of procedures to include **amplification**, meaning the addition of information that does not appear in the ST in order to aid comprehension (sometimes in the form of a footnote). The opposite procedure is known as **omission**. Similar to **amplification** is the procedure of **explicitation**, which consists of expressing directly that which was implicit in the ST. This procedure is common when the translator is confronted with **culture-bound** elements in the translation, or when the ST carries an ironic or satirical charge that is not easily reproducible in the TT. The translator may often find that part of the meaning or functional thrust of the ST is lost in translation. When this happens, recourse to **compensation** is common, meaning the attempt to restore that which has been lost, either inserting a similar element in another position in the text, or by using devices not present in the original. Thus a translator faced with dialect may use standard language and then add "he said in marked Havana dialect". These procedures are closely linked to the discipline of semantics, in which the relations between words in a given language are studied. From the point of view of translation, the differences in the semantic fields between languages are of primary relevance. Thus the connotative and denotative meaning of a word or group of words can be examined. **Denotation** means the basic meaning of a word (the one that generally appears in dictionaries); **connotation** is the added significance the word may carry (such as its association with a prestigious way of speaking, a specific region and so on).

The reader will become familiar with these and other relevant terms through using the manual; it is hoped that the explanations offered here and in the glossary will assist in understanding these terms and their relevance to translation.

Introducción: La Traducción en el Caribe

EL PORQUÉ DE ESTE MANUAL

El motivo inicial para escribir este manual fue completamente práctico: como profesores de traducción entre inglés y español en el Caribe, los autores estaban convencidos de la necesidad de tener un libro de recursos que contuviera material traducido, análisis, ejercicios e información relevantes para la región. No había ningún libro que cumpliera esas expectativas, obligando a los profesores y estudiantes de traducción a consultar obras con contenido predominantemente norteamericano o europeo, o a buscar en diferentes fuentes materiales traducidos y analizarlos por sí mismos. Este manual no resultó, pues, de un interés particular por recalcar el carácter distintivo de las variantes del inglés o el español hablado en el Caribe, sino más bien de la sencilla observación de que los estudiantes de traducción se sienten más motivados cuando trabajan en contextos que les son relativamente más cercanos.

Si bien la relevancia del contenido pudo haber sido el interés principal, el uso del inglés o el español caribeño ocupa y debería ocupar un lugar preponderante en todos los salones de clase – y en la mente del traductor – de la región. La eficacia sin par de la traducción como instrumento de análisis textual, que requiere atención minuciosa a la función y a la dinámica interna del texto origen, inevitablemente también sirve para resaltar las diferencias entre las variantes regionales de una lengua dada. En contextos completamente vernaculares estas diferencias son obvias, como se demuestra en los capítulos de literatura y cine de este volumen. Otras diferencias en las respectivas formas estándar pueden ser más sutiles y crear confusiones e incluso conflictos. Por ejemplo, en inglés la palabra *several* – sinónimo de "pocos, un reducido número de" en la variante británica, pero de "muchos, un gran número de" en inglés caribeño – resultó ser motivo de conflicto que llegó a hacer que algunos de los estudiantes caribeños dudaran de la competencia del autor inglés de este texto en su lengua materna.[1] Otro debate que causó alboroto fue el que generó la palabra *quite*, en contextos como *the film was quite good*, que todos los estudiantes del Caribe del Este identificaron con el significado "mejor que bueno", pero que en inglés británico por lo general significa "un poco menos que bueno". En español, por su parte, el coautor colombiano de este trabajo causó perplejidad en un bar español con el simple pedido "¿me regalas una cerveza, por favor?", que en su país de origen constituye una fórmula normal para pedir una cerveza, pero que en otros países sugiere que el hablante está pidiendo una cerveza por la que no tiene ninguna intención de pagar.

Otra ventaja de usar materiales regionales como fuente en la enseñanza de la traducción es la adquisición de conocimiento cultural mediante el contacto con textos provenientes del "otro lado" de la barrera lingüística, que obstinadamente prevalece en el Caribe. La tendencia dominante en los habitantes de la región a identificarse solamente con aquellos que hablan la misma lengua sobrevive, mientras ya se han deshecho de otros vestigios del pasado colonial, o luchan por erradicar los que quedan, lo que sugiere que muchos caribeños ni siquiera reconocen esta realidad a nivel consciente. Esto se ve reflejado tal vez de manera más obvia en la nomenclatura: una persona "española" en el Caribe anglófono es cualquier persona que hable español, aunque los mismos usuarios

 A TRANSLATION MANUAL FOR THE CARIBBEAN (ENGLISH–SPANISH)
UN MANUAL DE TRADUCCIÓN PARA EL CARIBE (INGLÉS–ESPAÑOL)

de esta nomenclatura errada concuerdan en que no les gustaría ser designados "ingleses" por el simple hecho de que ésta es su lengua materna. De igual forma, el término *the Caribbean*, en el lenguaje coloquial, todavía excluye a menudo a los territorios de habla no inglesa, si bien Belice y Guyana algunas veces son consideradas erróneamente "islas" para incluirlas en la categorización. Por otra parte, la presencia del territorio continental de Latinoamérica al lado de la región – o quizás al revés – hace que con frecuencia se considere el Caribe como una subregión o apéndice en la conciencia hispana, como lo evidencian los títulos de instituciones y eventos que incluyen la frase "Latinoamérica y el Caribe" y las alusiones de los territorios insulares a "nuestro continente". Incluso en Cuba, cuya visión es claramente universalista, el término "Caribe" se usa en ocasiones para referirse al Caribe no hispano, lo que deja entrever la propia afiliación del país con Latinoamérica.

Otros casos de nomenclatura tienden a mostrar las mismas divisiones coloniales limitantes del saber: en la víspera del nuevo milenio, sólo un reducido grupo de estudiantes en una clase de español en Barbados fue capaz de identificar a Ernesto 'Che' Guevara en la famosa foto tomada por Korda, considerada una de las imágenes fotográficas más icónicas de la historia (aunque el hecho de que menos tuvieron problemas para identificar al actor español Antonio Banderas sugiere que esto se le puede atribuir a la falta general de conciencia histórica, más que a una falta de conciencia específicamente regional). Solamente uno o dos de veinte sabía el nombre de la capital de Nicaragua (Managua), algunos más sabían la de Costa Rica (San José), mientras que ninguno sabía la de Honduras (Tegucigalpa). Todos sabían la capital de Francia, España, Jamaica, y Trinidad y Tobago.

Las Antillas, las Antillas francesas, las Antillas holandesas . . . ¿"las Antillas hispanas"? La extrañeza que causa esta frase y su uso poco frecuente (aunque en ocasiones se utiliza, principalmente en contextos académicos junto con "las Antillas españolas") demuestran la brecha presente en la autodefinición entre el Caribe hispano y sus vecinos, creada en gran medida por los procesos divergentes de colonización y descolonización y por la presencia de Latinoamérica. Consecuencia lógica de estas múltiples autodefiniciones es, por supuesto, que incluso el término "Caribe" se presenta como un asunto de continuas disputas. Esperamos que sea suficiente decir que la definición que los autores tuvimos en cuenta al escribir este libro fue tan amplia como nos fue posible y que va un poco más allá de la definición propuesta por el ex secretario general de la Asociación de Estados Caribeños, Norman Girvan: "la totalidad de la cuenca: todas las islas incluyendo las Bahamas, la totalidad del litoral incluyendo México, todo Centroamérica, Panamá, Colombia, Venezuela, Guyana, Surinam y la Guyana francesa".[2] Aunque para algunos pueda resultar controversial seguimos a Hillmann y D'Agostino al incluir la parte sur de la Florida y Miami en nuestra concepción del Caribe, ya que nuestro enfoque es sobre todo lingüístico y, específicamente, se basa en el flujo de la actividad traductora.[3] Debemos añadir que si bien este manual busca elogiar la diversidad y multiplicidad de la región, inevitablemente en ocasiones nos referimos al Caribe de forma que parece que homogenicemos una realidad que es irreduciblemente multicolor, llena de matices, compleja . . . Esperamos que se nos acepten estas simplificaciones como sacrificios inevitables al servicio de la economía de expresión.

Resumiendo, aunque este manual se plantea claramente como una herramienta práctica para adquirir habilidades traductoras, también quiere ser una modesta contribución hacia el conocimiento y entendimiento mutuo entre los países del Caribe anglófono y el hispano, al promover la comparación y el contraste en las áreas estudiadas en los capítulos que siguen.

INTERCAMBIOS ENTRE EL CARIBE ANGLÓFONO Y EL CARIBE HISPANO

A pesar de la persistencia de los esquemas coloniales de división dentro de la región, hay cada vez más áreas de afinidad entre los países del Caribe anglófono y su contraparte hispana que parecieran favorecer una cooperación y un intercambio más significativo en el futuro. A diferencia de las antillas francesas y holandesas, la mayor parte del Caribe hispano y el anglófono se clasifica como estados independientes. El deseo compartido de reafirmar y proteger esta independencia frente a intentos de control de los Estados Unidos, principalmente, ha llevado a un acercamiento entre Cuba, en particular, y algunos países del Caribe anglófono desde los años de la desconfianza que fueron el resultado del uso de Barbados como base para transportar tropas a Angola en 1975, el hundimiento de la lancha cañonera bahamesa en 1980 y su participación en Jamaica bajo Michael Manley y en Granada bajo Maurice Bishop. Ahora es común que cientos de estudiantes del Caribe anglófono se dirijan cada año a Cuba para estudiar. Los programas de intercambio de estudiantes con México, Colombia, Venezuela y Costa Rica, en particular, también han prosperado en los últimos años.

Además, el deseo de reforzar el crecimiento y la seguridad económica caribeña, en especial frente a iniciativas como el Área de Libre Comercio de las Américas, ha llevado a la creación de organizaciones que sobrepasan la barrera lingüística, como es el caso del CARIFORUM, que une a Haití y la República Dominicana a CARICOM, y la Asociación de Estados del Caribe que une al Caribe y Centroamérica con México, Colombia y Venezuela. Las alianzas comerciales estratégicas entre el Caribe anglófono y Latinoamérica son para algunos las únicas salvaguardas frente a la abrumante hegemonía norteamericana en un contexto de creciente comercio liberalizado. Estas alianzas generarán potencialmente grandes cantidades de traducción, ya que se requerirá inicialmente documentación bilingüe o multilingüe para cimentar su legitimidad y luego para mantener las actividades comerciales entre empresas específicas. Es este deseo de aumentar el intercambio comercial por encima de las barreras lingüísticas el que generará la mayor cantidad de oportunidades de empleo profesional para traductores capacitados en los años venideros.

En el área del turismo, todavía es común que las visitas de personas del Caribe anglófono a territorios predominantemente hispanohablantes (Isla Margarita, Puerto Rico, Miami) sean motivadas principalmente por el consumismo: el objetivo principal es compensar el costo del viaje adquiriendo suficientes cantidades de bienes que son más caros en sus países. El estatus hegemónico del inglés hace que el flujo de la traducción en este contexto, como es común, favorezca al angloparlante, quien en muchas ocasiones espera encontrar tanto información impresa en inglés como conocimiento de la lengua por parte de los locales para facilitar su experiencia.

Los visitantes hispanos al Caribe anglófono todavía representan una pequeña minoría de la totalidad de llegadas. No obstante, desde fuera puede parecer sorprendente que un país como Barbados ofrezca tan poca información en español, que después de todo es la segunda lengua oficial del país y de CARICOM, y que cuenta con muchísima mayor cantidad de hablantes en la región (64% del "núcleo" de la población caribeña – las antillas mayores y menores, además de las Guyanas, Surinam y Belice – son ciudadanos de Cuba, la República Dominicana y Puerto Rico).[4] Esto refleja otra vez la persistencia de un esquema mental del Caribe dividido por la lengua, pero también es por supuesto una consecuencia del dominio global de la lengua inglesa. Si bien es cierto que probablemente la mayoría de los hispanos que visitan los países anglófonos sepan el suficiente inglés para defenderse – la mayoría puede predecir sin temor a equivocarse que su visita sería pesada sin ese conocimiento – se sabe que los visitantes se sienten tentados a volver a un lugar si han tenido una "influencia" positiva en su experiencia turística: el sentimiento de que han sido bienvenidos a nivel personal y que el destino acoge a "gente como nosotros". Mejorar el conocimiento del español en la industria anglófona de la hospitalidad es una forma de elevar el grado de esta "influencia", así como lo es la creciente presencia del español (y otras lenguas) en páginas web y en la documentación local.

Sin embargo, la mayor incursión de hispanohablantes en términos numéricos en el Caribe anglófono no la representan los turistas, sino más bien los trabajadores que han emigrado a la región. Se cuentan en miles los ciudadanos de la República Dominicana que se han asentado principalmente en Antigua y San Cristóbal y Nieves, un fenómeno proporcionalmente significativo en un contexto de población reducida. Aún no se ha estudiado el efecto de grandes cantidades de hispanohablantes y la consecuente "hispanización" (o para ser más precisos "dominicanización") de algunas partes de estos países, mediante el establecimiento de tiendas y negocios que funcionan en parte o principalmente en español, pero una cosa es cierta: genera actos de traducción a diario, los inmigrantes se esfuerzan por integrarse al nuevo medio y la población anglófona existente busca entender y acomodar a los recién llegados. De hecho, bajo las circunstancias, se requiere que haya un flujo de comunicación sin obstáculos mediante el filtro de una traducción que sea tanto rigurosa como cuidadosa, si se quieren evitar fricciones y agitaciones sociales. Del mismo modo, no se puede subestimar el papel de la traducción como mediadora de las relaciones entre el gran número de doctores cubanos y sus pacientes en la región anglófona.

LA PEDAGOGÍA DE LA TRADUCCIÓN EN EL CARIBE

En el Caribe anglófono, como en el resto del mundo, la priorización del enfoque comunicativo en el aprendizaje de lenguas ha relegado la importancia de la traducción escrita, o la ha eliminado del todo, en el contexto del aprendizaje de lenguas extranjeras en la escuela secundaria durante los últimos años. A modo de ejemplo, el Currículo de Lenguas Extranjeras del 2002 para las escuelas secundarias en Barbados dice que "ya que la intención principal del nuevo Currículo de Lenguas Extranjeras es desarrollar la competencia oral, se recomienda que el tipo de evaluación sea dirigido a comprobar las habilidades para escuchar, hablar y leer, con menos énfasis en escribir"; y luego, de manera más explícita, "no se espera que se requiera traducción directa a la lengua meta por parte de los estudiantes". La preeminencia de la competencia oral, con razón vista como la clave para facilitar la integración regional a través de la pedagogía de las lenguas extranjeras, tiende, pues, a mover actividades como la traducción escrita a la periferia. La priorización de las habilidades orales también va de la mano de las expectativas propias de los estudiantes del Caribe anglófono en cuanto al aprendizaje de lenguas, ya que una gran mayoría tiende a identificar el dominio y la fluidez a nivel oral de la lengua extranjera como su objetivo principal.

Sin embargo, de modo similar a lo que ocurre en otros contextos fuera de la región, hay evidencias de que la educación universitaria en el Caribe trae de nuevo la traducción al centro de la pedagogía de las lenguas extranjeras, o al menos se asegura de que haya una vía para aquellos que desean desarrollar habilidades especiales en esta área. Este manual, proveniente del campus de Cave Hill de la Universidad de las Antillas Occidentales (UWI) en Barbados, es una pequeña contribución hacia ese movimiento. En el campus de la UWI en Jamaica (Mona), se ha introducido una especialización en traducción a nivel de pregrado, permitiendo a los estudiantes tomar un curso basado en la traducción en los tres niveles de la carrera de lenguas extranjeras. Esto les dará acceso preferencial al Master en Estudios de Traducción que ofrece la universidad.

Estas iniciativas enfocadas al desarrollo de la competencia en traducción, aunque loables, son mínimas si se las compara con los sistemas del Caribe hispano para la preparación de traductores. Esto es lógico, primero, por la creencia extendida de que la competencia en inglés o bien pone la carga de la traducción en el no anglófono, u obvia por completo su necesidad; segundo, porque la antigüedad relativa de las universidades hispanas en la región les ha dado más tiempo para cultivar sistemas efectivos. Así el programa de postgrado en traducción de la Universidad de Puerto Rico, compuesto de un Master en Traducción y un Certificado de Especialización a nivel post-master, ha estado preparando a profesionales desde 1970 y puede reabsorber a sus propios graduados como profesores.

No obstante, en el caso de Cuba, no sólo es la longevidad de los programas lo que ha facilitado el desarrollo de la traducción como disciplina en la educación universitaria, sino también el enfoque de su pedagogía de la lengua extranjera en general: *todos* los estudiantes cubanos de lenguas extranjeras a nivel universitario se preparan principalmente para ser traductores e intérpretes profesionales. Es decir, se asume que el objetivo principal de una persona que estudia inglés como carrera es poder traducir e interpretar de dicha lengua y hacia ella. Así, los objetivos del programa de cinco años de inglés como carrera de pregrado en la Universidad de La Habana (fundada en 1728) son los siguientes:

El Licenciado en Lengua Inglesa debe ser capaz de desempeñarse profesionalmente en dicha lengua, así como en una segunda lengua extranjera. [. . .] Este profesional debe dominar:

El proceso de traducción.
El proceso de interpretación.
La investigación lingüística.
El proceso de enseñanza de las lenguas extranjeras[5]

Por otro lado, las limitaciones económicas y políticas han hecho que el alto nivel de preparación formal llevado a cabo por las universidades y otras instituciones oficiales en Cuba no venga acompañado de oportunidades de inmersión en la lengua extranjera que sin lugar a dudas mejoraría aun más la calidad de sus profesionales, profundizando en el conocimiento cultural y cultivando la fluidez. Una forma de mitigar esta escasez en la exposición a hablantes nativos sería facilitar la incorporación regular de estudiantes de traducción del Caribe anglófono a una de las fases de los programas cubanos (o de otros lugares hispanos), una posibilidad que la Universidad de las Antillas Occidentales explorará en un futuro.

  A TRANSLATION MANUAL FOR THE CARIBBEAN (ENGLISH–SPANISH)
UN MANUAL DE TRADUCCIÓN PARA EL CARIBE (INGLÉS-ESPAÑOL)

LA PRÁCTICA DE LA TRADUCCIÓN EN EL CARIBE

La práctica de la traducción en el Caribe resulta tan diversa como la región misma. Es inevitable que la actividad y los servicios de traducción en Curaçao, donde mucha gente puede funcionar con la misma facilidad en papiamento, holandés, español o inglés según sea la situación, se organice de modo diferente a como se hace en el contexto de creol e inglés estándar de Jamaica. Un recuento minucioso de la práctica de la traducción en la región, por lo tanto, constituiría un volumen en sí mismo y sólo podría salir de estudios encargados en los países y una consulta mutua entre los compiladores. Para ejemplificar la diversidad de las prácticas, presentamos aquí un esbozo de la traducción en Trinidad y Tobago, primero, y en Cuba, después. En el caso del primer país, hay algunas evidencias que sugieren que el volumen de material traducido y el reconocimiento de la importancia de la traducción son más altos que en otros países del Caribe anglófono dada su extrema proximidad con Venezuela. Su situación estratégica hace que muchos organismos multilingües tengan sus sedes principales en la nación. Uno de ellos es la Asociación de Estados del Caribe que tiene una alta demanda diaria de traducciones. Desafortunadamente, como sucede con la mayoría de organismos y empresas en la región, no se cuenta con un personal interno de traducción: los documentos son preparados en inglés, francés o español, dependiendo del personal que esté a cargo en un momento determinado, y su traducción se encarga a traductores freelance. Sin embargo, se tiende a encargar el mismo **tipo de textos** a los mismos traductores (si los resultados de traducciones anteriores han sido de alta calidad), lo que les proporciona cierta estabilidad y un grado de relación constante con el organismo. El flujo de la traducción tiende a incrementar con la formación de nuevas agrupaciones y empresas que buscan un mercado tanto en el Caribe como en Latinoamérica. Trinidad se prepara para este incremento por medio de instituciones de capacitación tanto públicas como privadas. En el sector privado CILCO (Caribbean Institute of Languages and International Business) destaca por ofrecer tanto servicios de traducción como de capacitación para futuros traductores, ofreciendo un Diploma Asociado en Lenguas Extranjeras (Traducción Inglés <> Español), así como la posibilidad de certificarse por medio del Institute of Linguists (Gran Bretaña) o la American Translators' Association (Estados Unidos), ya que hasta ahora no existe ningún tipo de titulación de este estilo a nivel caribeño. En el sector público, una institución como COSTAATT (College of Science, Technology and Applied Arts of Trinidad and Tobago) ofrece servicios profesionales de traducción, aunque de nuevo por medio de algunos traductores freelance. Existe también una agrupación llamada Translators and Interpreters Association of Trinidad and Tobago (TIATT) que busca servir de enlace entre traductores, intérpretes y clientes. Aunque la creación de esta institución es un esfuerzo por reunir a los profesionales de la rama, la realidad es que muchos de ellos aún no hacen parte de la misma. En el estudio que los autores hicieron en Trinidad, descubrieron que si bien muchos están en principio interesados en formar parte de una organización de este estilo, no reconocen la importancia de hacerlo y por lo tanto siguen promocionándose y haciendo contactos a nivel individual.

En cuanto a los tipos textuales que se traducen, los legales son los más comunes, seguidos por los comerciales. Los textos legales son la base de los organismos que mencionamos antes y de allí su importancia. En cuanto a los comerciales, Trinidad sobresale en el Caribe como la isla quizás más industrializada. Cada vez más bienes de consumo se producen allí, especialmente los norteamericanos que buscan entradas al mercado tanto caribeño como latinoamericano, por lo que la documentación y las etiquetas de dichos bienes han de estar diseñadas tanto en español como en inglés.

Finalmente, la traducción e interpretación para la corte es otro campo específico que se va desarrollando en el país.

En el caso de Cuba, la actividad en traducción e interpretación es considerable debido al enfoque conscientemente internacionalista de la Revolución en cuanto a la cultura y al esfuerzo intelectual. Cuba es, pues, un importante centro para congresos internacionales, simposios y ferias para participantes de varios negocios y actividades profesionales, todos con servicio de traducción e interpretación dotado oficialmente. La agencia de noticias Prensa Latina, con base en La Habana y fundada en 1959, es otro ejemplo de esta escrupulosa atención a la traducción: aunque su interés principal es Latinoamérica, la página web de la agencia se puede consultar en español, italiano, portugués o inglés. En general, el considerable grado de organización en el área de traducción refleja tanto el relativo alto estatus dado a la traducción e interpretación como opción de carrera, como la amplia tendencia cubana a supervisar centralizadamente y absorber a los profesionales en las instituciones oficiales en todas las áreas. Casi todos los traductores e intérpretes cubanos siguen este sistema universitario y hacen sus prácticas en la Escuela Superior de Traductores e Intérpretes (ESTI), una entidad nacional que sirve de enlace entre los profesionales y los clientes que requieren sus servicios y que tiene programas y materiales integrados de capacitación tales como glosarios especializados y bases de datos para su personal interno. La gran mayoría de los traductores profesionales son miembros de la Asociación Cubana de Traductores e Intérpretes (ACTI). Los traductores literarios, que aun en países más grandes y con una economía más fuerte casi nunca se asocian formalmente con sus colegas, pueden también tener una membresía honoraria de un gremio especializado afiliado a la Unión Nacional de Escritores y Artistas Cubanos (UNEAC).

LOS ESTUDIOS DE TRADUCCIÓN Y EL CARIBE

El campo de los "Estudios de Traducción" ha progresado rápidamente desde que se estableció en los años 70, generando un crecimiento particularmente veloz en los últimos 10 o 15 años con nuevas aproximaciones y enlaces con otras disciplinas. Antes de los años 70, había una fuerte tendencia a percibir la traducción exclusivamente desde el punto de vista de la lingüística, donde los teóricos intentaban clasificar los "cambios" que ocurrían en el proceso de traducción de una lengua a otra, o establecer varios tipos de **equivalencia** que las traducciones deben buscar o producir. En los años 70 y 80, los teóricos de la traducción buscaban abrir las perspectivas de la disciplina proponiendo teorías funcionales que explicaban la práctica y los procesos de traducción en términos del *propósito* de la traducción. Desde la década del 90, los traductólogos han intentado contextualizar incluso más el proceso de producir y evaluar las traducciones por medio del examen de las relaciones de poder que llevan a encargar la traducción de ciertos textos pero no de otros, y de la interpretación de las estrategias utilizadas por los traductores en términos de esta relación de poder. En los últimos tiempos, esta preocupación por el efecto de las relaciones de poder en la producción de traducciones y la forma en que se producen se ha extendido a estudios de la práctica de la traducción y sus relaciones con fuentes específicas de desigualdad de poder, como las que se presentan en las sociedades coloniales y postcoloniales, o con relación a temas de género.

A través de su evolución, se ha tendido a pasar de enfoques prescriptivos que presuponían que había una forma "correcta" de traducir cierto texto, a indagaciones descriptivas de por qué y cómo se producen las traducciones y el espectro de posibles opciones que posee el traductor dependiendo de la función de la traducción, las presiones impuestas durante el proceso por varias figuras de poder (autores, agentes, editores, críticos literarios, la academia, grandes empresas, u otras instituciones que encargan las traducciones), y la ideología del traductor (entre otros factores). En el contexto de este manual, todo esto pareciera dejar abierta la principal pregunta pragmática que interesa al traductor en formación: ¿cómo debo traducir si quiero que mi trabajo sea profesionalmente aceptable? La respuesta provista por la base teórica esbozada arriba es que el traductor debería ser tan consciente como le fuera posible de todos los factores que condicionan y están integrados en el proceso de producir un texto meta dado a partir de cierto texto de partida. Por lo tanto, si bien los comentarios sobre traducciones específicas propuestos en este manual clasifican tipos de procesos de traducción de acuerdo con la terminología lingüística creada a finales de los 50 (pero que se utiliza ampliamente en la actualidad), nos hemos esforzado en la medida de lo posible en prestar la merecida atención al contexto en el que la traducción se ha producido, y a las implicaciones ideológicas que tienen tanto el contexto como el texto meta resultante.[6] Esto no excluye un enfoque que intenta ser predominantemente pragmático y vocacional cuando es necesario: cuando parece que se pueden inferir nociones prescriptivas, esto se debe en general a que las *expectativas* dominantes en el mundo comercial de la traducción dicen que cierto enfoque o solución probablemente debería usarse. Por ejemplo, en el capítulo sobre cine afirmamos que el subtitulador experto "debe evitar que los subtítulos sigan pasando cuando hay un cambio de ángulo de la cámara o que se revele información antes de que se introduzca de manera visual en la versión original". Resulta evidente que los subtituladores competentes a veces pueden decidir no respetar ambas normas porque otras exigencias así lo determinan: el traductor o traductora en formación puede, por supuesto, sentirse libre de transgredir, traducir "contra la corriente", si se siente motivado o motivada a hacerlo; el objetivo es sencillamente cultivar la máxima conscientización de cómo y cuándo estamos siendo transgresivos.

Sin embargo, debemos hacer énfasis en que este manual no pretende promover el conocimiento de ningún enfoque teórico a la traducción aplicándolo al contexto caribeño. Dada la coexistencia en la región de sociedades coloniales y postcoloniales y la complejidad lingüística, político-social e ideológica que esto acarrea, aplicar los enfoques recientes a la traducción como las teorías postcoloniales o las de "polisistemas" sería sin duda enriquecedor para las teorías, por un lado, y por el otro, de modo más general, para la comprensión contemporánea del Caribe. Hasta el momento en que tal obra se pueda contemplar, el objetivo un poco más humilde de este manual es contribuir a los presentes esfuerzos por comenzar a "trazar el mapa" de un corpus de estudios caribeños de la traducción que incorpore aspectos teóricos y prácticos de toda la región.

CONCEPTOS Y ESTRATEGIAS DE TRADUCCIÓN UTILIZADOS EN ESTE MANUAL

A lo largo del manual, el usuario se encontrará con una serie de términos en negrita que están relacionados con la traducción, aunque algunos de ellos hayan surgido de disciplinas afines. De hecho, la traducción es considerada hoy en día una interdisciplina que se nutre del estudio comparado de lenguas, la estilística comparada, la lingüística, los estudios culturales, la textolingüística, la sociolingüística y la terminología, entre otras, a la vez que proporciona nuevas visiones a dichas disciplinas. Los términos en negrita aparecen explicados en el glosario, al final del libro. Sin embargo, aquí presentaremos los más relevantes, de modo que el lector pueda armarse un marco teórico que le ayude a comprender la actividad traductora. Los alcances de este manual no nos permiten ser exhaustivos, pero el lector curioso puede consultar la bibliografía o la página web donde encontrará más referencias sobre los temas que aquí tratamos.

Cuando se recibe un texto para ser traducido, por lo general lo primero que el traductor hace es leerlo en su totalidad. El texto, sin importar su longitud es, pues, la unidad de traducción. Al leerlo, y con ayuda de la información que nos da el cliente, vemos de qué **tipo textual** se trata, analizamos si es un artículo científico o periodístico, o si es un contrato o un anuncio publicitario. No debemos olvidar que los **tipos textuales** no son excluyentes. Puede haber, por ejemplo, un artículo periodístico que trate un descubrimiento científico. Ciertas expresiones, palabras y estructuras nos ayudan a ver con qué clase de texto estamos trabajando. Analizamos la **coherencia** o cómo se relacionan las partes conceptualmente y la **cohesión**, es decir, cómo se relacionan unas partes del texto con otras (mediante marcas cohesivas como "además", "sin embargo", "éste", etc.). Analizamos también la **densidad informativa** o **concisión**, es decir qué relación hay entre la cantidad de palabras utilizadas y la cantidad de información que se da. Vemos también si el texto hace referencia directa o indirecta a otros textos (**intertextualidad**). Éstos y otros conceptos han sido adaptados de la textolingüística. Una vez leído y analizado el texto, pasamos a buscar textos similares en nuestra lengua (**inmersión textual**). El análisis contrastivo de los tipos textuales nos sirve para familiarizarnos con la terminología y la estructura general de los textos en un par de lenguas, que no siempre se corresponden.

Los textos se producen en un contexto y con un fin específico y la traducción tiene en cuenta estos elementos. A través del estudio sociolingüístico y funcional (**skopos**) de los textos podemos examinar quién creó el texto, en qué contexto y con qué fin. Encontraremos marcas que nos ayudarán a localizar el **registro social** o **sociolecto**. Con éste podemos determinar si el texto pertenece a un **dialecto**, si tiene elementos particulares que lo doten de alto prestigio (**acrolectal**) o si tiene marcas de conciencia de genero (**generolectal**). Por lo general, identificamos los textos con el habla de un grupo especializado (en términos de **tecnolecto** o **jergas,** por ejemplo). Nuestro cliente nos dará pistas sobre la función que tendrá nuestra traducción y esto a la vez nos ayudará a decidir cómo tratar estos elementos sociolingüísticos.

Una vez terminado este proceso previo podemos empezar a traducir. Algunos teóricos de la traducción han intentado describir y esquematizar los procedimientos utilizados por los traductores para lograr sus versiones. Quizás la aproximación más reconocida ha sido la de los autores franceses Jean-Paul Vinay y Jean Darbelnet, quienes establecieron siete procedimientos de traducción. Los autores los dividieron en dos grupos: los procedimientos de traducción directos y los oblicuos.

Los directos son el **préstamo**, el **calco** y la **traducción literal**. El **préstamo** supone que el traductor ha tomado una expresión de la LO y la ha trasvasado tal cual en el TM. Este procedimiento se utiliza generalmente cuando la expresión aún no existe en la LM o ésta hace referencia a costumbres u objetos exclusivos o provenientes de la cultura origen. Algunos ejemplos de palabras que por lo general se prestan en el par inglés-español son whisky (a pesar de que la Real Academia Española de la Lengua propone güisqui), happening, roti, tango o fiesta latina.

El siguiente procedimiento es el **calco**. Esta vez se toma prestada la composición de los elementos de la LO y se cambian por los de la LM. Así, podemos decir que *Governor General* es un **calco** de "Gobernador General", o "balompié" uno de *football*. Como se observa en este último ejemplo se ha descompuesto la palabra en sus dos componentes traduciéndolos por los preexistentes en español y manteniendo la estructura que es común en la LO pero no tanto en la LM. Algunos autores distinguen el **calco** del **préstamo** naturalizado. Para ellos este último se caracteriza por una asimilación fónica que conserva las bases de la LO: "fútbol" es un **préstamo** naturalizado de *football*.

El último de los procedimientos directos es la **traducción literal**. Algunos teóricos distinguen la traducción literal de la traducción palabra por palabra, pero aquí no trataremos esta distinción. La **traducción literal** es uno de los procedimientos que se utilizan con más frecuencia, pero hay que tener en cuenta que no siempre es factible usarlo, ya que las lenguas poseen diferencias estructurales y semánticas. *Three men came running* se traduce literalmente sin problemas por "Tres hombres vinieron corriendo". Pero *The Caribbean is seen as a safer choice than Europe,* por ejemplo, puede ser traducido palabra por palabra como "El Caribe es visto como una más segura elección que Europa". El contenido se entiende, pero estilísticamente deja mucho que desear. En primer lugar, hay divergencias en la posición de los adjetivos en inglés y español (*safer choice* frente a "elección más segura"); en segundo lugar, *choice* en este contexto puede querer decir "destino" (lo que nos recuerda que el significado de las palabras está ampliamente ligado al contexto). Por último, el español prefiere, en estos casos, la construcción con "se" a la voz pasiva ("es visto" frente a "se ve"). Una versión menos literal puede ser: "el Caribe se considera un destino más seguro que Europa".

Como se puede observar, es necesario realizar una serie de cambios a diversos niveles (léxico, sintáctico, gramatical, semántico, pragmático, etc.) para obtener una versión que pueda ser considerada natural, a la vez que estilística y pragmáticamente equivalente en la LM. Cuando la traducción literal no basta para lograr estos objetivos, se presentan los procedimientos oblicuos de traducción. Para Vinay y Darbelnet, éstos son: la **transposición**, la **modulación**, la **equivalencia** y la **adaptación**.

La **transposición** consiste en cambiar una parte del discurso (una categoría gramatical) por otra, manteniendo el contenido semántico principal de la expresión. Los autores distinguen entre la **transposición** facultativa y la obligatoria. La obligatoria ocurre cuando no es posible hacer una traducción literal al no existir una estructura idéntica en la LO y la LM, por ejemplo en el caso del cambio singular a plural: *furniture* > "muebles"; con el pronombre *it* en frases como *it was raining* > "llovía"; o con el artículo neutro como sujeto: "lo importante del acuerdo . . . " > *What is important about the agreement . . . / The important thing about the agreement . . . .* La traducción facultativa u opcional se presenta cuando aunque sea posible una traducción literal, las características estilísticas del texto transpuesto superen las de la traducción literal, como sucede con la posición de algunos adjetivos: *three little houses* > "tres pequeñas casas / tres casas pequeñas". Nótese que la posición de los adjetivos altera el estilo en las dos versiones del TM. Con otros adjetivos el autor no puede elegir: *The White House* > "La Casa Blanca". Algunos dialectos caribeños utilizan una estructura adjetival divergente de la estandarizada: *She white car = Her white car.*

La **modulación** se define como un cambio de punto de vista, es decir, proponer una misma realidad desde dos miradas diferentes. Si la **transposición** se basa en un cambio de categoría gramatical, la **modulación** lo hace en un cambio de categoría de pensamiento. Un ejemplo típico de **modulación** es el cambio de una frase negativa, por su opuesta positiva: *it's not difficult to get lost* > "es fácil perderse", o viceversa. Es importante notar que el significado primario se mantiene, aunque cambia la forma en que se expresa el evento. Otros tipos de **modulación** requieren cambios de un nombre abstracto por uno concreto, de la parte por el todo, de específico a general (*lion* > "felino"), de función a proceso, de animado a inanimado, o de metáfora a no metáfora.

El siguiente procedimiento es la **equivalencia**. Ésta se puede definir como la presentación de una expresión que surte un efecto similar en la L1 y la L2, sin utilizar necesariamente palabras que se correspondan una a una. El caso más común de equivalencias establecidas es el de la traducción de dichos populares, proverbios, onomatopeyas, y clichés: *Birds of a feather (flock together)* > "Dios los hace y ellos se juntan".

El último procedimiento que estudian los autores es la **adaptación**. En ocasiones algunos elementos de la cultura origen no son aceptados, compartidos o en ocasiones tan siquiera conocidos en la cultura meta, e introducirlos en nuestra traducción podría crear limitaciones a la lectura de un texto (el lector puede no encontrar sentido a lo que lee), o podría dar lugar a malentendidos. Al enfrentarse con elementos cargados culturalmente el traductor puede optar por traducir los elementos de modo que el lector se tenga que acercar a la cultura meta (**traducción extranjerizante**), o puede adaptar dichos elementos de modo que el texto se acerque al lector (**traducción domesticada**). En América Latina, por ejemplo, el deporte número uno es el fútbol o balompié, en el Caribe anglófono, predomina el críquet. Podemos imaginar una situación en que para denotar la alegría de un aficionado que ve a su equipo ganar, hayamos de cambiar en nuestro texto un deporte por el otro.

Otros autores han extendido la lista de procedimientos, incluyendo la **ampliación** que consiste en añadir información que no estaba en el TO, pero cuya inclusión mejora el entendimiento del TM (algunas veces se amplía en pie de página). El caso opuesto se denomina **omisión**. Parecida a la **ampliación** es la **explicitación**, que consiste en expresar directamente lo que el TO dejaba implícito. Este procedimiento es común cuando nos encontramos con expresiones culturalmente cargadas (**culture-bound**), o cuando el TO tiene cargas irónicas o satíricas que no son necesariamente captadas en la LM. En ocasiones cuando traducimos nos encontramos con que en nuestra versión hemos perdido parte del significado o fuerza funcional en un segmento del texto. Podemos recurrir a la **compensación**, es decir, intentar recuperar lo perdido en otra parte del texto o con métodos no usados en el TO. Por ejemplo, en la traducción de dialectos algunos traductores optan por traducir el dialecto por lengua estándar y añadir marcas como "dijo en dialecto claramente trinitario". Estos procedimientos están altamente ligados con la semántica. Dentro de esta disciplina se estudian las relaciones que se establecen entre las palabras de una lengua dada. Desde el punto de vista de la traducción, se pueden estudiar las diferencias en los campos semánticos existentes entre las lenguas. Además se puede estudiar el significado connotativo y denotativo de una palabra o un grupo de palabras. La **denotación** se refiere al significado básico de una palabra (el que por lo general aparece en los diccionarios); la **connotación** al significado añadido que ésta pueda tener (palabras que se asocian, por ejemplo, con el habla educada o con una región).

 A TRANSLATION MANUAL FOR THE CARIBBEAN (ENGLISH–SPANISH)
UN MANUAL DE TRADUCCIÓN PARA EL CARIBE (INGLÉS–ESPAÑOL)

A medida que avance en el manual, el lector se encontrará con éstos y otros términos y los ejemplos provistos ayudarán a una mejor comprensión de los mismos y de su utilidad para la actividad traductora.

CHAPTER 1

Tourism

INTRODUCTION

Translation students and practitioners in countries with developed tourist industries are frequently familiar with advertising in the sector and have keen sensibilities regarding appropriate tone and lexicon. Many Caribbean countries offer an abundance of freely available material (brochures, leaflets and promotional magazines) that can be used in preparation for translating to (re)familiarize oneself with the distinctive features of tourist advertising discourse in the target culture (hereafter this procedure will be referred to as **textual immersion**), and for reference during the translation process itself. As a sub-genre of advertising, the discourse of the tourist brochure fits into the category of prescriptive/persuasive rather than empirical/descriptive: its function is to persuade and seduce, rather than merely to inform. Translation of tourist discourse requires a subtle appreciation of appropriate use of the basic linguistic tools of the genre, such as vocative and exhortative locutions, cliché and hyperbole. Freedom to cultivate and use these expressive devices is frequently a liberating experience for the translator and particularly for the student, since they are discouraged in other types of discourse such as academic writing. More broadly, an awareness of culturally determined norms governing advertising discourse in particular societies is also required. More generally still, advertising for tourism inevitably raises the question of regional stereotyping. A useful exercise prior to **textual immersion** is to make a list of stereotypes that apply to the Caribbean region or to your country, if you are from the region, or of stereotypes held in your region or country about the Caribbean, if you are from outside it. As you familiarize yourself with the TL documentation you have gathered together, you can observe how it reflects, directly or indirectly, the list of stereotypes you have compiled. It will also help you to identify assumptions about the region of which you may have been unaware. Awareness of the stereotypes that frequently underlie texts in this genre may help to resolve issues of connotative meaning in the ST, which in turn will aid informed decision-making during the translation process.

Stylistically, the diversity of the tourist market provides interesting and subtle contrasts of **register** and tone: the "high-end" versus populist product, the hedonistic sun-and-sand holiday as against the "green" or "solidarity" tourist product. The frequency of colloquialism in tourist discourse often makes it gratifying to translate: as with cliché and hyperbole, the opportunity to take an excursion into the lower regions of societal and tonal **register** often makes a refreshing change for both the student and the professional translator. Grammatically, tourist discourse can be used to improve command of a number of common features of the genre: use of adjectives (tourist texts offer many good examples of descriptive versus restrictive positioning in Spanish); use of imperatives (the choice between *tú* and *usted* becomes crucial in this kind of discourse); phrasal verbs in English (the colloquial **register** supplies an abundance of these). As far as translation choices and procedures are concerned, the abundance of proper nouns and the frequency of wordplay or punning in tourist discourse offer the opportunity for translators and translation students to refine their skills in these areas.

INTRODUCCIÓN

Los estudiantes y profesionales de la traducción en países con industrias turísticas desarrolladas por lo general están familiarizados con la publicidad que se maneja en dicho sector y tienen sus sentidos muy agudos al momento de usar el tono y léxico apropiados. Muchos países caribeños ofrecen una gran cantidad de materiales que se consiguen gratuitamente (folletos, volantes y revistas promocionales). Ya sea como preparación para la traducción o como referencia durante el proceso mismo, estos materiales se pueden utilizar para (re)familiarizarse con las características específicas del discurso publicitario del turismo (nos referiremos a esta familiarización como **inmersión textual**). Al ser un subgénero de la publicidad, el discurso del folleto turístico se encuentra en la categoría de textos prescriptivos/persuasivos, más que en la de empíricos/descriptivos: tiene la función de persuadir y seducir, y no simplemente la de informar. La traducción del discurso del turismo requiere una apreciación aguda sobre las herramientas lingüísticas básicas de este género, como las locuciones vocativas y exhortativas, el cliché y la hipérbole. La posibilidad de adoptar y utilizar estos mecanismos expresivos constituye casi siempre una experiencia liberadora para el traductor y especialmente para el estudiante, ya que frecuentemente no son bien recibidos en otros tipos de discurso como el académico. En el plano general, se requiere ser consciente de las normas culturales que gobiernan el discurso publicitario en una sociedad determinada. En un plano aun más general, la publicidad del turismo inevitablemente plantea el tema del estereotipo regional. Un ejercicio que se puede realizar antes de la **inmersión textual** es hacer una lista de los estereotipos que se aplican a la región caribe o a su país, si se es de la región, o de los estereotipos que se tienen en su país sobre el Caribe, si no se proviene de él. Al familiarizarse con los textos en la LM que se han recopilado, observará cómo se reflejan, directa o indirectamente, estos estereotipos. También le ayudarán a identificar los supuestos acerca de la región de los que usted tal vez no se había percatado. Ser consciente de los estereotipos que subyacen a los textos de este género puede ayudar a solucionar problemas de significado connotativo en el TO, lo que a la vez servirá para tomar una decisión bien fundada durante el proceso de traducción.

Estilísticamente, la diversidad del mercado del turismo presenta contrastes interesantes y sutiles en el **registro** y el tono: el producto dirigido a las "altas esferas" en oposición al producto populista; las vacaciones hedonistas de "sol y playa" contra el producto turístico "ecológico" y "solidario". Es gratificante traducir este tipo de discurso debido a la gran cantidad de coloquialismos: como sucede con el cliché y la hipérbole, la oportunidad de adentrarse en los terrenos más bajos del **registro** social y tonal constituye un cambio refrescante para el estudiante y el profesional de la traducción.

Pasando al plano gramatical, el discurso del turismo se puede utilizar para mejorar el dominio de varias características en este aspecto: uso de adjetivos (los textos del turismo ofrecen buenos ejemplos de la posición descriptiva en oposición a la restrictiva de los adjetivos en español), el uso de los imperativos (la elección entre "tú" y "usted" resulta crucial en este tipo de discurso), los verbos con partículas en inglés (el **registro** coloquial ofrece una gran cantidad de ellos). En lo que respecta a los procedimientos y decisiones en la traducción, la gran cantidad de nombres propios y juegos de palabras o albures en el discurso turístico ofrece una oportunidad para que los traductores y estudiantes de traducción refinen sus habilidades en estas áreas.

I. SPANISH > ENGLISH

Text 1

Bus Turístico Vaivén
Un encuentro con La Habana[1]
El bus turístico Vaivén le permite recorrer La Habana de oeste a este, y viceversa. Desde la Villa Panamericana hasta el Hotel Las Praderas, viva los mayores encantos de la capital, incluyendo la famosa ceremonia del cañonazo.

Usted lo reconocerá muy pronto, pues en su diseño sobresalen imágenes de los principales sitios de interés capitalinos.

Disfrute de este interesante paseo con un solo ticket, válido por todo el día, que se adquiere en los buróes de turismo de Rumbos Cuba o en el propio ómnibus. Otra de sus ventajas es que puede abordarlo dondequiera que lo vea.

Bus turístico Vaivén, un servicio del Grupo de Recreación y Turismo Rumbos.

Para cualquier información contáctenos a través de los teléfonos . . .

Class Translation

[a.]The Vaivén Tour Bus
[b.]Rendezvous with Havana
The Vaivén Tour Bus [c.]**takes you on a journey through the ins and outs of Havana,** from the Villa Panamericana to the Hotel Las Praderas and back again, and gives you the opportunity to experience the most appealing features the capital has to offer, including the famous gun-salute ceremony or *cañonazo*.

[d.]**Look out for** our distinctive bus, colourfully decorated with images of Havana's most attractive locations.

Enjoy this [e.]**exciting ride** with just one ticket, which is valid for the whole day and can be bought from the Rumbos Cuba Tourist Offices or [f.]**on the bus itself.** [g.]**Another plus** is that you can board wherever you see the bus.

The Vaivén Tour Bus is provided by the Rumbos Tourism Recreational Group.

[h.]**For further information** call us at . . .

Commentary

Though the tone of this advertisement is less hyperbolic than many such texts, it nonetheless clearly aims to persuade or seduce the potential customer, as well as to inform. Despite the directness of the imperatives, the **register** is fairly high, in accordance with the relatively high-cultural nature of the product (the use of *usted*, *adquirir* rather than *comprar*, *contactar* rather than *llamar*, for example). It is therefore a useful exercise in striking the balance between elegant expression and the direct, persuasive tone appropriate to an advertisement.

a. The Vaivén Tour Bus Both "shuttle" and "coach" were considered, but ultimately it was felt "bus" had greater affinity with "tour".

b. Rendezvous with Havana The romantic and somewhat sophisticated associations of the Gallicism "rendezvous", while perhaps less forceful in the ST, seem to fit both the high-cultural nature of the product and the overall reputation of Havana as a romantic destination. "A Date with Havana" was rejected as too prosaic, while "A Havana Encounter" was preferred as an alternative to the confrontational-sounding "An Encounter with Havana".

c. takes you on a journey through the ins and outs of Havana This idiomatic formula was preferred to a more literal rendering because the ST's real purpose here is to explain the name *"Bus Turístico Vaivén"* (*bus que va y viene de vuelta*). Since the Spanish name is retained in the TT, this pun is lost and the tour's precise trajectory from east to west and back becomes less important (this factor also made elision of the first two sentences advisable). The idiom used gives a suitable impression of comprehensive coverage of the city. An even more colloquial – perhaps hyperbolic – formula suggested was "from the Villa Panamericana to the Hotel Las Praderas, experience the capital's greatest thrills . . .".

d. Look out for Retaining the ST's second-person future tense would have sounded stilted here in English. The imperative accords better with the overall tone of the ST and is an example of the principle of **compensation**, since an imperative had been eliminated in the first sentence (*viva los encantos*). The addition of "distinctive" and "colourfully" are examples of **amplification**, a device commonly used in translation of advertising material. An alternative formula suggested was "decorated with images of the capital's main places of interest, the bus is instantly recognizable".

e. exciting ride The chosen epithet sits more naturally with the noun than the immediate English cognate here, though some found it hyperbolic or misleading given the historical and informative content of the tour. The intensified "fascinating" was still felt preferable to "interesting", however, which was felt to be too bland in English.

f. on the bus itself The ST's use of the term *ómnibus* offers an opportunity to review the vast number of possible terms for different types of bus or public transport in Latin America and the Caribbean: *autobús, buseta, camello, camión, colectivo, guagua, micro, ómnibus*; ZR van, route taxi, maxi-taxi. Some of these terms are highly location-specific (or **culture-bound**) and would thus have to be used with caution.

g. Another plus More colloquial than the ST, but a common idiom in advertising and tourist discourse. The opening "what's more, . . ." was also considered, but rejected as over-emphatic in the context.

h. For further information As with the greeting or valediction in a letter, this is a formulaic rendering that rounds off the advertisement in a satisfying manner by meeting the reader's expectations about the way to end a text of this kind.

Text 2

Dominicana con todo[2]

Uno de los destinos más solicitados del Caribe es sin duda República Dominicana, entre otras cosas por sus playas paradisíacas, pero también por su famosa y difundida música típica: el merengue. Si a estas dos bondades se agrega el beneficio de no tener que ocuparse de gastos menores durante la estancia en esas tierras, entonces el éxtasis es completo.

Con este propósito, Iberojet y Aserca Airlines anunciaron dos ofertas con todo incluido en los hoteles contemplados en el programa: Iberostar Dominicana y Bávaro Resort, justamente ubicados en la playa que lleva este nombre, en la región de Punta Cana. En el primero de los hoteles el precio por persona en habitación doble es de 363 dólares con todas las comidas y bebidas nacionales, mientras en Iberostar Bávaro Resort es de 311 dólares, con acceso a media pensión (desayunos y cenas).

Los precios incluyen además del boleto aéreo, 4 días y 3 noches de alojamiento, traslados hotel-aeropuerto, impuestos hoteleros y todas las delicias de dos hospedajes cinco estrellas.

Para información adicional sobre otras opciones de alojamiento, ☎:

Published Translation

[a.]**Dominican with everything**

One of the most [b.]**sought-after destinations** in the Caribbean is no doubt the Dominican Republic, which is famous for, among other things, its [c.]**extraordinary beaches** and [d.]**well-known merengue, the country's widely popular, typical music.** [e.]**If you add to these two** [f.]**blessings, the benefit of not having to worry about minor expenses during your stay** [g.]**in that land, then** [h.]**your ecstasy will be complete.**

[i.]**With this purpose in mind,** Iberojet and Aserca Airlines have advertised [j.]**2 special offers with everything included** in the hotels mentioned in the program. The hotels – Iberostar Dominicana and Bavaro Resort – are both located on the beach bearing the same name, in the Punta Cana region. At Iberostar Dominicana, the price per person in double rooms is $363 with all meals and local beverages included; while at the Iberostar Bavaro Resort the rate is $311 including breakfast and dinner only. The rates also include the air ticket, 4 days and 3 nights' accommodation, hotel-airport transfer, hotel taxes, and all the delights of accommodation in a five-star hotel.

[k.]**For additional information on additional accommodation options, please** ☎:

For an alternative version of the TT, see
http://www.caribbeantranslationmanual.com/tourism.html

Commentary

Like TT 1, this text exhibits typical characteristics of tourist advertising discourse, combining to-the-point commercial information with hyperbole and cliché.

Where a published translation was discussed and alternatives suggested in the classroom, as here, local pressures on both the translation industry and the individual translator should always be borne in mind. In the case of a translation published in a magazine in a country such as the Dominican Republic, factors such as tight submission deadlines, limited access to training for local translators, dearth of affordable TL native-speaker translators and style correctors, and generally exiguous resources for ensuring quality control, should be set against any perceived deficiencies.

a. Dominican with everything The suggestion of a pun in the title, playing on *Dominicana* as the name of the country or as "a Dominican girl", is inevitably lost here. The glance at "*[República] Dominicana con todo [incluido]*" could have been at least partially reproduced, however, by "Dominican All In", which also has an internal assonance that adds catchiness.

b. sought-after destinations "Popular" was felt to be more a natural companion for the noun here.

c. extraordinary beaches "Unspoilt beaches" was felt to be an improvement on the published TT. As suggested in the introduction, while cliché may be discouraged in academic composition in the native language, it is frequently a necessary component of translation in advertising discourse. Sensitivity to the use of cliché in the SL, and the ability to use it judiciously in the TL, therefore need to be cultivated.

d. well-known merengue . . . music Though it can be argued that *famosa* and *difundida* express slightly different ideas in the ST, the inclusion of both "well-known" and "widely popular" comes across as tautological in the TT. Either "famous" or "well-known" on its own was preferred.

e. If you add . . . will be complete In the ST, the impersonality supplied by the pronominal verbs and definite article ("*el éxtasis*") is regarded as elegant and does not seem excessively detached and thus might arguably befit a "top end" tourist product such as a five-star hotel. Avoiding all personalization in English would seem forced, however, particularly since English tolerates this device to a high degree in tourist and advertising discourse (perhaps because no choice regarding formal or familiar address has to be confronted). While some form of direct address seemed appropriate, it was felt that the published TT's three personal pronouns generated excessive familiarity.

f. blessings This strikes an oddly religious note in English. "Attractions" was preferred.

g. in that land It was felt that **omission** was the best strategy for adapting this over-literal rendering.

h. your ecstasy will be complete This discordantly hyperbolic, literal translation was toned down by employing an appropriate cliché: "a perfect vacation is assured".

i. With this purpose in mind Modification of this somewhat laboured conjunctive clause to the much more direct "that's why. . ." improves flow. Elimination of the paragraph break is a natural consequence of this modification.

j. 2 special offers with everything included The context-specific term "all-inclusive" is clearly required here.

k. For additional information . . . please The repetition of "additional" is infelicitous here. Use of the formulaic "for further information. . ." as with the translation of Text 1, rounds off the TT in a satisfyingly predictable manner.

El Caribe de Guatemala[3]

El gran lago de Izabal, el mayor de Guatemala con 590 kilómetros cuadrados, es un enorme espejo de aguas bordeado de huertas de mangos, aguacates, mameyes y piñas que perfuman los aires con olores exóticos. De sus aguas profundas nace el río Dulce, que se aleja presuroso para zambullirse en la selva tupida. Allá en la jungla serpentea y suavemente se desliza entre meandros selváticos al son del griterío de los multicolores pájaros ribereños que sacuden el follaje. El río sigue su paso para ensancharse de gozo y selva y formar el Golfete ... A su vez, el río Dulce se peina las aguas en los manglares llenos de vida y se funde amoroso con las aguas de la bahía de Amatique, frente al mar Caribe.

Aquí, en el Caribe guatemalteco, entre palmeras de cocos que se mecen seductoras ante la línea suave de la costa, frente a un mar azul, se alza el pueblito de Livingston. Sus casas están llenas de sabor marino y de pan de coco. En Livingston, los viajeros sienten el saludo puro del sol y la caricia rejuvenecedora del mar, mientras hunden sus pies descalzos en la arena de conchas y caracolas quebradas, al ritmo cadencioso que cantan los afrocaribes bajo la enramada de palma.

The Guatemalan Caribbean[4]

[a]The huge Lake Izabal, 590 square kilometers and Guatemala's largest, is flanked by orchards of mangoes, avocados, [b]mameyes and pineapples filling the air with exotic fragrances. [c]The Dulce river rises here, to go burbling off and lose itself in the thick jungle. There, it meanders lazily through the tropical growth to the screaming delight of the colourful winged inhabitants of the foliage along its banks. [d]The Dulce continues its course to form the Golfete . . . Finally, it passes mangrove thickets seething with life, and flows out to meet the waters of the Amatique Bay, in the Caribbean.

Here, on the blue Guatemalan Caribbean, beside a seductively swaying fringe of coconut palms, is the little town of Livingston. Its houses smell of the sea and coconut bread and **[e]you feel the closeness of the sun and are rejuvenated by the cool caress of the waves, as your bare feet sink into the sand between shells and broken conches, while behind you is the lilting rhythm of Afro-Cuban songs played under shady palms.**

Commentary

This extract from a Guatemala Tourist Board leaflet promoting the Central American country's natural attractions focuses on its easternmost region, which includes a stretch of Caribbean coastline. The description moves geographically from west to east, and as it does so shifts from evocations of the natural exuberance of the jungle to a description of a Caribbean coastal town, with its inevitable palms and musical accompaniment. It is clear from the exoticizing invocation of these tropical commonplaces that the text is principally intended for prospective tourists from outside the region.

Typically in this area of discourse, particularly in Spanish, the ST style tends towards hyperbole, using a variety of metaphorical devices, especially personification or animation of inanimate natural phenomena (the river, the sun and the sea). The translator opts to reduce the density of metaphor, "flattening" the language or making it more prosaic in order to avoid an excessively convoluted or self-consciously literary TT. Strategies of **modulation** and **omission**, particularly, are used to this end. Simplification of metaphors or reorganization of their elements (a form of **modulation**) is a common procedure in translation generally, because the metaphorical dynamics of languages differ (thus, for obvious reasons, it is logical that the verb *torear* (lit. "to cape/fight a bull") can be used to mean "to dodge, sidestep, deal with someone skilfully" in Spanish, but not in other languages). Outright **omission**, however, is often not an option when translating genuinely literary texts such as novels or, particularly, poems, since specific metaphors form the substance of literary discourse, rather than merely constituting a conventional feature of style whose degree of incidence may vary from language to language, as in this instance.

a. The huge Lake Izabal . . . is flanked by The first instance of **omission**, as the ST offers no equivalent for the metaphor *"es un enorme espejo de aguas"*.

b. mameyes The retention of the Spanish plural suffix (as opposed to "mameys") is probably an oversight, though the translator may have deliberately chosen to reproduce the Spanish form for exotic effect, reasoning that most of the target readership would not recognize the English name either. The edible fruit of the mamey tree is also commonly known as the mammee (or mammy) apple in the anglophone Caribbean, but this name would also have left the great majority of readers in the anglophone world beyond the Caribbean none the wiser, as well as striking a dissonantly folksy note in its exotic surroundings.

c. The Dulce river rises here . . . along its banks The verb *nacer* is commonly used of rivers to mean "to rise, have its source", but here there is also a glance at its more general meaning, "to be born". It thus opens a sequence of verbs in the ST used to animate the river metaphorically, as if it were a living creature: it is born, it rushes away (*"se aleja presuroso"*) and it plunges into the jungle (*"para zambullirse en la selva"*). While the decision not to prioritize the metaphorical, animating character of the verbs in the TT is defensible for the reasons regarding metaphor suggested above, it can also be argued that the chosen equivalents "rise . . . burbling off and lose itself" rob the description of some dynamism.

In the following sentence the ST metaphorically equates the river to a snake: *"serpentea y suavemente se desliza"* ("snakes its way and softly slithers"). *Serpentear* is the common verb to describe the twisting course of a path or river in Spanish, just as English might have a river "snaking through the jungle". The translator may have reasoned, however, that even a metaphorical allusion to snakes in the jungle, however apposite, could be off-putting to many prospective visitors.

d. The Dulce continues its course to form the Golfete . . . the Amatique Bay, in the Caribbean The TT here sensibly omits the ST's highly figurative formula *"para ensancharse de gozo y selva"* ("before swelling with joy and jungle"). Equally, the wisdom of avoiding the personifications *"se peina las aguas"* and *"se funde amoroso"* can be easily appreciated by comparing the published TT with the excesses of a more literal rendering: "Finally, it combs its waters in the mangrove thickets seething with life, before merging lovingly with the waters of the Amatique Bay."

e. you feel the closeness of the sun . . . under shady palms The generally more familiar approach of tourist advertising in English is reflected by the TT's conventional use of direct address with the pronoun "you", as opposed to the ST's more discreet "travellers". The TT again opts to eliminate a personification, as the ST literally has the visitor "feeling the pure greeting of the sun", though the sea's "caress", a commonplace in both languages, is retained in the TT.

As well as eliminating personification, the TT also partially suppresses the only actual people present in this extract (it is, after all, an advertisement for Guatemala's natural, not human, resources), as the *afrocaribes* of the ST are transposed to an adjectival role describing the noun "songs". This is likely to have arisen from the frequently awkward necessity of adding a noun to the adjectival designation "Caribbean": though the terms "Caribbeans" and "Caribbeaners" have both been used, neither has general currency outside the region. Further complicating the issue is the use of *caribes*, as opposed to *caribeños*, possibly suggesting people of mixed African and Carib Indian descent ("Afro-Caribs" would perplex most tourists unfamiliar with the region). While the term "Afro-Caribbean" (or "Afro-Guyanese" etc.) is less problematic than "Afro-American" (now usually rejected in favour of "African American"), the translator may have reasoned that the need to specify the racial identity of the performers at all might seem dubious in English. Finally, the **explicitation** that the predominant musical style is "Afro-Cuban" is likely to be based on local knowledge.

II. INGLÉS > ESPAÑOL

Texto 1
Barbados

If you value traditional courtesies combined with a warm welcome from people who know how to have a good time, then Barbados is the place for you.

Come find an island steeped in history, with beaches that seem to never end, and discover some of the finest watersport opportunities in the Caribbean.

The island has its very own gold coast for swimmers, named after the fabulous sands. Visitors come from all over the world to take part in windsurfing, surfing and sailboarding competitions. Sports fans can also play golf and tennis and watch some of the world's best cricketers.

Published Translation
Barbados[5]

[a.]**Si usted valora la cortesía tradicional combinada con una cálida bienvenida** de unas gentes que saben mejor que nadie cómo divertirse, Barbados es el lugar indicado para usted.

[b.]**Tierra adentro encontrará una isla moderna con una apasionante historia.** En las costas, playas que parecen interminables, y un mar que le ofrece algunas de las mejores posibilidades del Caribe para practicar deportes acuáticos.

[c.]**La fabulosa calidad de la arena ha dado nombre a la costa dorada, el lugar ideal para practicar la natación.** A estas costas acuden visitantes procedentes de todo el mundo para participar en competiciones de windsurf, surf y vela. En la isla también podemos practicar golf y tenis y ver en acción a algunos de los mejores jugadores de cricket del mundo.

Visitors from Britain will find other reminders of home, from the wigs and robes worn in Parliament, to the statue of Nelson in Trafalgar Square. The architecture in the capital of Bridgetown and the second largest town, Speightstown, and names such as Brighton beach also offer many reminders of links between the two nations.

The biggest annual event in Barbados is the Crop Over Festival, celebrating the harvest of sugar cane, formerly the island's main industry. The five-week summer celebration is a fiesta of colourful floats, parades and people in costume dancing and enjoying themselves to the background of music and fireworks. It also offers the opportunity to taste the finest island cuisine, including the national dish of Flyingfish and Cou-cou. Everyone is encouraged to join in. Music lovers can hear the world's best artists at the annual Paint it Jazz festival.

Many of the grand homes built by the sugar kings are open to the public. Plantation mansions such as Sam Lord's Castle contain many of their original gilt and mahogany fittings. You can still see a working sugar plantation on Arbib Nature and Heritage Trail and all over the island you will find rolling green fields for a relaxed stroll.

If you prefer formal settings, there are the famous cliff-set Andromeda Gardens. The finest hotels are also positioned in beautifully planned tropical landscapes.

And if you're still raring to go when evening comes there is another Barbados of waterfront restaurants, nightlife, music, gaming – and more than 1,000 rum shops to consider.

[d.]**Los visitantes procedentes de Gran Bretaña encontrarán muchas cosas que les recordarán a su país, desde las pelucas y túnicas de los parlamentarios,** hasta la estatua de Nelson en la Plaza de Trafalgar. La arquitectura de Bridgetown, la capital, y de Speightstown, la segunda ciudad de la isla, y nombres como la playa de Brighton también constituyen claros recuerdos de los lazos que unen a estas dos naciones. Los isleños celebran el Festival anual de la cosecha de la caña de azúcar, que antiguamente era la principal industria de la isla. [e.]**Esta celebración se extiende a lo largo de cinco semanas durante el verano,** con gran diversidad de vistosos desfiles, cabalgatas y bailes de disfraces, además de música y fuegos artificiales. [f.]**También constituye una ocasión ideal para probar** la mejor cocina de la isla, incluyendo el plato nacional, el Pez Volador y "Cou-cou". Todos están invitados a participar. Los amantes de la música podrán escuchar a los [g.]**mejores músicos de jazz** del mundo en el festival anual Paint it Jazz.

[h.]**Muchas de las grandes mansiones construidas por los magnates del azúcar** están abiertas al público. Algunas de ellas, como el Castillo de Sam Lord, todavía conservan muchas de las decoraciones de oro y caoba originales. Aún es posible ver una plantación de azúcar en funcionamiento siguiendo la ruta del Arbib Nature and Heritage Trail, y en toda la isla [i.]**encontrará verdes campos** en los que pasear apaciblemente.

Si prefiere un ambiente más formal, [j.]**visite los famosos Jardines de Andrómeda, espectacularmente situados al borde de un acantilado.** Los mejores hoteles también están enclavados en hermosos paisajes tropicales.

Y si al caer la noche aún tiene ganas de nuevas emociones, existe otro Barbados de restaurantes situados a la orilla del mar, animada vida nocturna, música, juego... y más de 1.000 [k.]**ronerías.**

a. Si usted valora la cortesía tradicional combinada con una cálida bienvenida Aunque algunos anuncios utilizan la forma "tú", más familiar y cercana al destinatario buscando una relación relajada y amistosa, en este tipo de anuncios se prefiere la forma "usted" más formal y respetuosa. Esta elección resulta esencial debido al grupo de lectores-clientes al que va dirigido el anuncio y que en este caso se caracteriza por estar en la edad adulta y contar con recursos económicos suficientes para planear unas vacaciones en el Caribe. El texto comienza presentándole al lector ciertas cualidades que espera que se valoren y que hacen parte del estereotipo sobre las islas del Caribe. Aquí se utiliza el condicional aunque también existe la posibilidad de dirigirse mediante una pregunta, estrategia muy difundida en español para este **tipo textual** ("¿es usted de los que valoran la cortesía tradicional. . .? Si su respuesta es afirmativa, entonces Barbados. . .")

b. Tierra adentro encontrará una isla moderna con una apasionante historia El TO utiliza el imperativo *"Come find"*, la versión del TM prefiere dejarlo de lado debido a la formalidad que quiere preservar y a que en español es mucho más común el uso del futuro que del imperativo para lograr el efecto buscado. También, debido a que en el párrafo anterior se le dio prioridad a lo tradicional, la **ampliación** de "modernidad" causa problemas de **coherencia**. Por otro lado, lo moderno no hace parte de los estereotipos del Caribe a los que nos referimos en la introducción del capitulo, y ciertamente no se encuentra entre las prioridades del turista a quien va dirigido este texto.

c. La fabulosa calidad de la arena ha dado nombre a la costa dorada, el lugar ideal para practicar la natación El traductor ha decidido invertir el orden de la frase haciendo un cambio de sujeto y una **transposición** en el caso de *swimmers* > natación. También cabe mencionar que el nombre que recibe la playa no se debe a la calidad de la arena sino al alto costo de las viviendas de la zona: "costa de oro", más literal, mejora incluso la versión del TO. Pero la verdadera pregunta es si el traductor puede corregir, mediante la **omisión**, la **ampliación** o cualquier otro medio, la información poco precisa o errónea del TO.

d. Los visitantes procedentes de la Gran Bretaña encontrarán muchas cosas que les recordarán a su país desde las pelucas y túnicas de los parlamentarios Este segmento se aleja de la **traducción literal** considerando la cultura de la LM. El párrafo anterior culminaba con una referencia al críquet ("crícket" en la versión publicada). En el mundo anglófono *cricket* es una palabra culturalmente cargada, no necesariamente así en el mundo hispanohablante. También, la construcción *"worn in parliament"* se simplifica en español, pasando a ser directamente "de los parlamentarios". Este es un tipo de **modulación** que cambia el lugar por las personas que trabajan en él.

e. Esta celebración se extiende a lo largo de cinco semanas durante el verano En muchas ocasiones es preciso cambiar la categoría gramatical de un enunciado (**transposición**). Casi siempre esto obedece a la falta de correspondencia uno a uno entre las dos lenguas con las que se trabaja. El inglés en este caso tiene gran capacidad para crear una larga cadena de adjetivos que parecerían forzados en español.

f. También constituye una ocasión ideal para probar Este **tipo de texto** permite hacer uso de la **ampliación**. En este caso, "ideal" no aparece en el TO pero es un adjetivo que puede encontrarse en una gran variedad de contextos unido al sustantivo "ocasión". En semántica y otras disciplinas lingüísticas este fenómeno recibe el nombre de **colocación**.

g. los mejores músicos El TO contenía el término hiperónimo *artists*; el TM prefiere ser más específico. El caso contrario también se puede presentar (ir del término específico al general) por diversos motivos, entre ellos la censura o el grado de especialización de la audiencia al que va dirigido el texto. Otro ejemplo de **modulación**.

h. Muchas de las grandes mansiones construidas por los magnates del azúcar Es muy importante seleccionar el léxico que concuerde con el tono y la estructura de la LM. En el caso de "*grand homes*" se ha escogido la mejor opción ante "grandes casas" o "casonas".

i. Encontrará verdes campos Se presenta aquí el caso opuesto de la **ampliación**: la **omisión**. Cuando el texto está demasiado cargado de adjetivos que en realidad no añaden demasiado al contenido, éste es un mecanismo al cual recurrir.

j. visite los famosos jardines de Andrómeda, espectacularmente situados al borde de un acantilado Vimos antes algunas de las razones por las cuales se puede utilizar la **ampliación**. Otra razón es la falta de vitalidad en la que caería una **traducción literal** del TO. *Cliff-set* se pudo haber traducido como "situados al borde de un acantilado", pero la frase se quedaría en una mera descripción geográfica y no nos dice nada sobre la calidad de la localización. La versión en español devuelve la vitalidad casi cliché a este **tipo textual**.

k. ronerías El TO dictaba "*rum shops*". Al no tener un equivalente al español, se ha optado por usar un **calco**. Esta palabra pudo haber sido creada por el traductor, aunque dista mucho de ser una creación al azar. Se basa, como todos los **calcos**, en un análisis paradigmático para la creación de una nueva palabra, es decir en un análisis componencial interlingüístico que sigue el paradigma: *shop* = lugar donde se vende algo. Lugares donde se vende (y a veces se consume) algo: cafetería, panadería, heladería. Como se ve, el elemento en común es el sufijo "–ería" precedido por lo que allí se vende.

Para terminar, quisiéramos que el lector se fijara en la diversidad de extensión de los textos, donde el TM tiene casi un veinte por ciento más palabras que el TO. En el caso de una publicación en una página web esto no es necesariamente un problema, pero en ocasiones el traductor tiene que ceñirse a una extensión determinada, que se asemeje a la del TO, como cuando se publica el TO y el TM en las caras opuestas de un folleto.

Texto 2

The National Gallery of Jamaica
The Ultimate Visual Experience[6]

Many visitors to Jamaica miss out on what is certainly one of the island's most valuable treasures, the National Gallery of Jamaica. As the unofficial "cultural capital" of the Caribbean, Jamaica has produced a number of world-class artists that is quite disproportionate to its tiny size, and much of the region's best work is housed here.

The Gallery is located in the Roy West Building on Kingston's Waterfront, a winding promenade lined with palm trees and caressed by gentle sea breezes. The entrance to the Gallery itself is located on Ocean Boulevard, and once inside, visitors are welcomed by an eight-foot bronze representation of Jamaican reggae singer Bob Marley emerging out of an elongated tree trunk, representative of the artist's growth from a seedling who never separates from his roots. Christopher Gonzales' Bob Marley is a dramatic foretaste of the many other masterpieces that make up the nation's collection of fine art further inside.

Although the Institute of Jamaica has maintained a collection of Jamaican art since the late nineteenth century, it was not until 1974 that the National Gallery was founded as a division of the Institute of Jamaica. The main functions of the Gallery are to acquire and preserve Jamaican and Caribbean art, to mount and exhibit local and international works and to research and record the history and progression of Jamaican art. Originally located inside Devon House, in up-town Kingston, the National Gallery was moved into its present location in 1982 and since then has grown in size and stature, to house over two thousand works today.

[a.]The National Gallery of Jamaica (La Galería Nacional de Jamaica)[7]

Muchos visitantes de la isla no llegan a conocer lo que es sin duda uno de los más valiosos tesoros de la isla, la National Gallery of Jamaica (la Galería Nacional de Jamaica). Siendo de forma no oficial "la capital cultural" del Caribe, Jamaica ha producido un número de artistas de talla mundial que no guarda proporción con el tamaño de la isla. [b.]**Gran parte de los mejores trabajos artísticos del área se encuentran en este recinto, localizado en el edificio Roy West** del malecón de Kingston, [c.]**paseo marítimo delineado con palmas y acariciado por la suave brisa del mar.** La entrada a la galería se encuentra en el lado de la calle Ocean Boulevard (Paseo del Océano), y una vez en su interior, los visitantes se encuentran con [d.]**una estatua de ocho pies (2.4 metros)** de bronce del cantante de música reggae Bob Marley brotando del largo tronco de un árbol, representando el desarrollo del artista desde su comienzo [e.]**como si fuera una semilla, y que nunca se separó de sus raíces.** El Bob Marley de Christopher Gonzáles es un conmovedor aperitivo para las muchas otras obras maestras que constituyen la colección nacional de bellas obras que se encuentran en el interior.

Aunque el Institute of Jamaica (Instituto de Jamaica) ha contado con una colección de arte jamaicano desde finales del siglo diecinueve, no fue hasta 1974 que se constituyó la galería nacional como una división del Instituto. Las funciones principales de la Galería son adquirir y preservar arte jamaicano y caribeño, [f.]**montar exposiciones y hacer exhibiciones** de trabajos nacionales e internacionales, e investigar y registrar la historia y progreso del arte jamaicano. En un principio la galería estuvo localizada dentro de la Devon House (Casa Devon), en el Kingston residencial, desde donde se trasladó a su presente ubicación en 1982 y desde entonces ha crecido el número de sus obras y su peso cultural, incluyendo hoy en día más de dos mil obras.

Comentarios

Este texto cae dentro de la categoría de textos turísticos ya que posee las mismas cualidades que los presentados hasta el momento: es apelativo al mencionar las virtudes de un lugar que se debe visitar, pero a la vez es altamente informativo, lo que nos recuerda que los textos rara vez pertenecen a un sólo **tipo textual**.

a. **The National Gallery of Jamaica (La Galería Nacional de Jamaica)** El traductor ha decidido mantener el nombre original y agregar una traducción entre paréntesis. Esta estrategia se mantiene a lo largo del texto: "la calle Ocean Boulevard (Paseo del Océano)", "el Institute of Jamaica (Instituto de Jamaica)", "la Devon House (Casa Devon)". En los casos en los que el nombre en inglés aparece formando parte de una frase, se incluye el artículo definido que correspondería si la palabra estuviera en español. Este mecanismo es muy útil para transmitir al lector del TM información literal del TO. En este **tipo de texto** conviene usarlo la primera vez que se menciona un nombre pero si éste se repite se debe elegir entre dejar la versión inglesa o la española ya que de otro modo la **densidad informativa** se reduce y la lectura se vuelve tediosa y el texto redundante.

b. **Gran parte de los mejores trabajos artísticos . . . en el edificio Roy West** Se decidió reorganizar los contenidos de los dos párrafos del TO en uno sólo en el TM. También a nivel de la frase se ve un cambio en las relaciones. En el TO se separan las obras que están en la galería de su ubicación, el TM prefiere unir esta información en una sola frase.

c. **paseo marítimo delineado con palmas y acariciado por la suave brisa del mar** Ésta es una frase típica en la que los estereotipos de los que se habló en la introducción se reproducen.

d. **una estatua de ocho pies (2.4 metros)** En ocasiones donde las unidades de medida no concuerdan entre la cultura origen y la cultura meta la decisión del traductor depende de si prefiere hacer una **traducción domesticada** o una **traducción foránea**. En el caso de la domesticada el traductor tendrá en cuenta ante todo la cultura meta con lo cual omitirá o adaptará aquella información que sea relevante sólo para la cultura origen. En el caso que nos compete, las medidas en pies no son muy comunes en los países de habla hispana, en los que se usa el sistema decimal. Un traductor que quisiera domesticar su traducción simplemente mencionaría la medida utilizando el equivalente en metros. De otro lado, un traductor que quiera dar énfasis al carácter foráneo del texto podría omitir la información sobre el sistema decimal. Una posición intermedia es la representada por este ejemplo en el que los dos sistemas conviven al igual que sucede en el caso de los nombres de los lugares turísticos traducidos entre paréntesis.

e. **como si fuera una semilla, y que nunca se separó de sus raíces** En este caso el traductor ha optado por convertir una metáfora en un símil. Esta decisión, si bien no afecta mucho el contenido del texto, representa una extensión del mismo. El lenguaje poético se mezcla con el informativo y el apelativo. Ver comentarios al texto 3 Spanish>English de este capítulo.

f. **montar exposiciones y hacer exhibiciones** El lector hispano encontrará reforzada esta construcción. Cuando se monta una exposición necesariamente es para exhibirla. Se cae aquí en mantener la literalidad del TO aunque la traducción resulte redundante. Para solucionar este y otros problemas relacionados con la interferencia de la LO una etapa necesaria en la traducción es dejar reposar el texto traducido durante algún tiempo y luego volver a él y leerlo como si se tratara de un TO, y de ser posible lograr que alguien más haga una prueba de lectura del mismo.

Texto 3

Health Tourism[8]	**Turismo de salud[9]**

Health and tourism share a number of relationships. The taking of waters at mineral spas and hot springs has occurred since Roman times and the "taking to the waters" of the elites of 17th-Century Europe provided one of the foundations for the modern pleasure resort concept. In addition, the use of travel to improve an individual's health, for instance, through cruising or a change in climate has long been a motive for travel. However, with an increasingly health and fitness conscious western society, health tourism has developed as a small, yet extremely significant special interest market segment in some countries.

Health tourism has been defined by the United Nations *"as the provision of health facilities utilizing the natural resources of the country in particular, mineral water and climate."*

There are five (5) components of the health tourism market with each identifying a more specific segment.

1) Sun and fun activities
2) Engaging in healthy activities, but health is not the central motive (adventure and sports tourism activities such as hiking, cycling or golf).
3) Principal motive to travel is health (e.g., a sea cruise, or travel to a different climate)

4) Travel for sauna, massage and other health activities (spa resort)
5) Medical treatment.

La salud y el turismo comparten una serie de relaciones. [a.]**El uso del agua minerales en spas y cálidos manantiales** proviene de la época de los romanos y la "[b.]**ingestión de aguas**" de las élites europeas del [c.]**siglo XVII**, como fundamento de uno de los conceptos modernos de instalaciones de lujo. Además, los traslados por razones individuales de salud, por ejemplo, en busca de cambios climáticos, han sido motivo de viajes desde antaño. Sin embargo, al incrementar la conciencia de bienestar y salud de la sociedad occidental, [d.]**el turismo de salud se ha desarrollado como un segmento de mercado reducido, pero de gran interés en muchos países.**

El turismo de salud ha sido definido por las Naciones Unidas "como la provisión de instalaciones de salud utilizando [e.]**recursos naturales del país en particular, agua mineral y clima.**"

Hay cinco (5) componentes en el mercado de turismo de salud dentro de los cuales se identifican segmentos de mercado aún más específicos.

1) Actividades de sol y diversión
2) Participación en actividades saludables, [f.]**aún no siendo la salud el motivo principal** (actividades de aventura y deportes como las caminatas, el ciclismo o el golf).
3) El motivo principal para viajar es la salud ([g.]**Vg. un crucero por el mar o viajes a diferentes climas**).
4) [h.]**Viajes por saunas, masajes y otras actividades de salud (spas).**
5) [i.]**Tratamientos médicos.**

For many years a number of European governments bore the costs of its domestic visitors to European spas stating it was a component of national health delivery. By the late 1980s most of these governments discontinued the practice of paying for these treatments as they sought to contain health service expenditure.

Durante muchos años los gobiernos europeos asumieron el gasto de los visitantes domésticos de los spas europeos indicando que constituían un componente en el [j]servicio de salud nacional. [k]A finales de los años '80 la mayoría de estos gobiernos descontinuaron la práctica del pago de estos tratamientos al pretender limitar los gastos por servicios de salud.

Comentarios

Este es un tipo especial de texto del subgénero de turismo. Al ser parte de un libro de enseñanza está lleno de terminología relacionada con este sector, además de ser de corte académico.

a. El uso del agua minerales en spas y cálidos manantiales Lo primero que nos choca es la falta de concordancia. Pero esto probablemente más que una falla de traducción es un error tipográfico. Por mucho que se revisen los textos, especialmente si hacen parte de un libro de la longitud del que nos ocupa, es muy común encontrarnos con este tipo de fallos. Los correctores ortográficos de los procesadores de palabras nos pueden ayudar, pero tampoco son perfectos. La revisión de estos aspectos generalmente no la hace el traductor, sino una persona especializada en este tipo de labor.

"Taking of waters" por su parte tiene un equivalente en español: "tomar las aguas". Esto se refiere a darse baños en aguas de manantiales minerales, y tanto en inglés como en español son expresiones anticuadas, pero no por eso impertinentes en el contexto. En el TO se produce una relación adjetivo-sustantivo entre *mineral* y *spas* relación que se establece en el TM entre "agua" y "minerales". Esto nos indica que se ha cambiado el significado de la frase. Otra opción para transmitir el contenido de la frase podría ser: "El uso en spas de aguas ricas / agua rica en minerales . . .". En cuanto a *"hot springs"* se ha hecho un **calco** poco afortunado pues como expresión compuesta se puede expresar en español como "aguas termales" o "termas".

b. ingestión de aguas Como se expresó en el punto anterior, *"taking to the waters"* no se refiere a ingerir agua, sino más bien a darse un baño en aguas termales con fines terapéuticos. Ingestión se refiere exclusivamente a tomar por vía oral.

c. siglo XVII El uso de los números romanos es común en español para referirse a los siglos, congresos y otros eventos similares. Algunos de los estudiantes de español del Caribe anglófono no están habituados a esta numeración y tienen problemas para identificarla y producirla correctamente.

d. el turismo de salud se ha desarrollado . . . gran interés en muchos países La capacidad del inglés de añadir varios adjetivos y modificadores a un sustantivo no es semejante a la del español, lo que en ocasiones causa problemas a los traductores. La traducción que se presenta logra captar la mayoría de estos significados al agrupar el sustantivo compuesto "segmento de mercado" con el primer adjetivo, dejando para la segunda parte de la frase los demás modificadores que se condensan en "de gran interés". Como vemos la frase ha perdido fuerza pero ha ganado en naturalidad. Es un ejemplo de **omisión**.

e. recursos naturales del país en particular, agua mineral y clima Este es un ejemplo de la manera en que la puntuación puede afectar la comprensión de un texto. En esta lectura "en particular" antes de la coma se relaciona sintáctica y semánticamente con "país". Lo mismo sucede en la versión inglesa. Sin embargo, "en particular" en este contexto se refiere a "agua mineral" y "clima", por lo que la posición de la coma debe preceder la expresión. También aquí es necesario utilizar los artículos definidos correspondientes.

f. aún no siendo la salud el motivo principal Otro signo que puede cambiar el significado de las palabras y las oraciones es la tilde. En este caso se utilizó "aún", que es sinónimo de "todavía", lo que resta sentido a la frase. En este caso se usa "aun" que es sinónimo de "incluso" y "también", además de ser un enlace gramatical de valor concesivo como en este caso. Ver también algunas líneas antes "aún más específicos".

g. Vg. un crucero por el mar o viajes a diferentes climas La expresión *"verbi gracia"* (Vg.) no es muy común en libros de texto en español; se usa casi siempre la expresión completa "por ejemplo".

h. Viajes por saunas, masajes y otras actividades de salud (spas) Cuando en español oímos o leemos "viajes por" esperamos que el complemento sea el nombre de una zona geográfica. Si decimos "viajes de" esperamos un tipo de viaje (negocios, placer). Por lo tanto, el **calco** en esta expresión no es equivalente a su uso en español y debemos encontrar otra alternativa. Una posibilidad suponiendo que no tenemos problemas de espacio es **ampliar** la expresión a "Viajes en busca de saunas".

i. Tratamientos médicos El equivalente plural del inglés *"medical treatment"* es un gran acierto en esta traducción. Como en esta ocasión hay discrepancias entre el uso del plural en inglés y en español. Este es un ejemplo de **transposición** (singular por plural).[10]

j. servicio de salud nacional Aunque la manera en que se ha formulado el nombre de la entidad es completamente comprensible, éste se ha fijado en español como "servicio nacional de salud". Si bien es un leve cambio de posición de los adjetivos, la naturalidad sufre. Los traductores tienden a hacer bases de datos con este tipo de información ya que son nombres que aparecen en un gran número de documentos. Al igual que con las **colocaciones**, una buena forma de detectar cuál es la manera más común de agrupar ciertas palabras es realizando una búsqueda entrecomillada en cualquier buscador de la red.

k. A finales de los años '80 Aunque no hay consenso sobre el uso del apóstrofo, parece que se mantiene solamente en los nombres extranjeros de los cuales hace parte. Sin embargo, hay textos en los que se ve usado de diferentes maneras. Una es como aquí, delante de la década; otra es detrás de la misma. Algunos han escrito también el apóstrofo seguido de una "s". La más común parece ser aquella que no usa el apóstrofo. Diríamos pues "A finales de los años 80".

Read the following texts:

A. CIRCUITOS ECOTURÍSTICOS[11]

Cada día más y más personas quisieran alejarse de las multitudes buscando regresar a sus valores originales y reencontrarse con la naturaleza, quieren estar en contacto con lo mejor de nuestro planeta conociendo todos esos sitios especiales donde los tesoros naturales han sido conservados, buscando bosques, ríos, animales, frutas y flores de los cuales muchos se encuentran en peligro de extinción y estar en contacto con las tribus nativas que mantienen sus primitivas costumbres en su hábitat natural.

Venezuela tiene mucho que ofrecer para los amantes de la naturaleza. Estamos muy orgullosos de proponerles diferentes circuitos que incluyen los lugares más importantes tales como: Parque Nacional Mochima, la Cueva del Guacharo, Delta del Orinoco, el famoso Salto Ángel ubicado en el Parque Nacional Canaima. Todos estos circuitos se pueden entrelazar y de igual manera le ofrecemos la oportunidad de adaptarlos a sus requerimientos específicos. Seleccionamos los mejores servicios y posadas garantizando, con profesionalismo, que nuestro turismo de eco-aventura será una experiencia inolvidable.

B. BODAS EN CANCÚN: Nuestros Servicios[12]

El día más importante de tu vida por fin se acerca. ¿No te gustaría estar rodeado de palmeras, el mar, el sol, la playa . . .? ¿Poder realmente disfrutar de tu boda ya estando en la luna de miel, escaparse de todo el alboroto que conlleva una boda tradicional en la ciudad y volar como aves para tener una ceremonia íntima sólo los dos o poder compartir ese momento tan especial con familiares y amigos dándoles a todos la oportunidad de tomarse unas merecidas vacaciones?

Nosotros estamos aquí para ayudarte a hacer ese sueño realidad. Relájate y disfruta mientras nos encargamos de todos esos pequeños detalles para que tu boda sea especial y única. Somos un grupo de profesionales trabajando juntos sólo para ti.

Cuéntanos tus ideas, tus fantasías. Te ayudaremos a hacer la boda de tus sueños, y si no sabes por donde empezar te daremos muchas ideas para orientarte y te diseñaremos un paquete especial para ti o si prefieres puedes empezar por alguno de nuestros Paquetes de Boda ya preparados y elegir el que se adecúe más a tu gusto y presupuesto.

Nos encargamos de todo (¡menos de conseguir pareja!), desde los requisitos legales hasta el banquete: flores, sacerdote, fotografías, juez, video, música. . . todo lo que necesites para hacer que tu boda sea tan bonita y romántica que, ¡la recordarás por siempre!

Ponte en contacto con nosotros y prepárense para unir sus vidas en este paraíso que es Cancún. Pulsa aquí para recibir más información o bien envíanos un e-mail, o si lo prefieres, escríbenos a:

1. Analyse comparatively the **register** of the two texts, identifying features that illustrate your analysis and commenting on the appropriateness of the **register** to the product in each case. Include reference to the ways in which the reader is addressed in each text.
2. Exemplify and compare the use of cliché in each of the two texts.

  3. Translate both texts into English. Compare and contrast your translations with
     those of a partner.
  4. Analyse the uses of the Spanish gerund in the two texts and comment on how
     you have translated the phrases in which this verb form appears.

IV. EJERCICIOS PRÁCTICOS INGLÉS > ESPAÑOL
Lea las dos traducciones que ofrecemos del siguiente texto.

CARIBBEAN ROMANCE CRUISE[13]
This month's featured tour is the Caribbean Romance cruise. The Caribbean is a place
of eternal mysteries. It has pirate shipwrecks and ruins from past civilizations. Exotic
species of brilliantly plumed birds nestle among rare giant ferns and orchids. The islands
have rich heritages that have been influenced by British, French, Spanish and Dutch
cultures. Cruise east in search of romance – a hammock swaying in the tropical breeze,
a secluded cove on a picture-perfect beach, the enticing scents of myrrh, thyme, and
cloves. The itinerary for this 10-day cruise includes visits to some of the most exotic ports
in the Caribbean with enough time to sightsee, shop and enjoy. And for those tranquil
moments, there are also two full days at sea.

A. CRUCERO ROMÁNTICO POR EL CARIBE
El tour que le ofrecemos este mes es el Crucero Romántico por el Caribe. El Caribe es un lugar lleno de misterios. Tiene barcos piratas hundidos y ruinas de antiguas civilizaciones. Aves exóticas con brillantes plumas anidan en medio de fascinantes helechos gigantes y orquídeas. Las islas del Caribe tienen patrimonios históricos que han sido influenciados por la cultura española, la británica, la francesa y la holandesa. Tome un crucero por el Este en busca del romance: una hamaca balanceándose en la brisa tropical, una gruta apartada en una playa de ensueño, los aromas de mirra, tomillo y clavos, siempre apetecibles. El itinerario para este crucero de diez días incluye visitas a algunos de los más exóticos puertos del Caribe con tiempo suficiente para visitar los lugares de interés, ir de compras y disfrutar. Y para aquellos momentos tranquilos, también hay dos días completos en altamar.

B. CRUCERO ROMÁNTICO POR EL CARIBE
Este mes se ofrece el recorrido turístico en el Crucero Romántico por el Caribe. El Caribe siempre ha sido un lugar de misterios: tiene naufragios piratas y ruinas de culturas antiguas. Especies exóticas de aves con plumas brillantes se posan sobre estupendos y gigantes helechos y orquídeas. Las islas poseen un inmenso patrimonio que ha tenido influencia de los británicos, los franceses, los españoles y los holandeses. Aventúrese hacia el Este en un crucero en busca de romance – una hamaca que se balancea en la fresca brisa tropical, una apartada cala en una playa de película, las deliciosas fragancias de la mirra, el tomillo y el laurel. El itinerario de este crucero de diez días incluye visitas a algunos de los puertos más exóticos en el Caribe, dejándole tiempo para pasear, comprar y disfrutar. Y si gusta de momentos tranquilos, también puede relajarse dos días enteros en altamar.

1. Encuentre ejemplos de los siguientes procedimientos traductológicos:

   Ampliación.
   Compensación.
   Omisión.
   Colocación.

2. Analice cómo se expresa la función comunicativa del texto en el TO y qué medidas se toman para aumentar el efecto vocativo en español. ¿Las decisiones que se tomaron en las dos versiones a este respecto son válidas, suficientes o exageradas?

3. Compare las dos traducciones del texto e identifique sus deficiencias y aciertos. Analice también cómo la posición de los adjetivos afecta la naturalidad del texto.

4. Teniendo en cuenta los puntos anteriores haga su propia traducción y luego compárela con la de algún compañero o compañera, explíquele qué motivos tuvo para tomar sus decisiones.

CHAPTER 2

Commerce

INTRODUCTION

Trade and commercial activity in the Caribbean has historically been organized according to the colonial divisions of language and culture. The most important intra-regional linkages have thus generally been with territories that speak the same language – though the anglophone Caribbean shows a greater degree of structured internal linkage in this regard than its Hispanic counterpart – while the principal channel of trade with other parts of the world has either been with the former colonial powers or with North or South America, depending on the language of the territory. This evidently has much to do with the self-interest of these powers, but it is also a consequence of the commonality of practices and norms governing commercial exchange, and the obvious convenience of doing business in the same language. There is greater similarity between business norms and practices in Venezuela and Spain, it would seem, than in Venezuela and Jamaica. As a result of this, less than 10 per cent of the foreign trade carried out by the countries of the Association of Caribbean States (ACS) is with each other.

Liberalization of world trade, however, means that it makes increasing sense for the Caribbean to strive towards a greater degree of internal trade cooperation and integration. The plight of Caribbean banana growers is an example of the diminishing role of preferential trade with Europe generally, while the Free Trade Area of the Americas will expose the diminutive economies of the Caribbean territories to vast external forces. The much vaunted Caribbean Single Market and Economy (CSME) is an attempt to make common cause to shield against such forces within the anglophone Caribbean, while the ACS, by prioritizing trade, transport and tourism, aims to achieve similar collective strength on a larger, pan-Caribbean scale. Recent initiatives in this direction include the Business Forum of the Greater Caribbean, held annually since 2001, and ongoing attempts to create a Virtual Market of the Greater Caribbean, which would use information technology to mitigate difficulties arising from mutual ignorance of entrepreneurial culture, markets and bureaucratic issues such as customs procedures, all of which continue to hamper intra-regional trade across the linguistic and cultural divides.

Commercial translation covers a large number of textual typologies, ranging from invoices and letters, through annual reports and marketing surveys, all the way up to treaties and agreements between nations or groups of nations. Given the repetitive and norm-governed nature of trade, many such documents are conventional in character, making careful filing of paired types an important process for the translator who wishes to specialize in this field. Very careful attention to figures, amounts and their evolution is also an obvious concern of the commercial translator, particularly as source texts are nowadays often sent as computer files: it is very easy for the novice to skip over tables of figures, for example, in the mistaken belief that their punctuation is "international". As in other areas in which institutional activity is prevalent, commercial translation in the Caribbean context also requires care in the rendering of acronyms and official names of bodies and processes, of which there are a considerable number.

Attention to the function or **skopos** of the translation is also especially important in the area of commerce, since this may be somewhat disguised: an annual report for internal consumption by board members is likely to differ in both tone and content from an identically titled document published on the Internet, aimed principally at consumers and potential investors. This ambivalence of function is evidenced in coinages such as "advertorial", a hybrid textual type which combines the authoritative, ostensibly objective format and tone of a newspaper editorial with the persuasive function of an advertisement. Similarly, the skills of diplomatic translation may also be required in commercial correspondence, where an apparently informative message may disguise what is really a threat or a complaint.

The texts selected for this chapter are extracts from a trade agreement, two informative pieces from company web pages, an annual report and two analyses of extra-regional trade relations. As such, they are intended only as a basic introduction to the issues of commercial translation in the Caribbean. The web sites and publications of the ACS and of the Inter-American Development Bank, both of which habitually publish texts in several languages, are a useful source of further material.[1]

El Comercio

INTRODUCCIÓN

El comercio en el Caribe se ha organizado históricamente en concordancia con las divisiones coloniales de la lengua y la cultura. Los lazos más importantes dentro de la región han surgido entre territorios que comparten la misma lengua – aunque el Caribe anglófono muestra unos vínculos mejor estructurados que su contraparte hispánica – mientras que los principales canales comerciales con otras partes del mundo se han establecido con los antiguos poderes coloniales, o con Norte o Suramérica, dependiendo de la lengua del país. Por supuesto esto tiene mucho que ver con los intereses particulares de estos poderes, pero también es una consecuencia de las prácticas y normas compartidas que rigen los intercambios comerciales, y la ventaja obvia de hacer negocios en la propia lengua. Hay quizás mayor similitud entre las normas y prácticas de negocios entre Venezuela y España que entre Venezuela y Jamaica. Como resultado, menos del diez por ciento del comercio internacional de los países de la Asociación de Estados del Caribe (AEC) se lleva a cabo entre sus territorios miembros.

No obstante, la liberalización del comercio internacional ha hecho que cada vez tenga más sentido que el Caribe trabaje por una mayor cooperación e integración de su comercio interno. La difícil situación de las bananeras caribeñas es un ejemplo de la reducción del comercio preferencial con Europa en general, mientras que el Área de Libre Comercio de las Américas expondrá las pequeñas economías de los territorios caribeños a inmensas presiones externas. El tan mencionado Mercado y Economía Únicos del Caribe (CSME, por sus siglas en inglés) es un intento de hacer causa común entre los territorios del Caribe anglófono para protegerse contra tales presiones, mientras que la AEC, dándole prioridad al comercio, el transporte y el turismo, busca lograr una fuerza colectiva similar pero mayor, a escala pancaribeña. Algunas iniciativas recientes en esta dirección incluyen el Foro de Negocios del Gran Caribe, que tiene lugar anualmente desde 2001, y los intentos actuales de crear un Mercado Virtual del Gran Caribe, que usaría la tecnología de la información para sobrepasar obstáculos que surgen de la ignorancia mutua de la cultura corporativa, mercados y asuntos burocráticos tales como los procedimientos de aduana, obstáculos que siguen dificultando el comercio dentro de la región entre las divisiones lingüísticas y culturales.

La traducción comercial cubre un gran número de tipologías textuales que van desde recibos y cartas, pasando por informes anuales y estudios de mercado, hasta tratados y acuerdos entre naciones o grupos de naciones. Dada la naturaleza repetitiva y normativa del comercio, muchos de estos documentos son de carácter convencional, haciendo que el archivo cuidadoso de pares de documentos sea una importante herramienta para el traductor que quiera especializarse en este campo. Otra tarea del traductor comercial es prestar atención detallada a números, cifras y su evolución, especialmente porque ahora los TO se envían como archivos digitales: es muy factible que un novato se salte las tablas de cifras, por ejemplo, creyendo erróneamente que su puntuación es "internacional". Como en otras áreas en las que prevalece la actividad institucional, la traducción comercial en el contexto caribeño requiere cuidado en la manera en que se dan los acrónimos o siglas de los muchos procesos e instituciones oficiales.

También es importante en el área de comercio prestar atención a la función o **skopos** de la traducción, ya que puede que esté oculta: es muy probable que un informe anual para uso interno por parte de los miembros de la junta directiva tenga un tono y un contenido diferente que un documento con el mismo nombre para su publicación en Internet, dirigido a los clientes y los posibles inversionistas. Esta ambivalencia de función queda en evidencia en palabras acuñadas en inglés como *advertorial*, un **tipo textual** híbrido que combina el formato y tono fidedigno y supuestamente objetivo de un editorial en un periódico, con la función persuasiva de un texto publicitario (*advertisement*). De igual manera, se puede necesitar la habilidad para producir una traducción diplomática en la correspondencia comercial, donde un mensaje que es en apariencia informativo puede llevar consigo una amenaza o una queja.

Los textos que hemos seleccionado para este capítulo son extractos de un acuerdo comercial, dos textos informativos de las páginas web de una empresa, un informe anual y dos análisis de las relaciones comerciales fuera de la región. Como tales, su objetivo es sólo proveer una introducción básica a los elementos de la traducción comercial en el Caribe. Las páginas web y las publicaciones de la AEC y del Banco Interamericano de Desarrollo, entidades que comúnmente generan textos en varias lenguas, son una buena fuente para encontrar más material.[1]

I. SPANISH > ENGLISH

Text 1

Tratado de Libre Comercio y de Intercambio Preferencial entre las Repúblicas de Panamá y Nicaragua[2]	Treaty on Free Trade and [a]Preferential Trade Practices between the Republics of Panama and Nicaragua[3]
Artículo 19	Article 19
Cada Estado Signatario otorgará plena libertad de tránsito por todo su territorio a las mercancías destinadas al otro Estado, o procedentes de éste. Dicho tránsito no estará sujeto a discriminación ni restricción cuantitativa de ninguna especie.	Each Signatory State shall grant full freedom of transit through its territory for goods going to or coming from the other State. Such transit shall not be subject to any discrimination or quantitative restriction.
En los casos de congestionamiento de carga o de fuerza mayor, cada Parte Contratante atenderá equitativamente tanto a la movilización de las mercancías destinadas al abastecimiento de su propia población como a la de las mercancías en tránsito para el otro Estado.	When faced with [b]**freight back up** or [c]**situations of force majeur,** the Contracting Parties will provide [d]**equitable treatment for the movement of goods to its own population and to goods in transit to the other State.**
Las operaciones de tránsito se harán por las rutas legalmente habilitadas para este efecto y con sujeción a las leyes y reglamentos de aduana aplicables en el territorio de paso. No obstante ello, se procurará agilizar los procedimientos de las mercancías en tránsito. Las mercancías en tránsito,	Transit operations will be effected through the legally approved channels and be subject to the laws and customs regulations in effect in the transit territory. Nonetheless, efforts will be made to streamline procedures for goods in transit. [e]**Goods in transit, wherever they are going and even if not**

aún cuando no están incluidas en el libre comercio y el trato preferencial, quedarán exentas del pago de toda clase de derechos, impuestos o contribuciones fiscales y municipales, cualquiera que sea su destino, pero se mantendrán sujetas tanto al pago de las tasas aplicables por la prestación de servicios como al cumplimiento de las medidas de sanidad, seguridad y policía.

included in the free trade and preferential treatment agreement, will be exempted from payment of any kind of duties, taxes or national and municipal fees. They will, however, be subject to fees for services and to compliance with all health, security and law enforcement requirements.

Commentary

a. Preferential Trade Practices "Exchange" or even "Interchange" might have been temptations for a less adept translator when faced with the ST's *Intercambio*. Internet search engines, however, are a powerful tool for testing collocations, or the frequency with which words appear next to each other. A search for "preferential exchange" using one such engine, for example, reveals only one hit out of twenty in which the words appear in consecutive sequence. Even in this instance, the grammatical category of one of the terms differs from the ST here, since the exact hit is for "preferential exchange rate", in which "exchange" is used adjectivally. In instances where a specific formula is likely to have been adopted as a convention, performing a search will help to verify if the proposed translation has sufficiently general currency.

b. freight back up Another Panamanian web site using the same formula as the ST has "cargo congestion" in its English version.[4] This turns out to have far more general currency than the TT's formulation here, yielding six precise matches in twenty hits (that is, in which the words appear consecutively), as against zero out of twenty.

c. situations of force majeur More properly spelt "force majeure", this is a legal term typically referring to unforeseeable events such as natural disasters, wars or intervention by regulatory bodies that might prevent a party in a contract from fulfilling their obligations. Where it is established that failure to fulfill the contract is attributable to force majeure ("superior force") as defined therein, the defaulting party is protected from liability. As here in the TT, it commonly appears in prepositional phrases, though formulations such as "Event of Force Majeure" or "Act of Force Majeure" are more common than the TT's "situation".

d. equitable treatment for the movement of goods to its own population and to goods in transit to the other State This section illustrates the general tendency towards greater concision in the TT relative to the ST. A more literal rendering might have read "equitable treatment to both the movement of goods intended to supply its own population and to goods in transit to the other State". The string *"destinadas al abastecimiento"* is thus condensed down to the single word "to", giving a greater sense of economy that is common in English legal language when compared to its more florid Hispanic equivalent. In the first paragraph, the rendering of *"de ninguna especie"* as simply "any", rather than "of any kind", is illustrative of the same tendency.

e. Goods in transit . . . health, security and law enforcement requirements The TT wisely divides the ST's elongated, rather tortuous final sentence into two. This partition, together with the promotion of "wherever they are going" to a position earlier in the sentence with respect to the ST equivalent, reduces the ST's two subordinate clauses to one, thereby further assisting clarity.

Text 2

Comercialización[5]

Nuestros productos son comercializados a través de una amplia red de distribuidores dentro y fuera de Venezuela, quienes son aliados de EDIL y cuentan con personal calificado para ofrecerle la información que necesita acerca de los productos que mejor se ajustan a sus necesidades.

A través de nuestros distribuidores, ofrecemos un **Certificado de Garantía** por defectos de calidad en Mantos y Tejas asfálticas, cuya duración varía de 2 a 10 años.

Las garantías son entregadas en un formato especial estandarizado y son provistos únicamente por Distribuidores EDIL, quienes están autorizados para ello. Le recomendamos contactar a uno de nuestros aliados para garantizar que el producto que está adquiriendo es de nuestra marca y cuenta con todas las garantías.

Nuestras membranas poseen en su empaque una certificación de garantía, cuyo número de Lote nos sirve para identificar la formulación usada, los detalles del proceso productivo y los análisis de calidad seguidos, en caso de algún inconveniente con el producto.

Si usted o su empresa adquirió un producto EDIL y ha tenido algún inconveniente con el mismo, sólo debe comunicarse con el distribuidor autorizado al que contactó para la compra, y hacer uso de la garantía. También puede contactarnos directamente, enviándonos toda la información al respecto y un representante de nuestra empresa se comunicará con usted a la mayor brevedad.

Marketing[6]

[a.]**Our products are commercialized** inside and outside our country through an extensive dealer network, whose members are EDIL's allies. [b.]**These have qualified workers who offer you the information you need about the products that meet all your needs.**

Through our agents, we offer a **Warranty of Certification** for quality defects in roofing and asphaltic tiles. It has a variable duration from two to ten years.

[c.]**Warranties are delivered in a standard special format that are only given to EDIL's agents,** who are authorized to grant them. We recommend you to contact one of our dealers in order to guarantee that the product you are buying is manufactured by EDIL and to offer you all the warranties.

Every package has a Warranty of Certification. The batch number helps us to identify the combination used in the manufacturing process, details about the production process and the analysis of the quality of the product, in case there is an inconvenient with the product.

[d.]**If you or your company purchased an EDIL's product and you have had some inconvenient with it, you only have to re-contact the authorized distributor and use the warranty.** Also, you can contact us sending all the information about the problem and a representative from our company will contact you immediately.

For an alternative version of the TT, see http://www.caribbeantranslationmanual.com/commerce.html

Edil is a Venezuelan company that manufactures waterproofing products such as roofing tiles and asphalt surfacing materials for a variety of construction and engineering uses. It markets throughout the Americas and has distributors in the Caribbean in Aruba, Barbados, Curacao, the Dominican Republic, Jamaica, Puerto Rico and Trinidad and Tobago. The above extract forms part of a page of general information about the company. Though this page is offered bilingually, other areas of the site are exclusively in Spanish (such as the product descriptions) or only provide English versions for box labels on forms to be submitted to the site.

Various features of the TT betray their author's non-native competence in English, but it nonetheless conveys the necessary information and evinces some knowledge of appropriate translation strategies. From the point of view of corporate image, the TT would no doubt have benefited from revision by a suitably equipped native speaker. Nonetheless, the result is an interesting example of a TT that shows various types of interference from the SL and illustrates some of the pitfalls of translating out of the language of habitual use, making it a useful object of analysis.

a. Our products are commercialized For some reason, the translator chooses the cognate "commercialized" here, despite avoiding it with "marketing" in the title. For the former the *Oxford English Dictionary* (*OED*) has "1. exploit or spoil for the purposes of gaining profit; 2. make commercial". Since the primary sense carries negative **connotations**, "marketed" would be preferable here. In any event, "commercialize" does not collocate well with "products" in English, since in a business context the latter term already suggests something that is "commercial". Thus a university course might be considered a medium of enlightenment by an educator, but a "product" by an administrator seeking to increase revenue. Someone might then complain that the institution or the education system has become "commercialized", illustrating the negative **connotation** in English of something that acquires an excessively or exclusively commercial dimension that undermines some higher purpose.

b. These have qualified workers who offer you the information you need about the products that meet all your needs The first instance of a long sentence in the ST being divided into two in the TT (see also the succeeding paragraph and the penultimate paragraph in the TT). Dividing long periods may appear at first sight to be a prudent strategy when translating out of the language of habitual use, since it tends to break down the ideas in the ST into more manageable chunks. However, it can also in turn necessitate tricky modification of the scheme of deictic or anaphoric elements (demonstratives such as "these", as here, or pronouns such as "it", in the next paragraph). Equally, evaluation of whether the resulting TT is rendered unnaturally staccato can be problematic when translating into the foreign language. This procedure is thus best used sparingly in cases when native-speaker revision is not feasible.

For "worker", the *OED* offers "a person who works, esp. a manual or industrial employee". The industrial **connotation** is somewhat misleading here: while the manufacturing context might seem to justify this choice, it is of course unlikely that someone involved in manual or industrial production processes at one of EDIL's corporate allies would be assigned to answering customer queries, this being a different concept of "work" altogether. In any event *obrero* or *trabajador*, rather than *personal* would normally elicit "worker".

An alternative version of the first paragraph, in which the repetition of "need(s)" is also problematic, thus might read: "Our products are marketed in Venezuela and internationally through our corporate allies, who form an extensive network of distributors with personnel specially trained to provide information on the products that best suit your needs." As with other lexical items, the anglophone Caribbean appears to tolerate both North American "personnel" and British "staff".

c. Warranties are delivered in a standard special format that are only given to EDIL's agents The TT is syntactically ill-formed here, using the plural "are" for the singular subject noun "format". The questionable logic of the TT anyway suggests that "and" was intended after "format", in consonance with the ST's "y", but that "that" was erroneously substituted.

The TT initially offers "deliver" for *"entregar (una garantía)"*, then "grant" when it is alluded to anaphorically by the final *ello*. The former collocates more readily with "product" (for example, "we will deliver your product on the same day you make your order"), while the latter associates with nouns such as "licence" or "permit" ("we grant licences to selected companies that apply to distribute our product"). An alternative TT here might be: "Warranties are issued exclusively by authorized EDIL Distributors in a unique standardized format".

d. If you or your company purchased an EDIL's product and you have had some inconvenient with it, you only have to re-contact the authorized distributor and use the warranty The false cognate "inconvenient", which appears here and in the previous sentence, cannot be used as a noun in English. Moreover, substituting the cognate noun "inconvenience" does not resolve matters, since this suggests merely a minor discomfort caused by a circumstantial impediment: "Please use other door. We apologize for any inconvenience." In such an example, "inconvenience" would back translate as *molestia*: *Disculpen las molestias*. An alternative rendering for this sentence might be: "If you or your company encounters any problem with an EDIL product, therefore, simply contact the authorized distributor you purchased it from and use the warranty."

Text 3

<table>
<tr><td>

Latinoamérica[7]

El volumen consolidado exportado a la región mostró un crecimiento de 6,7%, impulsado por un positivo desempeño de los países de Centroamérica. En tanto, en Sudamérica, mostraron una interesante recuperación Brasil, Colombia y Ecuador.

La fortaleza de la marca y el creciente reconocimiento a la calidad de nuestros vinos premium quedó en evidencia con el

</td><td>

Latin America[8]

[a]**More stable political and economic environments underpinned sales trends in the Caribbean, Central and South America.** Brighter performances in Central American countries pushed consolidated sales to the region 6.7% higher, [b]**while in South America exports to Brazil, Colombia and Ecuador recovered well.**

Our strength of brand and an increasing perception of the quality of our wines prompted a 26% rise in premium wine

</td></tr>
</table>

aumento de un 26% que experimentó esta categoría en la región. El avance más interesante se obtuvo en la línea Casillero del Diablo. En 2003 continuamos progresando en el objetivo de potenciar las líneas de vinos finos, con capacitaciones al canal *on-trade*, la introducción de vinos en las cartas de restaurantes y una mejor rotación de los productos. Asimismo, se llevaron a cabo con éxito catas verticales de Don Melchor en la región.

sales to the region. ^c**Casillero del Diablo performed best. More effort went into encouraging the sales of our fine wines.** In 2003, ^d**we held on-trade master classes,** added wines to restaurant menus and offered increased product rotation. Vertical tastings of Don Melchor in many places also met with much success.

Commentary

Concha y Toro is a Chile-based wine producer and exporter that markets its products throughout Europe, Asia and the Americas, including the anglophone Caribbean. The company's web site has alternative versions in Spanish and in English. The text above forms part of the "Global Markets" section of the company's Annual Report for 2003. Since it is intended to convey a broad picture in a relatively short space, it does not contain a great deal of technical detail or dense financial information. Nonetheless, **textual immersion** in the language of annual reports in the TL (in this case English) is a good starting point when attempting such texts, which tend to use conventional combinations of terms.

a. More stable . . . Central and South America This sentence has no equivalent at all in the ST. Its addition to the TT may have resulted from the perception that non-Latin American readers – and potential investors or corporate allies – would be suitably reassured by this information, which perhaps seeks to counteract Northern Hemispheric preconceptions of unending political and social turmoil in the regions mentioned. Within Latin America, where the great majority of readers of the Spanish version are likely to be concentrated, the information would be either superfluous, or possibly regarded as inappropriately political.

b. while in South America exports to Brazil, Colombia and Ecuador recovered well The TT elides two sentences here, possibly because the insertion of the previous sentence opens the section with a suitably uncluttered statement, clearing the path for a longer second period.

This is a good example of the greater semantic area covered by *interesante* in Spanish, as against the narrower English cognate "interesting", sensibly avoided in the TT. The Spanish term often means, as here, "in the interests of, favourable to", rather than simply "provoking one's interest or curiosity". Thus *sería interesante que hablaras con Benítez* tends to mean that opportunities or fruitful collaboration may arise from the proposed consultation, not necessarily that you will be riveted by what Benítez has to say. "Positive" or "favourable" are alternatives for the adjective, though both would have generated a tautology if used adverbially here, since a "recovery" can rarely be anything other than positive or favourable.

c. **Casillero del Diablo performed best. More effort went into encouraging the sales of our fine wines** While the reduction of the first sentence from the ST's twelve words to a mere five is impressively economical, this and the decision to isolate the following sentence tend to produce a somewhat stilted result.

The rendering "more effort went into encouraging", for "*continuamos progresando en el objetivo de potenciar*", could be questioned on the grounds that it prioritizes the mere attempt rather than the result. A more positive tone might be struck by, "further progress was made toward strengthening sales of our fine wines".

d. **we held on-trade master classes** Evidently, some knowledge of the wine trade assists the translator in transposing *capacitaciones* to "master classes": a standard bilingual dictionary offers only the non-count noun "training" as an equivalent for the ST term. "On-trade" is a term used in the beverage industry to refer to establishments that have a licence to allow consumption on the premises (bars, pubs, clubs, restaurants), as opposed to "off-trade" outlets, where drinks can be purchased but must be consumed elsewhere. In the following sentence, a "vertical tasting" is one involving different vintages of the same wine, as opposed to a "horizontal tasting", in which wines from the same vintage, but from different producers, are sampled.

II. INGLÉS > ESPAÑOL

Texto 1

About us[9]

Accurate Communications is a professional consulting firm with over 15 years' experience in the areas of audiovisual services, business writing and translations, and business publications. During this period, we have worked side by side with Puerto Rico's most respected corporations, developing top quality media that reinforces their total quality and continuous improvement philosophies.

Please take a few minutes to look through our new web site. It reflects our commitment to offer our customers the latest and most effective products and services.

Contact us![10]

At Accurate Communications we don't believe in demo reels or fancy brochures, because we feel they only show a company's best work. Instead, we visit every customer and present actual projects completed for other customers. This doesn't mean that your company

Quiénes somos[11]

[a.]**Accurate Communications es una firma de consultoría profesional con más de 15 años de experiencia en las áreas de:** servicios audiovisuales, redacción comercial, traducción y publicaciones comerciales. Durante ese período hemos trabajado mano a mano con las organizaciones más prestigiosas de Puerto Rico, desarrollando materiales de primera calidad que apoyen sus filosofías de calidad total y mejoramiento continuo.

[b.]**Le exhorto a navegar unos minutos por nuestra nueva página.** Ésta refleja nuestro compromiso de ofrecer productos y servicios modernos y efectivos a nuestros clientes.

¡Contáctenos![12]

[c.]**En Accurate Communications no creemos en los demos, o en folletos lujosos, porque pensamos que sólo muestran el mejor trabajo de una compañía. En su lugar,** visitamos a cada cliente nuevo y [d.]**le mostramos trabajos verdaderos, realizados para clientes anteriores.**

secrets or proprietary technology will be exposed. Twelve years serving the top echelons of US and local corporations in Puerto Rico and abroad are proof of the way we protect confidential information.

But most importantly, we listen! We tackle every project with a clear and unbiased mindset, offering creative solutions that will embody your company's corporate identity, align with your strategic goals and fall within your specific budget.
Give us a call today, and discover the world of Accurate Communications.

Esto no quiere decir que sus secretos de negocio o tecnología propietaria estarán en peligro. Doce años sirviendo a [e]**la alta gerencia de corporaciones locales e internacionales establecidas** en Puerto Rico y en el exterior evidencian el cuidado con que protegemos la información confidencial.
¡Pero lo más importante es que escuchamos! Abordamos cada proyecto con una mente clara y sin prejuicios, ofreciendo soluciones creativas [f]**que proyecten la identidad de la compañía, se alineen con sus metas estratégicas** y se ajusten a su presupuesto. Llámenos hoy, y descubra el mundo de Accurate Communications.

Comentarios

a. **Accurate Communications es una firma de consultoría profesional con más de 15 años de experiencia en las áreas de** Una de las características de este subgénero de textos comerciales es que combina dos funciones comunicativas: los textos deben ser informativos y apelativos a la vez. Se parecen en esto a los textos publicitarios, pero tienen la ventaja relativa de disponer de mayor espacio. En esta frase vemos cómo la firma le da importancia a la función informativa (qué hace la empresa, hace cuánto funciona) que sirve a la vez para decirles a sus posibles clientes los motivos por los que deben trabajar con esta compañía (experiencia). El traductor ha decidido incluir dos puntos, aunque en realidad no son necesarios y cortan la fluidez de la frase.

b. **Le exhorto a navegar unos minutos por nuestra nueva página** Esta es la primera referencia directa al lector y posible destinatario del texto. El lenguaje que usa es más formal que otras expresiones equivalentes ("le invito"), o mandatos ("navegue"), ya que está dirigida a empresarios dispuestos a hacer negocios con ellos. Por otra parte, el uso del "le" demuestra una conciencia de género, en oposición al posible "lo". Finalmente, hoy en día la mayoría de los negocios se ven obligados a funcionar en Internet. Por lo tanto, deben adoptar el vocabulario y las herramientas necesarias para ser competitivos bajo esta forma de comunicación. El traductor debe ser un ágil navegador y mantenerse al día con el vocabulario relativo a la red en las dos lenguas. Aunque el inglés proporciona la mayoría de los términos del campo informático, muchas veces podemos encontrar una traducción de dichos términos que se rige por las reglas de construcción y uso del español. Los defensores del desarrollo del español en el campo informático piden que se usen los equivalentes en esta lengua cuando los hay y que se evite el **préstamo** innecesario. Los ejemplos más típicos se refieren a palabras como el mouse > el ratón, el e-mail > el correo electrónico, la web > la red, el avatar > el personaje digital, el backup > la copia de seguridad / de respaldo, el browser > el navegador, etcétera.

c. **En Accurate Communications no creemos en los demos . . . En su lugar** El sustantivo "demo" ya aparece en los diccionarios de español. Esta palabra es un **préstamo** del inglés en América Latina y el Caribe y por lo tanto se adapta a las reglas de concordancia de la lengua española: al terminar en "o" se espera que sea masculina. Sin embargo, en España y otras regiones es un sustantivo femenino por referencia apocopada a "la demostración". En cuanto a "en su lugar" se preferiría utilizar la expresión "en lugar de eso" ya que generalmente la primera se encuentra en oraciones en las que el posesivo se refiere a una persona y remite a frases hechas como "yo en su lugar . . .".

d. **le mostramos trabajos verdaderos, realizados para clientes anteriores** Muchos estudiantes de traducción tienen problemas con la palabra inglesa *actual*. En este caso nos encontramos con una traducción no muy feliz de dicha palabra. Preferimos la opción de "reales" pues al decir trabajos verdaderos viene a la mente la dicotomía verdadero/falso y el TO no se refiere a tal cosa. Un traductor debe ser consciente de las asociaciones y **connotaciones** que tiene una palabra, siendo éste otro elemento que influye la toma de decisiones.

e. **la alta gerencia de corporaciones locales e internacionales establecidas** Se ve aquí un ejemplo de la **adaptación** necesaria en los textos dependiendo de la perspectiva desde la que se escriben o traducen. La teoría **skopos** lleva esta afirmación al límite diciendo que los textos se traducen para un propósito (por ejemplo para un cliente o un grupo de lectores) y que este propósito permite que se hagan cambios radicales al TO. En este caso el TO incluía sólo Estados Unidos; la traducción lo volvió más general llamándolo "internacional".

f. **que proyecten la identidad de la compañía, se alineen con sus metas estratégicas** Queremos resaltar el uso del artículo definido "la" en la primera parte de la frase y el posesivo "sus" de la segunda. Aunque el español tiende a usar el artículo definido cuando es clara la relación entre lo poseído y el poseedor, escogeríamos el posesivo también en la primera parte pues tiene la función de acercar al destinatario del texto y cumplir así la función apelativa. Este texto utiliza esta función de forma explícita en algunas ocasiones (generalmente entre signos de exclamación) pero se puede criticar de extenderse demasiado sobre las bondades de la compañía, y no utilizar las herramientas del lenguaje para acercar al destinatario. Nótese el uso del subjuntivo en este tipo de construcciones.

Texto 2

The Greater Caribbean and the European Union: after the Madrid Summit[13]	[a]Gran Caribe y Unión Europea: Después de la Cumbre de Madrid[14]
The complexity of the trade agenda for the Greater Caribbean reflects the diversity of the region. The countries which enjoy and share the Caribbean Sea offer a sample of several cultures, languages, religions and histories. These peculiarities are coupled with the different structures and sizes of their economies, as well as a geographical	La complejidad de la agenda comercial del Gran Caribe está en concordancia con la diversidad de la región. Los países que disfrutan y comparten el Mar Caribe son una muestra de múltiples culturas, idiomas, religiones e historias. **[b]Estas particularidades se conjugan con las diferencias en las estructuras y el tamaño de sus económicas,**

location which make the region a complex mosaic of interests and agendas.

In this context, one of the most salient elements of the region's foreign policy has been the ongoing deepening of relations with the European Union (EU), which is unquestionably one of the world's largest trade and political partners. This process has become relevant and dynamic in view of the strengthening of implementation mechanisms, and more particularly, the outcomes of the Madrid Summit in May 2002.

así como su situación geográfica para crear un complejo mosaico de intereses y agendas.

En este contexto uno de los elementos más sobresalientes de la política externa regional ha sido la constante profundización de las relaciones con la [c] **Unión Europea (UE),** [d] **sin lugar a dudas uno de los socios políticos** y comerciales más importantes del mundo. [e] **Este proceso ha ganado relevancia y dinamismo** [f] **mediante la consolidación de los mecanismos que lo instrumentan** y especialmente por los resultados de la Cumbre de Madrid de mayo del 2002.

Comentarios

a. Gran Caribe y Unión Europea: Después de la Cumbre de Madrid Al tratarse de un título se omiten los artículos definidos en la primera parte. Sin embargo, esta práctica es tan normal como mantenerlos. También vale la pena anotar que después de dos puntos el español prefiere la minúscula. Esta regla ortográfica fue propuesta hace relativamente poco tiempo por lo que aún se encuentran mayúsculas como en el presente ejemplo. También se podría decir que se incluyen aquí por tratarse de un título en el que las palabras de contenido (en oposición a las gramaticales, como las preposiciones y artículos) son resaltadas con mayúsculas. Aunque es más común en español no resaltarlas.

b. Estas particularidades se conjugan con las diferencias en las estructuras y el tamaño de sus económicas Muchas veces este tipo de documento se encarga a traductores independientes y las fechas tope de entrega dejan muy poco tiempo para la revisión. En este caso se utiliza el adjetivo plural "económicas" cuando debería usarse el sustantivo correspondiente "economías", claramente un error tipográfico. Estos errores pueden ser evitados si se trabaja en conjunto con un revisor o lector de la lengua meta. También existe una gran variedad de programas informáticos que hacen el papel de revisores, aunque los resultados obtenidos al utilizar estos programas no son suficientes para garantizar la total calidad de la traducción en cuanto a su tipografía. Se sugiere que se utilice un revisor humano y uno electrónico para mejorar este aspecto. Por otra parte, la excelente elección de las otras palabras en esta frase contrasta con el error mencionado, como lo hace el hecho de singularizar "tamaño" y optar por el impersonal "se" en lugar de la pasiva.

c. Unión Europea (UE) El inglés se caracteriza por utilizar una gran cantidad de siglas para nombres de compañías (IBM), organismos del gobierno (FBI) o internacionales (UN). En algunos casos el español mantiene las siglas del inglés, pero en otros, especialmente cuando se trata de organismos internacionales se tiende a hacer que las siglas correspondan al nombre de la organización en español. En este caso EU, se convierte en UE. El traductor debe conocer los nombres de los organismos e instituciones y sobre todo enterarse de cuándo las siglas cambian, cuándo se mantienen y qué género tienen en español.

d. sin lugar a dudas uno de los socios políticos Este segmento se habría podido traducir literalmente como "que es sin duda uno de los socios políticos . . .". Cuando la traducción pasa de la literalidad por motivos gramaticales (posición de los verbos, adjetivos etc.) se puede decir que utilizamos la técnica de **transposición**, pero cuando los cambios se deben más a razones de índole estilística, es decir que el cambio es opcional pero se cree relevante para el contexto y el tono del texto, utilizamos la técnica de **modulación**. (Ver: Conceptos y estrategias de traducción utilizadas en este manual, en la Introducción al mismo).

e. Este proceso ha ganado relevancia y dinamismo Vemos aquí un pequeño cambio semántico. En el TO se utiliza *become* cuya **traducción literal** sería "convertirse". Este verbo implica un cambio de estado de algo que no era algo que es. "Ganar" por otro lado no implica tanto un cambio de estado como una intensificación. En este caso el cambio se ve validado por el contexto en el que aparece la frase. Esto nos recuerda que las palabras no tienen solamente una traducción sino que sus equivalentes dependen del modo en que ellas se organizan en el discurso.

f. mediante la consolidación de los mecanismos que lo instrumentan Uno de los principales problemas con los que se enfrentan los traductores es el uso de los adjetivos en inglés. Algunas veces el problema consiste en la capacidad del inglés de agregar numerosos adjetivos, otras veces, como aquí, se utilizan sustantivos con función adjetival. En este caso vemos cómo el traductor resuelve la frase mediante el trasvase a una relativa.

Texto 3

E-commerce. Recommendations by the Joint Committee:[15]

1. FTAA countries should encourage the existence of close cooperation, domestically and within the hemisphere, among governments, business and citizens – the stakeholders – in identifying and addressing all the factors necessary to reduce the digital divide and take full advantage of digital opportunities.

2. FTAA countries should cooperate within the hemisphere to encourage the establishment of public/private partnerships geared towards citizens and businesses, and designed to:

a) broaden access to, and promote development of, information infrastructures,

b) encourage the use of information technologies and e-commerce,

c) promote digital opportunities resulting from the growth in electronic commerce by framing laws and regulations that govern

Comercio electrónico. Recomendaciones del Comité Conjunto:[16]

1. Los países del ALCA deberían alentar la existencia de una estrecha cooperación, internamente y dentro del Hemisferio, entre los gobiernos, empresas y ciudadanos – los actores – a fin de identificar y abordar todos los factores necesarios para [a] **reducir la brecha digital y aprovechar al máximo las oportunidades digitales.**

2. Los países del ALCA deberían cooperar, dentro del Hemisferio, para propiciar el establecimiento de asociaciones entre los sectores público y privado destinadas a los ciudadanos y empresas, y diseñadas para:

a) [b] **ampliar el acceso a, y promover el desarrollo de, infraestructuras de la información;**

b) alentar el uso de las tecnologías de información y del comercio electrónico;

c) promover las oportunidades digitales derivadas del desarrollo del comercio electrónico, a través de la formulación de leyes

the main aspects of international electronic commerce among the countries of the hemisphere, and
d) advance the use of information technologies to meet social needs, such as education and medical care.

3. FTAA countries should promote policies aimed at closing the digital divide, by supporting the continued development of e-commerce within small and medium enterprises (SMEs) and rural sectors, and should provide for the corresponding training programs . . .

8. Concrete actions should be identified domestically to stimulate the production of local information and online content, to be accessed via the Internet.

y reglamentos que rijan los aspectos principales del comercio electrónico internacional entre los estados del Hemisferio; y
d) impulsar el empleo de tecnologías de información a fin de satisfacer necesidades sociales, tales como educación y asistencia médica.

3. Los países del ALCA deberían promover políticas tendientes a reducir la brecha digital, [c] **apoyando el desarrollo continuo del comercio electrónico dentro de las PyMEs** y los sectores rurales, y deberían proveer los respectivos programas de capacitación . . .

8. Se deberían identificar acciones concretas internas que estimulen [d] **la producción de información y contenido en línea locales a ser accesada a través de Internet.**

Comentarios

a. reducir la brecha digital y aprovechar al máximo las oportunidades digitales Los términos no se limitan a palabras aisladas sino que pueden estar formados por dos o más palabras. En este caso "brecha digital" es un término ya aceptado cuyo significado surge de la unión de los significados de los elementos que lo conforman. Cuando los términos no existen o no están estandarizados en la LM el traductor puede arriesgarse a hacer construcciones de este tipo para resolver sus inconvenientes terminológicos.

b. ampliar el acceso a, y promover el desarrollo de, infraestructuras de la información Esta es una estructura típica del inglés en la que se utiliza una construcción preposicional y se interrumpe con otra del mismo tipo. En español generalmente se soluciona terminando la primera construcción y añadiendo la segunda al final con el complemento requerido (por ejemplo un posesivo o un pronombre): "ampliar el acceso a infraestructuras de la información y promover su desarrollo".

c. apoyando el desarrollo continuo del comercio electrónico dentro de las PyMEs El traductor ha decidido omitir en el TM la **explicitación** que hace el TO de las siglas en inglés para este término. Otra opción hubiera sido escribir "pequeña y mediana empresa" y entre paréntesis las siglas. Sin embargo al tratarse de un término ampliamente utilizado se puede omitir teniendo en cuenta el **tipo de texto** que se traduce y sus lectores potenciales.

d. la producción de información y contenido en línea locales a ser accesada a través de Internet Es una construcción bastante complicada y tiene otro ejemplo de interferencia, esta vez a nivel tanto de palabra como de oración. En la versión presentada el adjetivo "local" concuerda con "información y contenido en línea" y los modifica. En español, cuando esto se da, la construcción requiere que el adjetivo vaya en plural como sucede aquí. Otra opción, si esto no afecta radicalmente el significado de la oración, es mover el adjetivo a una posición anterior. En este caso se sugeriría "producción local de información y contenido en línea". Aunque no significa exactamente lo mismo, en este contexto su significado se acerca lo suficiente al TO (ayudado por *domestically*) y además simplifica la lectura y comprensión de la frase. Ahora bien, si analizamos la oración del TO vemos que el adjetivo "local" y su relación con los sustantivos que modifica puede tener una doble lectura: por un lado puede modificar a los dos sustantivos, por otro, puede modificar sólo al primero. Debido al contexto y el significado del segundo sustantivo, nos inclinamos por la segunda opción: "producción de información local y contenido en línea". Pasamos ahora a "accesada" diciendo que surge de una interferencia cada vez más aceptada. La Real Academia de la Lengua se ha vuelto cada vez más consciente de la necesidad de actualizarse constantemente y de dar cuenta de los términos que se incorporan al idioma, especialmente de aquellos que provienen del ámbito tecnológico y científico. Sin embargo, la Academia también aboga por la búsqueda de soluciones que el español propone para cierta terminología que se toma prestada sin ser necesario, como discutimos en los comentarios del texto 1 de esta sección. Esto no sólo a nivel de palabra: en el caso que nos concierne, la misma idea se hubiera podido expresar por medio de "accesible" dentro de una relativa. Esto nos lleva a fijarnos en la interferencia a nivel de la frase, una **traducción literal** de *"to be accessed"*. Nuestra sugerencia sería "que sea accesible a través de Internet" o "a la que se pueda acceder en Internet".

III. SPANISH > ENGLISH EXERCISES

1. Reverse translation gap-filling. Reverse translation exercises, also called "re-translations", treat the TT as if it were a ST. Using the Spanish translation below to inform your deductions, fill in the gaps in the English ST (the number in the middle of the gap indicates how many words appear in the actual ST). Consult the web site and compare your version to the real ST, noting any specific translation procedures you detect in the Spanish TT. Add any relevant entries to your commercial glossary.

OMC- Exámenes de las Políticas Comerciales Órgano de Examen de las Políticas Comerciales: Costa Rica (año 2000) Informe de la Secretaría (extracto)[17]	WTO Trade Policy Reviews Trade Policy Review Body: Costa Rica (Year 2000) Secretariat Summary (extract)[18]
El sector de los servicios no se vio afectado por cambios importantes entre 1995 y 2000. El turismo sigue siendo una de las actividades que atrae más *divisas e inversiones* (a), pero las ineficiencias de larga data que existen en algunos sectores de servicios imponen costos innecesarios a otras actividades.	No major changes affected the services sector between 1995 and 2000. Tourism remains a main magnet for ______4______ (a), but long-standing inefficiencies in some other service areas impose unnecessary costs on other activities.
El Estado *mantiene derechos monopólicos* (b) en las actividades de seguros, telecomunicaciones y distribución de energía.	The State ______3______ (b) on insurance, telecommunications and energy distribution. Notwithstanding growing private

Pese a una participación privada cada vez mayor en el sector de la banca, los bancos de propiedad estatal, favorecidos por las reglamentaciones vigentes, siguen dominando el sector. *Al encontrarse ante una vigorosa oposición de grupos de interés* (c), el Gobierno no pudo obtener la aprobación de la legislación que consideraba de capital importancia para modernizar algunas actividades de servicios fundamentales, en particular las telecomunicaciones.

Las presiones en favor de la reforma derivan de *la brecha cada vez más amplia existente entre* (d) una legislación que tiene una antigüedad de varios decenios, la evolución de la tecnología y los nuevos imperativos del mercado. Las negociaciones en materia de servicios en el marco de la OMC *podrían dar un nuevo impulso al proceso de reforma* (e), pero esto requeriría crear una mayor conciencia pública de la necesidad de mejorar la calidad y reducir los costos de *los servicios bancarios, de seguros, de telecomunicaciones y de distribución de energía* (f).

participation in the banking industry, state-owned banks, favoured by current regulations, still dominate the industry. ______7______ (c), the Government was unable to pass legislation it considered of prime importance to modernize key service activities, notably telecommunications.

Pressure for reform arises from ______4______ (d) decades-old legislation, changing technology and new market imperatives. WTO services negotiations could ______8______ (e) but this would require building up wider public awareness of the need to improve the quality and reduce the cost of ______7______ (f).

See http://www.caribbeantranslationmanual.com/commerce.html for full English version.

2. Numbers and quantities

i) Read the following report on the Venezuelan economy, then select the correct word or phrase from the options below in order to complete the English version accurately. Where more than one option is valid, discuss which is preferable from a stylistic point of view. Finally, compare your answers to the published translation on the web site.

2003: Un año para no repetir[19]
En el 2003 la cantidad de bienes y servicios producidos en Venezuela *cayó 10.1%* (a), con lo que el ingreso por habitante *se redujo en 11.7%* (b). [. . .] Para recuperar el ingreso por habitante que tenía Venezuela al cierre de 1998 (que no era particularmente grande) el país va a necesitar *crecer 5% anual durante los próximos nueve años* (c).

La inflación a nivel del consumidor *cerró en 27.1%* (d), pero otros índices más representativos del consumo venezolano (dado

2003: A year not to be repeated
In the year 2003, the amount of goods and services produced in Venezuela ______a______, whereby the per capita income ______b______. [. . .] In order to recover Venezuela's 1998 per capita income (which was not particularly high), the country is going to need ______c______.

Consumer-level inflation ______d______ but other more representative consumption indices in Venezuela (inasmuch as it

que es difícil conseguir los productos a los precios controlados) estuvieron muy por encima: Al por mayor, 48.7%, Núcleo inflacionario 37.5%, y Alimentos (aun a pesar del control) 36.4%. Todo esto en un país en donde, a pesar de los informes del INE, existe un número de desempleados e informales *superior al 70%* de la fuerza laboral (e), y en donde los salarios formales mínimos subieron en promedio 10.5% (sí, *aumentos de 10% en Julio y de 20% en Octubre* (f), dan un promedio en el año apenas superior a 10%).

Miguel Ángel Santos, Economista Jefe de Venamcham

is difficult to obtain products at controlled prices) were far above that level: the wholesale index reached 48.7%, the inflationary nucleus was 37.5% and food staples (in spite of controls) rose to 36.4%. All this in a country where, contrary to the reports issued by the National Statistics Institute, the number of unemployed and informally-employed _____e_____ of the total labour force, and where minimum formal salaries rose on average 10.5% (yes, _____f_____ gave an average barely over 10% throughout the year).

Miguel Ángel Santos, Chief Economist of Venamcham

See http://www.caribbeantranslationmanual.com/commerce.html for full English version.

a)
   i)   fell to 10%
   ii) fell by 10%
   iii) fell 10%
   iv) dropped to 10%

b)
   i)   reduced itself by 11.7%
   ii) was reduced by 11.7%
   iii) reduced itself to 11.7%
   iv) dropped to 11.7%

c)
   i)   to grow 5% annually for the next nine years
   ii) to grow by 5% annually during the next nine years
   iii) to grow to 5% annually over the next nine years
   iv) to grow 5% per year during the coming nine years

d)
   i)   shut off at 27.1%
   ii) closed down by 27.1%
   iii) closed at 27.1%
   iv) finished up by 27.1%

e)
   i)   exceeds 70%
   ii) existing at above 70%
   iii) is superior to 70%
   iv) is greater than 70%

f)
   i)   increases of 10% and 20% in July and October respectively
   ii) raises of 10% through July and 20% through October
   iii) a climb of 10% in July and 20% in October
   iv) wage hikes of 10% in July and 20% in October

IV. EJERCICIOS PRÁCTICOS INGLÉS > ESPAÑOL

Lea y traduzca el siguiente texto.

Business Writing and Translations[20]

For the inexperienced writer, there's nothing more frightening than a blank sheet of paper. Yet, while few corporate managers have backgrounds in journalism, they're expected to produce crisp, elegant and effective copy that will get their message across while reinforcing their corporate image. Furthermore, in Puerto Rico, they're expected to be able to do that in both Spanish and English.

For years Accurate Communications has assisted managers at Puerto Rico's top corporations in the production of effective copy for press releases, magazine and newspaper articles, corporate brochures, employee handbooks, speeches and general translation projects.

And now the Internet makes it easier than ever. Just send us your copy by e-mail. You'll receive a crisp, error free translation, without ever leaving your desk, that will accurately convey your message.

1. Compare su versión con la de sus compañeros. Intenten discutir y dar sus explicaciones sobre las decisiones que tomaron a nivel de palabra, frase y oración. Luego compárela con la versión en la red: http://www.accuratecommunications .com/redaccion-com.html

2. Invente un producto y unos destinatarios. Haga la presentación de su empresa en un párrafo. ¿Cómo cambiaría el párrafo dependiendo de los destinatarios? Discuta. Luego intercambie su párrafo con el de algún compañero o compañera para que hagan la traducción de su texto. Cuando reciba la traducción, revísela y observe qué hubiera hecho diferente. ¿Encuentra algunos aspectos en los que pudiera mejorar? ¿Está mejor redactada y más clara que el TO? ¿Comparte la traducción y su TO el mismo propósito? ¿Va dirigido el texto en las dos lenguas al mismo tipo de destinatario?

3. Siglas: Complete este cuadro con las siglas de los organismos o instituciones y las palabras a la que se refiere la sigla tanto en inglés como en español:

Inglés	Español
1. CARICOM	
2.	AEC Asociación de Estados del Caribe
3.	Comunidad Andina de Naciones
4.	Comisión Económica para América Latina y el Caribe

5. WHO	
6.	ONUDI
7. International Monetary Fund	
8.	ALCA
9. PAHO Pan American Health Organization	
10.	ALADI

See http://www.caribbeantranslationmanual.com/commerce.html for complete table.

4. Adjetivos: Resuelva la traducción de estos textos del inglés al español prestando especial atención a los usos y la posición de los adjetivos:

Texto 1: CDB intends to be the leading Caribbean development finance institution, working in an efficient, responsive and collaborative manner with our borrowing members, towards the systematic reduction of poverty in their countries, through social and economic development.[21]

Texto 2: One regulatory problem dealing with Internet activities has been that many Internet sites are in Caribbean jurisdictions where regulatory regimes are different from those in other countries or states with respect to gaming. In addition, secrecy and less restrictive rules on financial services allow owners and operators of Internet gaming to operate offshore banks and financial entities that control the monetary payments for the cybergames.[22]

5. Interferencias: Reconstruya estas frases en español en donde se nota una interferencia del inglés:

a. Hoy en día los grandes empresarios dicen que – y seguramente tienen razón – ningún negocio, por pequeño que sea, puede sobrevivir sin tecnología.

b. Los negocios en el Caribe pueden, si así se lo proponen, entrar fuertemente en la escena mundial.

c. Gracias a los nuevos acuerdos, esperamos, el Mercado Común del Caribe ganará cada vez más fuerza.

d. El mercado ha avanzado más, pero mucho más de lo que se esperaba.

e. El acuerdo está firmado por, y beneficia a, todos los países del Caribe.

CHAPTER 3

Journalism

INTRODUCTION

Few forms of written discourse are subject to so many and such varied constraints as newspaper journalism. The vast majority of newspaper texts by definition must be topical and therefore produced at speed. Nevertheless, extreme caution is required since a flawed text released into the public domain becomes a ticking bomb that can severely damage the prestige of maligned parties or of the publication in which it appears. Press reports must be lucid, concise and factually accurate (can any newspaper claim never to have published a retraction or an apology?). Opinion pieces should be forceful but measured, forestalling both accusations of demagoguery or sensationalism and the ever-present threat of libel actions. The assumed position of impartiality occupied by the news media in itself creates further pressure, since in many countries newspapers are read only by the relatively educated – precisely those who are most aware that wholly disinterested news is an impossibility because ideology inevitably shapes what is reported and with what emphasis. To this suspicion on the part of the readership must be added the very real but often invisible constraints generated by many newspapers' dependence on corporate advertising and on the financial backing of powerful individuals or groups of shareholders.

This long list of exigencies bearing on the process of creating journalistic copy makes its translation a particularly challenging – and therefore valuable – exercise. The premium on space obliges the translator to be disciplined since it frequently not only precludes the option of explicatory **amplification** – often the recourse of the indolent – but actually necessitates **omission** or compression of parts of the ST (in order to cultivate this discipline, practice translations for journalism should be undertaken as if the TT is destined to appear in newspaper format and can only therefore cover an identical or similar physical area to the ST). Recognition and judicious resolution of ambiguity becomes crucial in order to avoid unwitting manipulation of the ST. In order to detect and deal appropriately with ideological **connotation**, the translator should ideally be equipped with a sophisticated knowledge of contemporary geopolitical issues, an awareness of the overall journalistic culture to which the source medium belongs and the specific ideological tendency of that medium. Furthermore, the very nature of news journalism, which is disseminated internationally but is often highly localized in content, requires that the translator respect conventions in the target culture regarding, for example, the retention of foreign terms to designate the many **culture-bound** features that frequently arise (such as *burkah, loya jirga, intifada, sharia, junta, jihad, glasnost* or *perestroika*) and whether these are sufficiently assimilated to avoid typographical indications (such as italicization) that they are foreign borrowings. Where possible, translators should obtain in-house stylistic norms when translating for specific media.

As elsewhere, the majority of Caribbean newspapers use a combination of locally generated copy and syndicated material from news agencies, sometimes generating stylistic inconsistencies. Furthermore, use of vernaculars for column pieces, alongside standard Caribbean and news agency "international English" in reports, has certainly become commonplace in the anglophone Caribbean. As with literature, therefore, translation of journalistic discourse can offer opportunities to employ localized colloquial forms where the context makes this advisable. This diversity of styles, coupled with the equally varied contexts of the numerous reports, columns, editorials and reviews, makes the bilingual newspaper a particularly challenging and fruitful arena of activity for the translator.

El Periodismo

INTRODUCCIÓN

Pocas formas de discurso escrito enfrentan tantos y tan variados obstáculos como el periodismo. La gran mayoría de los textos periodísticos deben por definición ser actuales y por lo tanto se deben producir rápidamente. Sin embargo, se requiere extremada cautela ya que un texto con fallas que sale a la luz pública se puede convertir en una bomba de tiempo que puede dañar el prestigio de las partes involucradas o del periódico que lo publicó. Los reportes de prensa deben ser lúcidos, concisos y ceñidos con precisión a los hechos (aunque ¿existe algún periódico que no haya tenido que publicar una disculpa o una retracción?). Las columnas de opinión deben tener fuerza pero también mesura, anticipando acusaciones de demagogia o sensacionalismo y la amenaza constante de demandas por difamación. La propia posición asumida de imparcialidad crea otro obstáculo, ya que en muchos países sólo los relativamente más cultos leen los periódicos – precisamente aquellos que saben que una noticia sin parcialidad no puede existir pues la ideología modifica aquello que se reporta y el énfasis que se le da. A este recelo por parte de los lectores se debe añadir el obstáculo real, aunque muchas veces oculto, generado por la dependencia del periódico al respaldo de un grupo de accionistas o individuos poderosos, así como a la publicidad corporativa.

Esta larga lista de exigencias en el proceso de crear un artículo periodístico hace que el ejercicio de traducirlos sea particularmente difícil, y por lo tanto valioso. La limitación de espacio obliga al traductor a ser disciplinado ya que no sólo excluye frecuentemente la opción de **ampliación** explicativa – a menudo el recurso del perezoso – sino que obliga a la **omisión** o condensación de partes del TO. Para cultivar esta disciplina las prácticas de traducción para periodismo deben suponer que el TM aparecerá en formato de periódico y que por lo tanto sólo puede cubrir un área física idéntica o similar al área del TO. Reconocer y resolver juiciosamente la ambigüedad es crucial para evitar la manipulación involuntaria del TO. Para detectar y manejar apropiadamente la **connotación** ideológica, se recomienda que el traductor tenga un alto conocimiento de los asuntos geopolíticos contemporáneos, que sea consciente de la cultura periodística a la que el medio del TO pertenece y su tendencia ideológica específica.

Además, la naturaleza misma del periodismo, diseminado a nivel internacional aunque muchas veces con un contenido altamente local, requiere que el traductor respete las convenciones establecidas en la cultura de llegada relacionadas, por ejemplo, con la retención de términos extranjeros para designar muchas características cargadas culturalmente que con frecuencia aparecen (*burkha, loya jirga, intifada, sharia, jihad, glasnost* o *perestroika*) y si éstas ya se han asimilado lo suficiente en la LM como para no necesitar indicaciones tipográficas (como las bastardillas) de que son préstamos lingüísticos. En donde sea posible, los traductores deben conseguir las normas estilísticas de la compañía para la que trabajen.

Como en otras latitudes, la mayoría de los periódicos caribeños utilizan una combinación de materiales generados a nivel local así como aquellos distribuidos por agencias de noticias, lo que en algunas ocasiones genera inconsistencias estilísticas. Es más, en el caso del Caribe anglófono resulta común encontrar columnas escritas en **dialecto** al lado de otras en las que se usa el inglés "internacional" de las agencias de noticias. Por lo tanto, como con la literatura, la traducción del discurso periodístico ofrece oportunidades para emplear formas coloquiales localizadas cuando el contexto así lo recomiende. La variedad de estilos así como de contextos de las numerosas noticias, columnas, editoriales y reseñas, convierte al periódico bilingüe en un área que presenta grandes retos pero a la vez trae grandes satisfacciones para el traductor.

I. SPANISH > ENGLISH

Text 1

Prensa colombiana critica a Shakira[1]

La cantante colombiana Shakira, considerada la figura musical del año en su país, recibió hoy un "tirón de orejas" del diario El Tiempo porque se volvió "ciega, sorda y muda" al no atender a periodistas ni a sus admiradores. "Sin pretender invadir su intimidad, que merece respeto, no podemos dejar de expresar una sensación de frustración y pasmo por la conducta de la artista", precisó el periódico en su página editorial.

"Déjate de vainas, Shakira. Vuelve a ser esa muchacha sonriente y amable que se parecía a las que hoy te esperan a la salida de tu casa para expresar su cariño", agregó el diario.

Shakira llegó la semana pasada a Barranquilla, su ciudad natal, acompañada de su novio Antonio de la Rúa, hijo del ex presidente de Argentina. El frente de la casa de Shakira, que se congestionó en el pasado de admiradores, periodistas, fotógrafos y camarógrafos, permanece ahora desierto, sin curiosos ni seguidores.

Class Translation

Colombian Press criticizes Shakira

Singer Shakira, considered the top musician of the year in her native Colombia, was today [a]**given a dressing down** by the *El Tiempo* daily because [b]**she seemed to have gone "blind, deaf and dumb"** as she ignored both reporters and fans. "Without wanting to invade her privacy, which should be respected, we can't help but express a feeling of frustration and amazement at the singer's behaviour", the paper lamented in an editorial.

"[c]**Stop putting on airs, Shakira.** [d]**Go back to being just like those smiling, friendly girls who today wait for you to come out of your door to express their affection for you**", the paper added.

Shakira arrived last week in her home town Barranquilla accompanied by her boyfriend Antonio de la Rúa, son of the former president of Argentina. [e]**The area in front of Shakira's house**, which was once packed with admirers, reporters, photographers and cameramen, is now deserted, with no sign of onlookers or fans.

Commentary

This is an example of "meta-journalism", in which a newspaper reports the appearance of another newspaper text as an event. By quoting directly from the primary text, an editorial piece, the meta-text appropriates the editorial's content and opinionated tone while maintaining the appearance of objective, informative reporting. Two styles must therefore be translated: that of the quoted primary text – which here is indignant, exhortative, emotive – and that of the meta-text, which is purely informative. This juxtaposition is useful in laying bare the contrasting conventions and challenges presented by the two styles.

a. given a dressing down It is unclear whether the quotation marks in the ST indicate self-conscious use of a colloquialism by the author of the meta-text, or an actual quotation from the primary text. In any event, the fairly bland formula in the TT was felt appropriate only if the translation were being made for an international news agency. Far more expressive regional suggestions were "given a good cussing" or "a good 'tongue-lashing'" (though the expression used in the ST is not limited to the Caribbean, the later use of "*déjate de vainas*" clearly indicates that regional colloquialism is used as an expressive strategy in the primary text, thereby allowing **compensation** at this point of the TT).

b. she seemed to have gone "blind, deaf and dumb" The ST's use of *volverse* communicates a nuance that is not easy to reproduce in English. The normal verb of "becoming" used for loss of faculty is *quedarse* (*sordo, ciego, mudo, paralítico, calvo,* and others). While *volverse* does not imply willful change in the way that *hacerse* does (as in *me hice el sordo*), it can be used to indicate negative evolution over time, as in *se volvió muy testarudo/reaccionario con la edad*. The addition of "seemed to" was felt to strike an appropriately sardonic note in the TT here. Since the ST here ironically **paraphrases** the eponymous refrain of Shakira's "Ciega, sordomuda" (from her 1998 album *¿Dónde están los ladrones?*), it was felt that the three adjectives should appear in the same order in the TT, as some anglophone readers would doubtless be familiar with the meaning of the song title and thus pick up the reference. An older translator might well have been tempted to have put "deaf, dumb and blind", echoing the well-known refrain of The Who's "Pinball Wizard" ("That deaf dumb and blind kid / Sure plays a mean pinball").

c. Stop putting on airs, Shakira Though the ST seems to invite localized regional alternatives here, the only one that occurred to the group was "stop the shite, Shakira". While this contains an alliteration that is arguably felicitous, its **register** clearly dips too low into the realm of the taboo to be appropriate for the editorial page of a daily newspaper. The chosen formula constitutes an **explicitation** of the more general Colombian Spanish idiom, legitimized by the context. The phrase *dejémonos de vainas* has particularly common currency in Colombia because of the 1980s television series so titled. Clearly, the echo of this title in the ST is entirely **culture-bound** and failure to reproduce it must simply be logged as inevitable **translation loss.**

d. Go back to being just like those smiling, friendly girls who today wait for you to come out of your door to express their affection for you Here the TT compresses the ST by **omission** of the somewhat tortuous comparative string "*que se parecía a las que hoy te esperan*", instead rendering as if the ST had read simply *vuelve a ser como esas muchachas sonrientes y amables que hoy te esperan*. The gain in syntactic clarity was felt to outweigh any loss of nuance.

e. The area in front of Shakira's house This **amplification** (as opposed to merely "the front of Shakira's house") assists clarity. While it was felt "the front" could sometimes designate the area in front of a house, rather than the façade itself, it only seems to have this function when preceded by a preposition in English (as in "at the front of the house", "in front of the house", "out front").

Text 2

Hacerse el sueco[2]

Haciéndose pasar por un profesor de literatura sueco en Cuba, un ladrón planea el espectacular robo de una joya, mientras se dedica a robar a cubanos y turistas en las calles de La Habana.

Está hospedándose en la casa de un ex policía retirado, estricto y patriótico, el cual no se imagina que tiene al tan buscado ladrón bajo su propio techo. Pero el experimentado y escurridizo ladrón termina enredándose con la hija del policía, una linda cubanita que estudia literatura en la universidad de La Habana.

Hacerse el sueco es una comedia costumbrista que plasma la realidad de La Habana actual, explorando las carencias de una sociedad sometida a notables privaciones con un sentido del humor que le permite jugar con alegatos críticos.

Su director, Daniel Díaz, ha elaborado un guión simpático, humano y descriptivo de La Habana de barrio, de la Cuba destartalada y desconchada en la que se defiende la pobreza con dignidad frente a la pillería de supervivencia y el deslumbramiento de las comodidades capitalistas.

En medio de todo, se destaca el valor de la amistad, la honestidad y el amor que no conoce fronteras.

Class Translation

Hacerse el sueco

[a.]**Posing as** [b.]**a Swedish professor of literature** [c.]**visiting Cuba,** a thief plans a spectacular heist to steal a precious stone while sticking up locals and tourists alike on the streets of Havana.

He is boarding in the house of [d.]**an uptight and fervently patriotic retired policeman,** who has no inkling he is harbouring the much wanted criminal under his very roof. The slippery and experienced thief, however, ends up getting involved with [e.]**the policeman's daughter,** [f.]**a beautiful literature student at the University of Havana.**

[g.]*Hacerse el sueco* **– a pun meaning both "playing dumb" and "pretending to be Swedish"** – is a comedy of everyday life that portrays the contemporary reality of the Cuban capital, laying bare the privations suffered [h.]**with a sense of humour that allows it to include a degree of implicit criticism.** Director Daniel Díaz Torres has written a lively script full of human interest and social commentary on the Havana of the neighbourhoods – the worn down and ramshackle side of Cuba where poverty with dignity is valued above getting by with scams and trickery or being dazzled by capitalist luxuries.

Above all, the film highlights the value of friendship, honesty and the kind of love that transcends all borders.

Commentary

a. Posing as Both "passing himself off as" and "masquerading as" were considered here. However, "posing" was felt to be especially apposite because it more strongly connotes an "upwardly mobile" deception, pretending to be something better or more prestigious than one is, rather than merely something different.

b. a Swedish professor of literature The lack of gender inflections in English would have generated ambiguity had this been rendered "Swedish literature professor": it would have been unclear whether the thief was claiming to be Swedish and a literature professor, or a professor of Swedish literature (the film reveals that the former best covers his initial claim, though he also later claims knowledge of Swedish literature in an attempt to impress the policeman's daughter). Even a circumlocution such as "a literature professor visiting Cuba from Sweden" would have left his claimed Swedish nationality less than fully clear.

c. visiting Cuba This **amplification** from the more obvious "in Cuba" is based on the knowledge that the thief does not claim to be teaching in Cuba, but merely researching in order to return to Sweden with his findings.

d. an uptight and fervently patriotic retired policeman The choice of "uptight", rather than the less colloquial direct cognate "strict", is again based on direct knowledge of the referent (the character in the film). The comic impetus of the film is generated by the friction between the policeman's desire to keep a firm grip on his domestic situation and the irresistible elusiveness and complexity of that situation, suggested in the ST by the words *escurridizo* and *enredándose*. The additional comic **connotations** of the epithet "uptight" justify the use of **explicitation** here. The **amplification** "fervently patriotic" is employed for similar reasons.

e. the policeman's daughter The possibility of using the CE colloquialism "a police" (for a policeman) was entertained. Even if the translation were destined for a local medium, however, this option was ultimately disregarded because here it would generate an unacceptable incongruity of **register**: use of the apostrophized Anglo-Saxon genitive was felt to belong firmly outside the dialectal realm inhabited by "a police". Dialect would have "the police daughter", creating problems of consistency elsewhere in the TT unless a thoroughgoing dialectal rewrite, or **domestication**, were undertaken.

f. a beautiful literature student at the University of Havana The **omission** of *cubanita* seemed advisable, since any reader would infer the nationality of the policeman's daughter to be Cuban unless specified otherwise. The ST's use of the diminutive suggests the inclusion of the term at all is not to clarify nationality, but to suggest a recognizable physical type to Spanish-speaking readers. To this extent, it can be classified as a **culture-bound** element: a mental picture of the type in question cannot be triggered with equal economy in English, simply because most anglophone readers, even in the Caribbean, are less likely to have a clear impression of what a young Cuban woman might typically look like. Other terms suggesting locally recognizable physical types or attributes like *mulatica*, *trigueña*, "red man/girl" cause similar problems, compounded further when social factors intervene as in "skettel/ghetto girl", "rude boy" etc.

g. *Hacerse el sueco* – a pun meaning both "playing dumb" and "pretending to be Swedish" This explicatory gloss was felt to be inevitable given the highly **culture-bound** character of the ST idiom here. Though it is popularly believed that the Spanish expression is derived from the presence of lost-looking northern European tourists in 1960s Spain – making it especially apposite in the context of the film, which draws on the stereotype of Scandinavians as civilized, bland and innocuous – the idiom in fact turns out to be a product of a false etymology involving the Latin word *soccus*, a type of shoe used by comics in the Roman theatre as part of the attire that distinguished them from tragedians (the same Latin term gave rise to the Spanish *zueco*, "clog" in English). *Hacerse el sueco* thus came to mean to "play the buffoon" or to behave like a theatre comic, who would entertain by pretending not to understand what the audience was saying.

h. with a sense of humour that allows it to include a degree of implicit criticism This gloss effectively interprets this tricky section of the ST to mean that the light comic touch of the film is used as a "Trojan Horse" to sneak a somewhat critical portrayal of contemporary Cuba past the censors. While this interpretation may be consistent with the history of Cuban film censorship, the ST is ultimately unclear here. Where the ST is allusive in a manner that makes comprehension uncertain, or at least would confuse readers from the TT culture, **explicitation** in the service of **acceptability** can be legitimate. It is of course the translator's responsibility to ensure that suppression of any ambiguity does not constitute outright manipulation of the ST.

Text 3

Dolor ciudadano[3]

Mientras que ser político sea un negocio, Panamá no caminará hacia el desarrollo, ni habrá justicia social. Me puedo imaginar la pelea del "quítate tú, para ponerme yo", me voy y fundo otro partido o me voy porque no votaron como yo quería. Esta situación, es vergonzosa para el país, frente a los foros internacionales. ¿Dónde se quedaron los valores de ciudadano; de éstos que aspiran a ser elegidos o reelegidos como servidores públicos? ¿Cuándo los políticos entenderán y aceptarán que una vez elegidos son servidores públicos; no "patrones" y que no son dueños del erario de la Nación?

¡Reflexión!!! Ya está bueno; no vivimos en una cueva, miren esto da vergüenza, cuando le preguntan a uno, cosas desagradables de la tierra que lo vio nacer. Están tan corroídos por las ansias de poder, soberbia, vanidad, que ya no tienen vergüenza ni decoro; sólo son unos "pobres entes" dignos de lástima; ruego a Dios Nuestro Señor que tenga compasión de su pobre alma enferma.

¡Saben qué! no salgan del país, por lo menos le hacen un favor a éste.

Verónica Matías
Oviedo, FL

Commissioned Translation

[a.]A Citizen's Lament[4]

As long as being a politician continues to be a business, Panama will not move towards development and there will be no social justice. I can just imagine the squabbling: "[b.]**I want you out so I can get in**", or "I am going to form another party", or "I am leaving because the people did not vote to suit me". This situation is embarrassing for the country, especially in international forums. Where is the sense of civic responsibility on the part of those who seek to be elected or re-elected as servants of the people? When will politicians understand that when they are elected they are the servants of the people and not their masters and that the public treasury is not their personal bank account?

Let's reflect for a minute: [c.]**We are not living in the Dark Ages.** It is really shameful to be asked such embarrassing questions about the land of your birth. These politicians are so corrupted by the lust for power, by pride and vanity that they have lost all sense of shame and decency. They are just poor souls who deserve our pity. May God have mercy on their poor, sick souls.

You know what? [d.]**They should never leave the country.** At least they can do us that one favour.

Verónica Matías
Oviedo, FL

Commentary

Though some bilingual newspapers do include translations of letters to the editor, it is generally not common to be asked to translate this epistolary form of journalistic text professionally. Nonetheless, translating examples of this genre can be a highly productive exercise because of the frequently opinionated character of their discourse, in which irony, fulmination and exhortation are common features. As in the case of letters of complaint, control of tone is crucial to the effectiveness or otherwise of many letters to the editor, making them useful testing grounds for the translator who, while mastering aspects such as adequate comprehension of the ST and broadly appropriate stylistic choices in the TT, may continue to neglect subtler issues of **connotation**.

In this instance, the Barbadian translator has tended to tone down the more extravagant style of the Panamanian author of the letter, normalizing punctuation and employing somewhat more sober diction. This perhaps reflects the prevalence and importance of sobriety of expression and the assertion of solid common sense as features of Barbadian dialectical style, at least in print, as against the more exhortative and openly indignant tone to be found in many Latin American instances of the genre.

a. A Citizen's Lament In the classroom, the title "Citizen Pain" was offered by two translators, who felt its punning echo of the classic film title *Citizen Kane* was the kind of device that sub-editors favour when adding headings to readers' letters. Significantly, both were educated outside the Caribbean; the title was unknown to those brought up exclusively within the region.

b. I want you out so I can get in. The idiom *quítate tú, para ponerme yo*, designating both ruthless competitiveness and egotistical self-promotion, was coined by Dominican salsa legend Johnny Pacheco as the title and refrain of a song made famous by the Fania Allstars in the early 1970s. It was later used as the title of a Mexican-Spanish television film in 1982, and that of a Spanish television series since the late 1980s. The Puerto Rican poet José Raúl González, asked to clarify the derivative expression *resuélvete tú pa' ponerme yo* by the translator of his poem "Chamaco's Corner", in which it appears, offered this graphic gloss: *Canción de salsa vieja: "quítate tú pa' ponerme yo". O sea, en la calle, salta del camino porque yo vengo a plantar bandera, yo soy más guapo que tú.*

The obvious applicability of the idiom to Latin American public life is reflected by a web search, which generates as many hits relating to shameless, power-hungry opportunism in the political sphere as it does to its musical origins. As such, it is comparable to *dejémonos de vainas*, discussed above, in being so commonplace in the popular consciousness as to incur inevitable loss of resonance when rendered in another language. "Get out so I can get in" was suggested in class as an alternative to the commissioned translation, with the repetition being felt to offer at least a suggestion of a song title or commonplace expression.

c. We are not living in the Dark Ages This **modulation** or conceptual recasting of the literal "living in caves" retains the metaphor of darkness as equivalent to that which is primitive or underdeveloped, but alludes much more specifically to a historical period regarded as relatively unenlightened and politically fragmented (the "back translation" into Spanish would be *la Edad de las tinieblas*). The question of whether metaphors that

equate darkness with the primitive or unenlightened are racist has centred on expressions relating to colonial Africa, such as "the Dark Continent" or Conrad's *Heart of Darkness*. Since "the Dark Ages" were precipitated by the expansionist activities of competing Germanic tribes in Europe and North Africa, there would seem to be no risk of equating dark skin colour with primitive behaviour here.

d. They should never leave the country The translator shrewdly interprets this imperative as an exhortation aimed at the politicians, though the implied interlocutors of the rest of the letter are clearly fellow readers of the newspaper and its editors (as is evident from the rhetorical question "*¿Cuándo los políticos entenderán . . . ?*"). The normal device for exhorting indirectly would be the addition of *que*, as in *que no salgan del país*. While this sudden change of addressee is not inconsistent with the spontaneous style of the rest of the letter, it may also be the result of an editorial excision of a cue indicating the change. In any event, by opting for "they" instead of "you", the TT follows the discursive logic of the rest of the letter by retaining the fellow readers or the editor as the implied addressees.

II. INGLÉS > ESPAÑOL

Texto 1

No US solutions likely to reduce crime problems.[5] (extract)

A WEEK ago it was reported that the United States of America has recorded another year of decline in reported crimes, on a national basis. This seems to suggest that the responsible American authorities know what successful strategies to utilize in curbing crime, unlike the situation that obtains in Jamaica, since our crime figures make for despondent reading.

One cannot, however, transpose successful strategies in one culture to another culture and expect similar results as other elements may work against such. A rehash of the major American crime strategies and an application to Jamaica will show why this is so. The first major strategy executed in the US was and continues to be the high levels of deportation of foreign nationals, especially Caribbean ones, but not exclusively so as Colombian nationals also rank high. The US deports the highest number of convicted aliens (a strange term, as if they came from Mars), and is not hesitant in also deporting long-standing residents

Traducción de Jairo Sánchez

[a.]**Las soluciones propuestas por EE.UU. no sirven para reducir delitos. (extracto)**

[b.]**LA SEMANA pasada se anunció que Estados Unidos ha tenido otro año de reducción en los delitos registrados.** Esto parece sugerir que las autoridades norteamericanas a cargo saben cuáles son las estrategias que funcionan en la lucha contra el crimen, al contrario de lo que sucede en Jamaica, pues [c.]**nuestros índices de criminalidad son descorazonadores.**

Sin embargo, no se pueden transponer las estrategias exitosas de una cultura a otra y esperar resultados similares, ya que otros elementos pueden estar en contra de ellas. Un recuento de las principales estrategias americanas y su aplicación a Jamaica nos mostrará por qué esto es así. La primera estrategia ejecutada por los EE.UU. fue, y continúa siendo, una alta tasa de deportación de extranjeros, especial pero no exclusivamente de origen caribeño, ya que los colombianos también constituyen un grupo importante. [d.]**Estados Unidos deporta el mayor número de convictos extranjeros (lo que ellos llaman *"aliens"***

who have committed crimes but never took the trouble to naturalize.

This policy has worked wonderfully for the Americans but has transferred these problems to countries like the Dominican Republic, Jamaica, Guyana and Trinidad and Tobago, which now face a serious rise in new types of crimes, like kidnapping in Trinidad and Tobago.

como si fueran monstruos de ciencia ficción) y no duda en deportar a los residentes que hayan cometido delitos pero que nunca se preocuparon por naturalizarse.
*ᵉ·***Esta política ha funcionado a las mil maravillas para los americanos** pero ha transferido los problemas a países como República Dominicana, Jamaica, Guyana y Trinidad y Tobago, quienes ahora afrontan un aumento considerable en nuevas modalidades delictivas, como el secuestro en Trinidad y Tobago.

Comentarios

Los artículos periodísticos, como todo texto, están escritos desde cierta perspectiva. Aunque se quiera mantener la ilusión de objetividad, no debemos olvidar que los textos están cargados de cierta ideología que los subyace y que ésta se hace patente cuando se analiza quién escribió el texto, para quién lo hizo y cuál fue su propósito.

Este extracto es la introducción de un artículo en el que se comenta una noticia que apareció en un periódico estadounidense (meta-texto), y sus posibles aplicaciones al contexto de Jamaica. El tono que ha decidido utilizar la escritora posee tintes de ironía. Ella critica, aunque no abiertamente, la tendencia que tienen ciertos países (especialmente aquellos en vía de desarrollo) de copiar el modo de hacer las cosas de los estadounidenses. También pone en duda la efectividad de las medidas tomadas por EE.UU. para resolver sus problemas.

Desde una perspectiva norteamericana, la noticia de la reducción de delitos es totalmente positiva. Desde la perspectiva de otros países la solución planteada no resuelve el problema, sólo lo envía a otra región. Esto muestra cómo el contexto desde el cual escribimos y traducimos (incluyendo nuestras creencias, presupuestos y prejuicios) influye en la manera en la que lo hacemos.

Estilísticamente, los escritos periodísticos en el Caribe anglófono pueden variar en su **registro**, desde la mayor formalidad hasta un estilo totalmente coloquial. Este fenómeno no es muy común en el Caribe hispanohablante.

a. Las soluciones propuestas por EE.UU. no sirven para reducir delitos Tal vez una de las partes más importantes de una nota periodística es su título. El titular debe dar una idea de lo que trata el artículo, pero también debe ser llamativo y breve. Por esto muchos de los titulares contienen juegos de palabras. La ambigüedad es también una importante aliada de la titulación. Una forma de hacer esto es sacar una parte de la noticia del contexto, o eliminar cierta información. En este caso la información completa sería "Las soluciones propuestas por EE.UU. no sirven para reducir delitos en Jamaica". En nuestra versión al español hemos optado también por darle una nueva perspectiva a la información: pasamos de "*No . . . likely*" a un "no" rotundo, para ejemplificar cómo la ideología del traductor también se refleja en el texto. En cuanto a "crime" debe tenerse en cuenta que se trata de un **falso amigo** y por lo tanto no puede traducirse como "crimen" en todas las instancias.

b. LA SEMANA pasada se anunció que Estados Unidos ha tenido otro año de reducción en los delitos registrados La estructura del pasivo tiende a utilizarse con más frecuencia en inglés que en español, en escritos de este tipo es bastante común cambiarla por el "se" impersonal. En cuanto al vocabulario, nótese el uso de la jerga periodística (**tecnolecto**) que incluye verbos relacionados con "decir" generalmente en el pretérito y algunas frases hechas. Para traducir un texto periodístico se recomienda usar la **inmersión textual**. Se ha optado por omitir "*on a national basis*" debido a que cuando se habla de un país se da por sentado que se está haciendo referencia a su totalidad. El español tiende a ser menos tolerante con este tipo de redundancias. Más adelante se omite *crime* en "*American crime strategies*" por razones similares. En cuanto a "*long-standing residents*" se podría haber explicado pues no hay una palabra para esto en español, pero no se debe olvidar que en periodismo los escritos están limitados a cierto número de palabras, lo que en ocasiones lleva tanto al escritor como al traductor a eliminar parte de su TO.

c. nuestros índices de criminalidad son descorazonadores El artículo en cuestión trata sobre la criminalidad. De allí que un gran número de expresiones y vocablos se refieran a este tema y se repitan, dándole **coherencia**. Entre ellos podemos encontrar "criminalidad", "delito", "lucha contra el crimen" y "modalidades delictivas". Mientras que el español se preocupa por la variedad, el inglés se conforma con *crime y crimes*. Como el texto analiza estadísticas también hay vocablos pertenecientes a esta área: "tasa", "índice", "un grupo importante", "el mayor número de". Debido a que los textos periodísticos tratan temas tan diversos, se puede hablar de una interdisciplinaridad. Es preciso estar atentos al tema tratado y, si es el caso, utilizar diccionarios especializados.

d. Estados Unidos deporta el mayor número de convictos extranjeros (lo que ellos llaman "*aliens*" como si fueran monstruos de ciencia ficción) En nuestras traducciones nos encontramos frecuentemente con juegos metalingüísticos. Estos son tal vez los más difíciles de traducir, ya que se basan en reflexiones sobre el sistema de la lengua. En este caso la palabra problemática es *alien* debido a su ambigüedad semántica, pues quiere decir "extranjero" y "alienígena". Extranjero en español no tiene dicha ambigüedad. Se optó por añadir un comentario ligeramente explicativo y modificar el juego de palabras, acercando el texto al mundo del lector, quien probablemente podrá relacionarlo con alguna de las cuatro películas que hasta ahora se han hecho.

e. Esta política ha funcionado a las mil maravillas para los americanos Junto con el comentario sobre los *aliens*, el uso de expresiones coloquiales y la exageración contribuyen en este texto a darle el toque familiar e irónico que buscaba la autora. Antes se vio *rehash*, pero al no haber una expresión similar en español coloquial, se llevó a un **registro** más alto. Cuando esto sucede a veces es preciso recurrir a la **compensación** en otra parte del texto.

Texto 2

Ex-Customs man on eight drug charges.[6]

A FORMER Guyanese Customs officer is facing eight drug charges in Barbados.

JSG was remanded to Glendairy Prison when he appeared in the Oistins Magistrates' Court on Wednesday.

G, 44, of Pleasant View, Cave Hill, St Michael, was not required to plead. He is to return to court on October 22.

He is charged with importing, trafficking, possession with intent to supply, and simple possession of marijuana, as well as importing, trafficking, possession with intent to supply, and simple possession of cocaine.

G was slapped with the charges on Tuesday after allegedly being caught with the illicit drugs.

According to Barbados Nation, the former Customs officer was detained when he arrived at Grantley Adams International Airport on a flight from Guyana.

The drugs were said to have a street value of $716,000.

Traducción de Jairo Sánchez

Ex agente de aduana con ocho [a]cargos por tráfico.

[b]**A UN EX AGENTE de aduana guyanés** se le han imputado ocho [c]**cargos relacionados con drogas** en Barbados.

JSG fue remitido a la cárcel de Glendairy tras su aparición el miércoles en la Corte de Magistrados en Oistins, Barbados.

[d]**G, de 44 años, residente en Pleasant View, Cave Hill, St Michael,** no tuvo que declarar. Debe volver a la corte el 22 de octubre.

[e]**Se le acusa de importe, tráfico, posesión con intención de distribuir y posesión simple de** marihuana, como también de importe, tráfico, posesión con intención de distribuir y posesión simple de cocaína.

[f]**A G se le imputaron los cargos** el martes pasado según se dice después de haber sido capturado con las drogas ilícitas.

[g]**Según el diario *Nation* de Barbados,** el ex agente de aduana fue detenido [h]**al llegar al Aeropuerto Internacional Grantley Adams** en un vuelo procedente de Guyana.

[i]**De ser vendida en la calle, se estimó que el valor de la droga sería de unos $716.000.**

Comentarios

Nos encontramos aquí con un breve texto que hace uso del vocabulario jurídico pertinente, sin pasar a ser demasiado especializado. El texto también nos remite a un artículo de otro periódico (**intertextualidad**). Los párrafos son breves y contienen una gran **densidad informativa**.

a. cargos por tráfico Aunque se puede argumentar que *"drug charges"* no es equivalente a "tráfico", hemos decidido utilizar esta fórmula por dos razones. En primer lugar, una **traducción literal** del título daría "cargos por droga(s)", frase poco común en español, por lo que preferimos aquella que tiene más **frecuencia de coocurrencia**. En segundo lugar, como mencionamos anteriormente, los títulos son sólo indicativos de la noticia que sigue. Aquí la versión en inglés es mucho más directa y completa que la selección que hicimos; ha ocurrido una pérdida en la traducción. Si este fuera un texto con efectos legales no se permitiría tal pérdida (ya que estrictamente no tiene ocho cargos por tráfico) y el traductor tendría que buscar mecanismos para recuperar la información, bien mediante una explicitación, bien recurriendo a una nota de pie de página.

b. A UN EX AGENTE de aduana Como se mencionó en la introducción, las normas de publicación en cuanto a estilo y formateo las impone el periódico para el que se trabaja. Lo más común en periódicos bilingües es que las dos versiones tengan el mismo formato, por lo que mantenemos las mayúsculas en este caso. Por otro lado, en inglés nos encontramos con dos términos *ex* y *former* cuyos equivalentes en español corresponderían a "ex" y "antiguo". Sin embargo, la segunda opción del español no resulta ser tan común como su versión inglesa, pues hace referencia en la mayoría de sus acepciones a algo que existe desde hace mucho tiempo. En el caso en que la acepción es similar a "ex" hay que ser precavidos pues no siempre coinciden ("un antiguo maestro", "un ex maestro"). Se ha optado por mantener el prefijo ex (sin guión) en los dos casos, aunque en traducción y en la escritura en general se aprecia la variedad en el vocabulario. Otra forma de solucionar la traducción hubiera sido mediante una frase relativa adjetiva como "un agente que solía trabajar para la aduana", pero se sacrificaría la **densidad informativa** que caracteriza a este texto. A esto hay que añadir el cambio de perspectiva gramatical en la formulación de la frase (**transposición**): el TO usa la voz activa y la traducción la pasiva refleja.

c. cargos relacionados con drogas Se presenta una segunda traducción más cercana al TO.

d. G, de 44 años, residente en Pleasant View, Cave Hill, St Michael Hay que tener en cuenta que la estructura presentada en inglés (apellido, número de años, dirección) es mucho más breve pero está preestablecida. En español no sucede lo mismo y por ende es preciso explicitar mediante la preposición en el primero de los casos, y el sustantivo en el segundo. En este caso, al tratarse de direcciones, se recomienda hacer una **transferencia** directa del inglés, sin buscar la **traducción literal** de los nombres de las calles. Esta **transferencia** se hace también en el caso de los nombres propios (a excepción del nombre del Papa y de algunos reyes), nombres de periódicos y revistas, entre otros.

e. Se le acusa de importe, tráfico, posesión con intención de distribuir y posesión simple de Nos encontramos con un escrito interdisciplinario en el que se mezclan las formulas del periodismo con las del tema tratado en el artículo, en este caso el derecho. Una **traducción literal** de *supply* puede ser suministrar, pero al ser una frase hecha se prefiere la traducción reconocida que es la que se presenta aquí. Los buscadores de Internet son de gran utilidad para ayudar al traductor a encontrar dichas frases. En este caso, por ejemplo, se puede hacer una búsqueda con las palabras entrecomilladas "posesión con intención" dando como resultado que en el 90 por ciento de los casos viene seguida de "de distribuir"; el otro 10 por ciento lo ocupan "de distribución" y "de venderla o venderlo". Mediante este tipo de búsquedas nos aseguramos de que nuestra traducción utiliza los términos más comunes y vigentes.

f. A G se le imputaron los cargos En español se ha optado por utilizar la fórmula jurídica más común con el verbo "imputar" que no tiene las connotaciones gráficas que tiene *slap* (dar una palmada/cachetada) en el presente texto. En inglés hay una gran variedad de palabras que pueden remplazar la utilizada en el TO, por ejemplo *served, faced, confronted, accused, presented,* aunque la más común y neutra es la primera de esta lista.

g. Según el diario Nation de Barbados Es común encontrarse con el fenómeno de la **intertextualidad,** pues al remitirse a otras fuentes se le da mayor credibilidad e imparcialidad a la noticia. En el caso de que se cite parte de un texto de una fuente que esté traducida, se recomienda utilizar la traducción reconocida, en lugar de crear una nueva traducción: supongamos que en un artículo periodístico aparece una cita de Walcott, es preferible en este caso buscar alguna de las traducciones que ya circulan que aventurar una nueva.

Por otro lado, como se dijo anteriormente, este nombre al ser el de un periódico, no se traduce pero sí se incluye una explicación de lo que el nombre *"Nation"* significa en este contexto, es decir un "diario".

h. al llegar al Aeropuerto Internacional Grantley Adams La forma de *when* + pronombre + verbo en pasado se traduce eficientemente en español mediante "al"+ verbo no conjugado. En cuanto al nombre del aeropuerto, se ha optado por traducirlo manteniendo las mayúsculas por ser un nombre propio.

i. De ser vendida en la calle, se estimó que el valor de la droga sería de unos $716.000 En este caso vemos cómo un sustantivo adjetivado en inglés (*street*) se convierte en una frase entera en español, una forma de ampliación que fuerza la reestructuración completa de la frase. Nótese el cambio en la puntuación utilizada para separar los miles, así como el hecho de que no se nombra el tipo de moneda en que se hizo el cálculo.

Texto 3	*Traducción Encargada*
Minister wants authorities to publicly hang murderers.[7]	[a.]**Ministro pide a las autoridades que se ejecute públicamente a los asesinos.**[8]
Friday July 23 2004	Viernes 23 de julio de 2004.
PORT-OF-SPAIN, Trinidad (CMC). A religious minister has called on the Trinidad and Tobago authorities to publicly execute convicted murderers as a deterrent to criminal activities on the island.	PUERTO ESPAÑA, Trinidad. (CMC). Un ministro religioso ha pedido a las autoridades de Trinidad y Tobago que se ahorque en público a los asesinos convictos para [b.]**disuadir a los criminales de practicar actividades ilícitas en la isla.**
Pastor Elmore Anthony made the call on Tuesday, while officiating at the funeral service of Police Constable HCJ, who was killed in a maxi-taxi last week by a lone gunman, who went on to rob the other six passengers in the vehicle.	El pastor Elmore Anthony hizo la petición el martes mientras oficiaba el servicio funeral del agente de policía HCJ, asesinado [c.]**en un *maxi-taxi* la semana pasada por un hombre armado** que luego asaltó a los otros seis pasajeros que se encontraban en el vehículo.
"I hope the day will come when hangings will be carried out at Woodford Square instead of the privacy of the prison", he said, noting that many killings were being carried out by people "without remorse".	"Espero que llegue el día en que los ahorcamientos se efectúen [d.]**en la plaza Woodford** en lugar de en la privacidad de la prisión", dijo, anotando que [e.]**mucha gente mataba "sin remordimiento".**
"Some people believe they are God's gunmen to release us from mortality when they want to rob you, when they want your money, want your car and want	"Algunas personas creen que son los pistoleros de Dios que vienen a [f.]**librarnos de nuestra mortalidad cuando quieren robarnos, cuando quieren nuestro dinero,**

your jewelry," he told mourners including National Security Minister Martin Joseph and Police Commissioner Trevor Paul.

Pastor Anthony said it had become easy "to take a gun and shoot somebody as life seems to some people to have no value".

The Police Second Division on Monday offered a TT$20,000 reward for information leading to the arrest of J's killer.

J was the second police officer killed in the last two weeks. On Monday, Police Constable AC was buried a week after he was bludgeoned to death while searching for an escaped prisoner.

More than 140 people have been murdered here so far this year.

nuestros autos y nuestras joyas", les dijo a los dolientes entre quienes se contaban el Ministro de Seguridad Nacional Martin Joseph y el Comisionado de Policía Trevor Paul.

El pastor Anthony dijo que ahora era fácil "tomar un arma y dispararle a la gente ya que [g]**para algunas personas la vida parece carecer de valor"**.

La Segunda División de Policía ofreció el lunes una recompensa de 20.000 dólares de Trinidad y Tobago [h]**para quien proporcione información que lleve a la captura del asesino de** [i]**J, el segundo policía asesinado en las últimas dos semanas.** El lunes, el oficial AC fue enterrado una semana después de haber sido muerto a palos mientras [j]**perseguía a un prisionero que había escapado.**

Más de 140 personas han sido asesinadas aquí en lo corrido del año.

Comentarios

El contenido de este texto periodístico se inscribe en un contexto en el que la pena de muerte está vigente en un país. En el caso del Caribe ninguno de los países pertenecientes a la ONU han firmado el segundo protocolo facultativo destinado a abolir la pena de muerte (CCPR-OP2-DP). Un traductor que esté contra la pena de muerte puede encontrarse en una situación en la que se le pida traducir textos que van contra sus principios. De ser así tiene toda la libertad para rehusarse.

a. Ministro pide a las autoridades que se ejecute públicamente a los asesinos La mayoría de los diccionarios incluyen "pastor" como la traducción de *minister* cuando se trata de la acepción religiosa de esta palabra. Sin embargo, se ha mantenido aquí "ministro" por dos razones. Por un lado la palabra puede significar "pastor" cuando va acompañada del adjetivo "religioso" como sucede más adelante en el texto. Por otra parte, el TO deja en el título la ambigüedad entre la **connotación** religiosa y la política de la palabra en cuestión, ambigüedad que se quiso mantener en la traducción. Como se mencionó anteriormente, la ambigüedad en los títulos de los artículos periodísticos es uno de los recursos con que cuentan los periodistas para despertar la curiosidad en el lector para que éste lea la nota. Al contar con dos expresiones que equivalen a *minister* en su sentido religioso ("pastor" y "ministro religioso") el traductor tiene la libertad para dar variedad léxica a su texto, una característica que se aprecia mucho tanto en español como en inglés, pero más en la primera lengua.

Pasando a las expresiones verbales vemos dos cambios de énfasis que probablemente tengan que ver con la percepción del mundo de parte de la traductora. El primero de ellos tiene que ver con la traducción de *want* por "pedir". El verbo "querer" hace énfasis en el sujeto, el verbo "pedir" es ditransitivo y por lo tanto hace énfasis en lo que se pide y en a quién se le pide. Es posible que este cambio se dé gracias a que para la traductora no es muy natural que un pastor desee la muerte de otro ser humano. El segundo cambio es la forma del "se" impersonal. Por razones similares a las expuestas anteriormente se ha cambiado el énfasis del agente de la acción a la acción misma.

Por último, se ha cambiado "ahorcamiento" por el hiperónimo "ejecución" por ser más general y así reforzar la ambigüedad de la que se habló arriba. Esta información se compensa en el cuerpo del texto.

b. disuadir a los criminales de practicar actividades ilícitas en la isla Peter Newmark, en su *A Textbook of Translation,* citando a Vinay y Darbelnet, llama **transposición** al cambio en la categoría gramatical que muchas veces es indispensable a la hora de traducir. Newmark menciona varios tipos de **transposición** así como razones para usarla. Se usa la **transposición** cuando una estructura en la LO no tiene equivalente en la LM, o aun cuando la tenga, si dicha estructura no resulta natural para el contexto. En este caso el cambio que se da es de un sustantivo *deterrent* a un verbo "disuadir". Es cierto que en español existe "disuasión" pero utilizarlo en esta frase haciendo una **traducción literal** hubiera restado naturalidad al texto. La decisión de usar el verbo lleva consigo otros cambios como la **modulación** que conlleva usar el agente por la acción (el criminal por lo criminal). En los casos en los que usamos la **transposición** nos vemos enfrentados a lo que podríamos llamar una reacción en cadena de cambios. El último en nuestra cadena se refiere a no poder utilizar el adjetivo "criminal" para evitar la redundancia, forzando a la traductora a buscar otro término que encaje en la frase dotando a la traducción de un significado lo más parecido al TO.

c. en un *maxi-taxi* la semana pasada por un hombre armado Se han mencionado antes (ver Comentarios al Texto 1 en la sección dedicada al turismo español > inglés) los diferentes nombres que reciben varios tipos de transporte en el Caribe y Latinoamérica. En este caso, el término es específico de la cultura de partida y se ha decidido hacer una **transferencia** directa. Aunque el lector no esté familiarizado con el término el contexto le ayudará a deducir que es un tipo de transporte masivo, en este caso el equivalente a *ZR* en Barbados por ejemplo, o "colectivo" en Colombia. Como se mencionó en la introducción, las marcas tipográficas como las bastardillas sirven para enfatizar que el término es extranjero y tiene por lo tanto una carga cultural específica en la cultura origen. En cuanto a *"lone gunman"*, se buscaron varias alternativas entre las que se cuenta "pistolero solitario" que es quizá la traducción más literal. Sin embargo se descartó por las asociaciones que despierta el término: "pistolero" recuerda las películas del oeste, y por la misma línea podemos llegar a la famosa serie *El Llanero Solitario*. Por estas razones se ha decidido omitir "solitario" y remplazar el término "pistolero" por su equivalente más neutral "hombre armado". Haber mantenido la **traducción literal** hubiera despertado las **connotaciones** anteriormente mencionadas y por lo tanto le hubiera restado la solemnidad que el caso amerita. No obstante, más adelante la traductora utiliza el término "pistolero de Dios" justificado debido al uso metafórico de la expresión.

d. en la plaza Woodford Se ha optado por hacer una **transferencia** parcial del lugar mencionado: *Square* > plaza. Si bien *Woodford Square* es un nombre propio y las reglas en general dictan que se debe transferir este tipo de nombres, en el caso que nos atañe "plaza" nos evita tener que hacer una **ampliación**. Se debe tener en cuenta que un factor que determina la **transferencia** total de un término es el hecho de ser reconocido como tal en la cultura meta. Así, si nos enfrentamos a *Times Square* dejaríamos la totalidad del nombre de la LO en la LM.

e. mucha gente mataba "sin remordimiento" En la versión inglesa del texto la sección entre comillas modifica al sustantivo *people*. En esta traducción las comillas hacen referencia a la acción más que a la persona. Se ha cambiado la perspectiva y el énfasis, manteniendo, eso sí, la idea general. Estos cambios se pueden deber a varias razones, entre las que se puede contar la limitación de espacio que tiene la traductora, aunque esto no ocurre en el resto del texto. Es un cambio de perspectiva, un tipo de **modulación** de la persona a la acción.

f. librarnos de nuestra mortalidad cuando quieren robarnos, cuando quieren nuestro dinero, nuestros autos y nuestras joyas El desplazamiento de la segunda persona plural en inglés al de la primera en español cambia la estructura semántica de la frase. Es posible que la traductora haya intentado reproducir el efecto de oralidad de un sermón en español en el que la repetición en plural por parte del pastor tiene el efecto de unión entre los presentes.

g. para algunas personas la vida parece carecer de valor Traducciones alternativas son "para algunas personas la vida parece no tener valor", "parece que para algunas personas la vida no tiene valor alguno". Como se ve en las dos alternativas propuestas el orden de las palabras cambia la percepción de la frase por parte del lector. En la primera se mantiene la lógica del TO; en la segunda "parecer" ya no se relaciona de la misma manera con "la vida". Además, la primera alternativa se libra de la cacofonía que se crea entre "parecer" y "carecer".

h. para quien proporcione información que lleve a la captura del asesino Todos los textos cuentan con expresiones fijas que nos ayudan a reconocerlos como pertenecientes a un tipo especial de discurso. Incluso los textos artísticos que se caracterizan por su unicidad tienen ciertas expresiones arquetípicas (Érase una vez . . .). Estas frases generalmente tienen como equivalente en la LM una expresión fija también que de ser traducida con otras palabras interrumpiría el ritmo de lectura al llamar la atención sobre la construcción gramatical o la elección de vocabulario, por ejemplo. Para ilustrar este punto compárese la frase citada con ésta: "para la persona que dé información que ayude al arresto del criminal". Si bien la información básica es la misma, y no hay nada agramatical en ella, la frase no fluye dentro del **tipo de texto** que estamos manejando.

i. J, el segundo policía asesinado en las últimas dos semanas La traductora ha optado por condensar dos párrafos en uno, ayudada por el hecho de que la información con la que concluye el primero de ellos, el nombre de la víctima, sirve de comienzo para el segundo. En este caso se omite el verbo "ser" en la segunda frase y se remplaza por una coma. Esta técnica puede ser utilizada siempre y cuando la estructura de los párrafos no pierda **coherencia**.

j. perseguía a un prisionero que había escapado Se ha cambiado el significado de la frase al escoger el verbo "perseguir" como equivalente de "buscar". Si bien estos dos verbos pueden funcionar como sinónimos en una variedad de contextos, en éste particular se añade información que no está explícita en el TO. "Perseguir" tiene implícito el hecho de que alguien huye y se le sigue para alcanzarlo o alcanzarla, por este hecho tiene el matiz de velocidad; "buscar", por otro lado, se refiere simplemente a intentar encontrar, careciendo del matiz mencionado. La elección que ha hecho la traductora no es gratuita ya que se ve reforzada por el adverbio "mientras", además de darle vivacidad a la historia. Cabe anotar la traducción del adjetivo *escaped* por una frase relativa adjetiva que es una forma de **transposición** muy común cuando se traduce del inglés al español.

III. SPANISH > ENGLISH EXERCISES

1. Read the following opening of a letter to the letters page of the Miami newspaper *El Nuevo Herald* and answer the questions below:

Vendo cocaína . . .[9]

La verdad, no vendo cocaína: sólo quería llamar la atención, primero, de la persona que en *El Nuevo* recibe la correspondencia y, luego, la suya, lector. Seré breve: soy un abogado colombiano, residente en Barranquilla, quien ha estudiado el tema del narcotráfico. El día que todos los gobiernos del mundo decidan despenalizar el narcotráfico, ese día el problema de los narcóticos se acaba.

   i) What do you think is likely to be the **skopos** or function of the full text?
   ii) Which expressive features are prominent in this opening and what kinds of linguistic structures and rhetorical devices are likely to appear in the rest of the letter?
   iii) What further arguments might the author use to support his contention that drug trafficking should be legalized? If necessary, research in the library or on the net the arguments used by proponents of legalization.
   iv) Consider your own position on legalization and summarize it in a short paragraph in English.
   v) Read the full text of the letter at http://www.caribbeantranslationmanual.com/journalism.html and see how well your answers to ii) and iii) above predicted its content. Translate the letter.
   vi) Find someone whose answer to iv), above, contrasts significantly with your own and exchange your translation with them. See if either of you can detect any differences in your translations attributable to your contrasting positions on the issue discussed.

IV. EJERCICIOS PRÁCTICOS INGLÉS > ESPAÑOL

1. El siguiente texto es el desarrollo del comentario periodístico del Texto 1 analizado arriba. Tradúzcalo teniendo en cuenta que debe haber **coherencia** y se debe mantener el tono entre su texto y el arriba traducido. Analice qué expresiones le ayudan a dar el tono de ironía al texto y cómo las ha traducido usted.

DEPORTATION STRATEGY[10]

If Jamaica was to apply the deportation strategy, the first question one would have to ask is since it is mainly Jamaicans who are committing these serious crimes, apart from a few Nigerians and Colombians, who can we deport? What is more, to where would we deport them? Lime Cay or other small islands seem unlikely, given their weekend traffic, while Cayman has already been reclaimed by the British, since independence. I wonder if we could ask the Americans to take some of them in Guantanamo Bay since they already have Al-Qaeda operatives there and seem determined to expand it.

The second major strategy has been stiffer and more mandatory sentencing guidelines in their court systems, a la the "three strikes you are out" type. This had caused a record high prison population, which leads into the third strategy, which is the building of many more maximum security prisons.

This was possible through the creation of fiscal surpluses (prior to Bush) and widespread co-operation with the private sector in privately-run prisons.

In Jamaica, given that existing maximum security prisons, G.P. and at Spanish Town, are already stretched beyond capacity, and given the debt situation, there is no way that five or more new maximum security prisons will ever be built in the next decade. Worse, if we were to actually impose more custodial sentences, there would be every likelihood of mass prison troubles a la Brazil.

The fourth US strategy is not well-known but it is being used. It is called "racial profiling", where minority groups are targeted and, when convicted, sentenced to longer stretches than the majority racial groups. This means that a disproportionate number of blacks and Hispanics are found in the prison population than a similar racial cohort in the general population census figures.

2. Compare dos noticias similares expuestas en dos periódicos de diferente corriente. Analice cómo se manipula la información de acuerdo a la ideología del autor/periódico y discuta cómo las creencias del traductor pueden afectar el texto a traducir.

CHAPTER 4

The Creative Arts I: Literature

INTRODUCTION

Though the literary output of the Caribbean is vast and diverse, it is typically character-ized by the need to retell the history of the region, to assert its cultural specificity – either through the use of language or through the content of the narratives – and to point up socio-economic, political, racial and regional issues. As far as language use is concerned, the Caribbean is made up of a plethora of dialects ranging from established variants that may now be used in a wide variety of contexts, such as Jamaican Creole, to those that are still vilified and persecuted as deformations of English, French or Spanish. The language of literature thus has an important role to play in validating such variants as vehicles of communication, leading to authors such as Gabriel García Márquez, Velma Pollard, V.S. Naipaul, Rosario Ferré, Earl Lovelace, Ana Lydia Vega, Juan Bosch, Jean Rhys or Derek Walcott being recognized internationally and celebrated with pride in the region as bear-ers of its cultural and linguistic specificity.

When translating Caribbean literature, therefore, one of the most salient aspects is the prevalence of regional usage. The translation of dialect has been approached in a variety of ways: there are those who advocate the use of a dialectal form in the TL that is equivalent to the dialect of the SL. Others regard such equivalence as impossible, arguing that transfer into a standard form is the best option, since dialects derive from historical processes that are never identical from one language to another. Finally, others suggest a middle path through the use of an artificial dialect in the TL that reproduces more liter-ally the form of the ST, since this form also carries a part of the meaning.

Another essential aspect of Caribbean literary texts is their tendency to denounce historical injustices perpetrated against the people of the region. Some do this explicitly, others through metaphors of power, as exemplified in the short stories analysed in this chapter. In order to understand fully these issues it is necessary to study the history of the region and the biography of the author being translated. For this reason it is preferable that the translator be either a Caribbean person or an expert Caribbeanist. However, largely as a result of vested interests and economic factors, most Caribbean texts are translated outside the region. On the one hand, there are a limited number of texts that are adjudged to "deserve" translation, since such texts have to be recognized both as regionally significant works and as economically viable products (that is, they should sell a certain number of copies). On the other hand, when a text has been adjudged "deserv-ing" of translation, the commissioning of the translated text is usually negotiated directly with major publishing houses, since these can ensure the widest possible distribution. These major publishing houses are headquartered in Spain, in the case of translation into Spanish, and in the United Kingdom and the United States, for translations into English. Thus García Márquez is generally translated in the United States, while Naipaul, Walcott and Lovelace tend to be translated in Spain.

But what is literary translation and how is it different from other types of translation? This question has been an area of intense debate among translation theorists and practitioners. The answers are complex and have always varied according to the prevailing notions of translation generally, and of **fidelity** in translation. Given the necessarily limited scope of this manual, what follows is a general description of only two of these notions, which are particularly relevant since they constitute opposite poles of the debate.

The first and earlier approach posits an opposition between the creative writer and the translator. This has a number of implications, the most obvious of which is the relegation of the role of the translator: the writer is the true artist, while the translator should simply transcribe the created work in another language. In this conception, therefore, the translator's role is submissive. Second, and by extension, the translator should be an invisible entity who simply serves to connect the ST with readers in the TL. This invisibility presupposes that the translated text should read like an original text produced in the TL, so that any element that makes the reader aware that they are reading a translation is condemned. Finally, the notion of **fidelity** is understood as the prohibition on modifying any aspect of the original author's creative genius. However, this requirement generates a contradiction that has led to the rejection of this approach by some theorists: how can the author's idiosyncratic or even experimental use of his or her language be reflected if the translation must "read like an original" in the TL, given that this latter obligation inevitably means normalizing the discourse of the TT to make it more "readable"?

The second approach views the translator as a creative artist on a level with the author of the ST. The implications of this approach are as follows: when translating, the translator is seen as actively recreating the ST, rather than copying it, and thus produces a new work of art in its own right. The translator's role is creative when decision-making arises from an understanding of the source and target cultures, of the literary canons within the two language contexts, and of the resources used in each language to create an artistic work, as opposed to other types of discourse (journalistic, legal, etc.). According to this approach, therefore, the translator is no longer invisible and the target text makes no attempt to disguise its identity as a translation, but its status is in no way diminished as a result. **Fidelity** is thus understood in a much broader sense as faithfulness not to the structure and meanings of the ST, but rather to its **communicative** and pragmatic function. This leaves the translator free to modify to an extent that would have been inconceivable in the past.

The translation process can thus be viewed from two different perspectives: the translator may choose to make a **domesticating** or a **foreignizing** translation. In the first instance, the text is translated as if it had been written in the context of the target culture, so that elements of the source culture may even be replaced by functional equivalents in the target culture (thus "he was eating a donut" might be replaced by *comía una arepa*). This type of translation presupposes that the translator should prioritize the reader of the TT. When the translator implicitly prioritizes the ST author, a **foreignizing translation** results, in which the reader of the TT is obliged to enter the world of the ST author, elements of the source culture are retained and in some instances the grammar of the TL may be modified so that it more closely resembles that of the SL. Finally, these conceptions raise the issue of the translator's ideological position. Advocates of the foreignizing approach contend that the process of **domestication** tends to suppress cultural differences in the service of economic concerns, arguing that major publishers demand domesticated translations, with maximum normalization of style, in order to stress the "universal" appeal of renowned authors and to increase sales by prioritizing readability above all other concerns. This agenda, it is argued, thus also tends to dictate that only texts that are susceptible to **domestication** are translated and disseminated in other languages. Such theorists hold that in literary translation, as elsewhere, translators must make ideologically responsible choices by cultivating maximum awareness of the political and socio-economic implications of their work.

While these conceptions represent opposite poles in the debate, the majority of literary translators tend to oscillate between them, drawing on each according to their specific needs and objectives.

In this chapter, two Caribbean literary texts are presented with their respective translations, together with commentary on their most salient and problematic aspects. Unlike other chapters, a reception study on the translation into English is also discussed, while in the into-Spanish section a reader survey of the English ST was used to clarify **connotations** of various expressions, structures and names before the translation was made. These surveys constitute just two examples of another facet of the translator's role: the translator as researcher. While such research may be carried out before, during or after producing the translation, it is ideally ongoing throughout the process. Most people have an image of the translator as a figure shut in a room with a pile of dictionaries. Translators are of course much more than this: their role also includes a considerable research component, involving recourse to other texts and, particularly, consultation with native speakers of the TL, who after all are the intended recipients of the translation. For this reason, a translator should not work in isolation; rather he or she should seek out contacts in order to clarify doubts, refine drafts and understand **connotations** (particularly outside the mother tongue) to achieve a result of the highest possible quality.

La Creación Artística I: La Literatura

INTRODUCCIÓN

La creación literaria en el Caribe es vasta y diversa pero arquetípicamente se basa en la necesidad de expresar la historia de la región, de reivindicar los temas culturales – bien mediante el lenguaje, bien mediante el contenido de las historias – y de enfatizar los temas socioeconómicos, políticos, raciales y regionalistas. En cuanto al uso del lenguaje, el territorio caribeño está compuesto por una plétora de **dialectos** que van desde los ya reconocidos como el creol de Jamaica, que se usa en una amplia gama de contextos, hasta los que aún son juzgados y castigados como denigraciones del inglés, el francés o el español. El lenguaje literario, por su parte, tiene un importante papel en la aceptación de las variantes como medios válidos de comunicación y es este hecho el que ha llevado a autores y autoras como Gabriel García Márquez, Velma Pollard, V.S. Naipaul, Rosario Ferré, Earl Lovelace, Ana Lydia Vega, Juan Bosch, Jean Rhys o Derek Walcott a ser reconocidos internacionalmente y acogidos en la región como muestra orgullosa de la cultura y el habla caribeña.

Uno de los aspectos que más sobresalen a primera vista al enfrentarse a un texto literario caribeño es su uso extendido de variantes regionales. La traducción del **dialecto** ha generado varias posturas: algunos creen que se debe encontrar un **dialecto** en la LM que equivalga al **dialecto** de la LO. Otros piensan que esta postura es imposible de seguir porque los **dialectos** surgen de procesos históricos que no se repiten de una lengua a otra, y por lo tanto abogan por la traducción del **dialecto** al lenguaje estándar. Por último, otros opinan que una solución intermedia es crear un **dialecto** artificial en el TM de modo que se recree más literalmente la forma del TO, teniendo en cuenta que la forma también hace parte del significado.

Otro aspecto que es evidente es que los textos literarios caribeños denuncian las injusticias históricas hacia el pueblo. Algunos lo hacen de forma directa, otros mediante metáforas de poder, como observaremos en los cuentos presentados en esta sección. Para acercarnos a un entendimiento a fondo de estos problemas es preciso estudiar la historia de la región y la historia de los autores que traducimos. Para esto lo ideal sería que el traductor fuera parte, o que se hubiera especializado en estudios de la región. Sin embargo, la mayor parte de los textos producidos en el Caribe son traducidos en países fuera del territorio. Esto se debe principalmente a motivos económicos y de interés. Por un lado, los textos que "merecen" traducción son limitados pues deben primero ser reconocidos como obras relevantes dentro de la cultura regional, pero también deben ser económicamente viables, es decir que deben vender un determinado número de copias. Por otro lado, cuando un texto ha demostrado "merecer" traducción, los contactos por lo general se hacen directamente con las grandes editoriales debido a que son éstas las que mayor salida le pueden dar a un producto. Las grandes editoriales tienen sus bases en España, para el caso de la traducción al español, o en el Reino Unido o Estados Unidos para la que se hace al inglés: por ejemplo, las traducciones de Gabriel García Márquez se hacen generalmente en Estados Unidos, las de V.S Naipaul, Derek Walcott y Earl Lovelace normalmente en España.

  A TRANSLATION MANUAL FOR THE CARIBBEAN (ENGLISH–SPANISH)
UN MANUAL DE TRADUCCIÓN PARA EL CARIBE (INGLÉS-ESPAÑOL)

Pero, ¿qué es exactamente la traducción literaria? y ¿cómo se distingue de otro tipo de traducciones? El intento de responder estos interrogantes ha generado grandes debates tanto entre los teóricos de la traducción como entre los mismos traductores. Las respuestas no son simples y siempre varían dependiendo de las concepciones que se han tenido de la traducción y de la **fidelidad** a lo largo de la historia. Debido a los alcances del presente manual nos limitaremos a presentar a grandes rasgos sólo dos de estas concepciones, las que a nuestro parecer son las más relevantes por presentarse como polos opuestos:

La primera concepción, también primera en términos históricos, es la que presenta la dicotomía creador/traductor como opuestos. Esto tiene varias implicaciones: primero le da menos importancia a la labor del traductor. El creador es el verdadero artista – el traductor sólo debe encargarse de copiar lo creado y ponerlo en otra lengua. Su labor, por tanto, es sumisa. Segundo, el traductor debe ser un ente invisible que sólo sirve de vínculo entre el TO y sus lectores en la LM. Bajo esta invisibilidad está sobreentendido que el texto una vez traducido se debe leer como un texto producido en la lengua meta; se critica cualquier indicio que le permita al lector darse cuenta de que se encuentra ante una traducción. Por último, la noción de **fidelidad** se entiende bajo esta concepción como la imposibilidad de alterar en cualquier modo la genialidad del autor original. Sin embargo, este requisito genera una contradicción que ha llevado a algunos teóricos a rechazar esta concepción: ¿cómo se refleja el uso idiosincrásico o incluso experimental de la lengua por parte del autor si la traducción tiene que leerse "como si fuera un original" en la LM, ya que esto último supone una inevitable normalización del discurso del TM para que resulte más fácilmente "legible"?

La segunda concepción es la que concibe al traductor como creador y artista al mismo nivel que el autor del texto en la lengua de partida. Las implicaciones de esta concepción son las siguientes: el traductor al verter el texto origen a su propia lengua hace una re-creación activa de dicho texto; no es una copia, es una obra de arte también. Su labor es creativa donde la toma de decisiones proviene del entendimiento de las culturas de salida y de llegada, de los cánones literarios de las dos situaciones lingüísticas, y de los recursos que utiliza cada lengua para crear una obra de arte, en oposición a otro **tipo de textos** (el periodístico, el legal y otros). Además, bajo esta concepción, el traductor deja de ser invisible y el texto se lee como una traducción, pero no por esto su estatus es menor. Otro punto importante es la **fidelidad**, que se entiende como un concepto mucho más amplio y generalmente se basa no ya en la estructura y significados del texto origen sino en su función comunicativa o pragmática. Es esta noción la que le permite al traductor hacer cambios que hubieran sido impensables años atrás. Bajo esta concepción podemos acercarnos al proceso de traducción desde dos ángulos: podemos hacer una **traducción domesticada** o una **traducción foránea**. En el primero de los casos, el texto es traducido como si hubiera sido escrito dentro del contexto de la cultura de llegada, y en el TM incluso se puede llegar a cambiar los elementos de la cultura de partida por sus correspondientes funcionales en la cultura de llegada (podemos cambiar *he was eating a donut* por "comía una arepa", por ejemplo). Este tipo de traducción se basa en que el énfasis que realiza el traductor está puesto en el lector del TM. Cuando el énfasis se pone en el autor del TO, lo que tenemos es una **traducción foránea**: en ella el lector del TM se ve obligado a meterse en el mundo del autor del TO, manteniendo los elementos culturales de la cultura de partida y en algunos casos alterando la gramática de la LM para que se parezca más a la de la LO. Por último, estas concepciones traen a colación el posicionamiento ideológico del traductor. Los que promueven la aproximación foránea de la traducción arguyen que la domesticación tiende a suprimir las diferencias culturales en aras de consideraciones económicas. El argumento es que las editoriales más importantes exigen traducciones domesticadas, con máxima normalización de estilo, para hacer énfasis en el carácter "universal" de los autores reconocidos e incrementar las ventas al dar prioridad, por encima de otras consideraciones, a la facilidad de lectura. Se argumenta que esta estrategia, por lo tanto, tiende a dictar que sólo se traducen y distribuyen en otras lenguas aquellos textos que sean susceptibles de domesticación. Estos teóricos piensan que en la traducción literaria, como en todo tipo de traducción, los traductores deben tomar decisiones ideológicamente responsables, teniendo en cuenta al máximo las implicaciones políticas y socioeconómicas de su labor.

Si bien estas concepciones representan los extremos, la mayoría de los traductores literarios oscilan entre una y otra, haciendo uso de los beneficios de cada una a su conveniencia y de acuerdo a sus necesidades y objetivos.

En el presente capítulo presentaremos dos ejemplos de textos literarios caribeños con sus correspondientes traducciones y comentarios sobre los aspectos más relevantes o problemáticos. A diferencia de otros capítulos del presente manual, incluimos un estudio que se realizó en el primer texto (español > inglés) para verificar la apreciación y recepción del texto traducido (estudio a posteriori). En el segundo texto (inglés > español) se llevó a cabo una encuesta previa a la traducción (estudio a priori) que ayudó al traductor a aclarar las connotaciones de ciertas expresiones, estructuras y nombres.

Estos son sólo dos ejemplos de otra faceta del traductor: el traductor como investigador. La investigación se puede llevar a cabo antes, durante o después de realizar la traducción, pero lo ideal es que se haga en todas las etapas del proceso. Muchas personas cuando piensan en un traductor se imaginan a una persona encerrada en un estudio con diccionarios. El traductor es mucho más que eso. Su trabajo comprende también una gran parte investigativa, de acercamiento a otros textos pero especialmente a los hablantes de la lengua, pues son ellos para los que se hace la traducción. Un traductor no puede estar aislado, siempre busca contactos para resolver sus dudas, para mejorar sus versiones, para enterarse de connotaciones que pueden tener las palabras (en especial aquellas que no son de su lengua materna), en fin, para lograr un producto de la mayor calidad posible.

I. SPANISH > ENGLISH

Text 1

"La nochebuena de Encarnación Mendoza", por Juan Bosch (extracto)[1]

– ¿Tú ta seguro que fue aquí, muchacho? – Preguntó el sargento. – Sí, aquí era – afirmó Mundito, bastante asustado ya.

– Son cosa de muchacho, sargento; ahí no hay nadie – terció el número Arroyo.

El sargento clavó en el niño una mirada fija, escalofriante, que lo llenó de pavor.

Published Translation

"Encarnación Mendoza's Christmas Eve", trans. by John Gilmore (extract)[2]

"[a.]You sure it was here, boy?" asked the sergeant.

"[b.]Yes, he was here," Mundito insisted, frightened enough already.

"[c.]The boy making sport, sergeant, nobody there," chipped in Private Arroyo.

The sergeant transfixed the child with a chilling stare which filled him with terror.

 A TRANSLATION MANUAL FOR THE CARIBBEAN (ENGLISH–SPANISH)
UN MANUAL DE TRADUCCIÓN PARA EL CARIBE (INGLÉS–ESPAÑOL)

– Mire, yo venía por aquí con Azabache –empezó a explicar Mundito – y lo diba corriendo asina – lo cual dijo al tiempo que ponía el perrito en el suelo – y él cogió y se metió ahí.

Pero el número Solito Ruiz interrumpió la escenificación de Mundito preguntando:

– ¿Cómo era el muerto?

– Yo no le vide la cara – dijo el niño, temblando de miedo – solamente le vide la ropa. Tenía un sombrero en la cara. Taba asina, de lao . . .

– ¿De qué color era el pantalón? – inquirió el sargento.

– Azul, y la camisa como amarilla, tenía un sombrero negro encima de la cara . . .

Pero el pobre Mundito apenas podía hablar; se hallaba aterrorizado, con ganas de llorar. A su infantil idea de las cosas, el muerto se había ido de allí sólo para vengarse de su denuncia y hacerlo quedar como un mentiroso. Seguramente en la noche le saldría en la casa y lo perseguiría toda la vida.

"d. **Look, I did be coming along here with Blackie,**" Mundito began to explain, "and e. **I put he to run along so**" – he put the little dog on the ground as he spoke – "and he go 'long and go through there".

But Private Solito Ruiz interrupted Mundito's dramatization, asking "What the dead man look like?"

"I din't see he face," the boy said, trembling with fear. "I only see he clothes. He got a hat over he face. He stop so, pon he side . . . "

"What colour pants?" the sergeant asked.

"Blue, and the shirt like it yellow, and he got a black hat pon top he face . . . "

But poor Mundito could scarcely talk; he stood there terrified, wanting to cry. To his childish way of thinking, the dead man must have gone off by himself to take revenge for being reported, and to make him look like a liar. Surely he was going to appear to him at home at night and haunt him for the rest of his life.

Part A: Commentary

This piece of dialogue is a useful illustration of the principles of **compensation** and of **communicative paraphrase** in translation. The translator has taken the totality of the dialogue in Bosch's short story as a distinct mode of discourse that generates particular literary effects. He has sought to reproduce these effects – the recreation of the rural plantation milieu of the story, the relative social status of the different characters and the tonal **register** they adopt – by incorporating features that generate them in the TT at different points from in the ST. The nature of spoken discourse accounts for this prevalence of compensatory techniques in the TT above: it is in the spoken **register**, particularly, that languages diverge in their modes and mechanisms for communicating nuance.

In this instance, the translator has clearly reasoned that the historical and social parallels between the plantation territories of the Hispanic and anglophone Caribbean regions justify the adoption of an anglophone Caribbean colloquial discourse in rendering the speech of Bosch's Dominican country-dwellers. As suggested in the Introduction above, this decision poses a number of overlapping questions for the translator to resolve:

- Should the dialogue merely insinuate spoken **register**, or be a thoroughgoing transcription of utterances Caribbean people would really use? This is of course a decision the author of the ST also had to confront.

- Will the juxtaposition of this markedly "familiar" discourse with other necessarily alien or "exotic" features of the translation generate excessive incongruity, or risk banality or caricature?
- Should the spoken discourse of a particular anglophone territory be inferable from the translation, or is a "neutral" or hybrid form preferable?

The degree of success achieved by the translator in resolving these questions, dependent as they are on matters of balance and context, can only be accurately evaluated by taking the translation of Bosch's story as a whole. A questionnaire-based reception study designed to offer such an evaluation – though by no means definitively – is offered in Part B of this section. Accordingly, this commentary in Part A addresses only in passing these wider questions pertaining to the appropriateness of the idiom chosen. Rather, it is principally limited to an account of the translator's use of **compensation** and of **communicative** strategies for supplying idiomatic flavour to the dialogue. Where possible, the specific anglophone Caribbean syntactic or lexical feature used by the translator has been identified and discussed. Strategies and mechanisms for translating textual features other than dialogue are discussed in the usual fashion.

In the classroom, this commentary can serve as a model for an analysis by students of any written transcription of spoken discourse in an anglophone or Spanish-speaking context, examples of which abound in literature and in the printed press. In this regard, Professor Richard Allsopp's *Dictionary of Caribbean English Usage* is an invaluable resource with which anglophone students, especially, should be strongly encouraged to familiarize themselves. Study and discussion of the front matter of the *Dictionary* will help situate Caribbean English in the global linguistic scheme and assist in dispelling any latent prescriptive notions:

> The putting together of words in an organized way, the grammatical feature known as syntax, is for most people the core, and for many the whole of what is generally meant by "grammar". For these many, English grammar is determined in England, distorted in America and destroyed in Caribbean talk. Leaving that argument on one side and taking "grammar" to be nothing more or less than the set of principles and conventions by which language operates, one can consider rationally the grammar of Caribbean English. (*DCEU*, xlviii)

This appeal to rationality, though obvious to professional linguists and translators, may well be salutary in the case of language students in the Caribbean and elsewhere, who are regularly chided for committing "grammatical" errors that on closer examination turn out to be misjudgements of **register** or code-appropriateness.

a. You sure it was here, boy? The formulation of questions without inverting subject and verb (as in "What time it is?"), or omitting the verb altogether, as here, is a feature of Creole syntax prevalent in **mesolectal** (mid-prestige) and even **acrolectal** (high prestige) levels of CE (evident also in "What the dead man look like?", below). While colloquial Caribbean Spanish question forms can differ from other variants in the position of the subject pronoun, this tends to happen when an interrogative pronoun or adverb is involved – not the case here – as in: *¿Qué tú piensas?* or *¿Cómo tú estás?* (as against *¿Qué piensas tú?* or *¿Cómo estás tú?* or *y tú, ¿qué piensas?*). Since no inversion occurs in the ST here, the use of non-inversion in the translation is clearly compensatory.

b. "Yes, he was here" Though not immediately apparent, this is a **transposition** or gloss of the ST: it is clear the subject of *era* cannot be the fugitive, as the TT has it, since the ontological *ser* is used, rather than the situational *estar* the TT seems to infer. The ST in fact incorporates implied cleft constructions:

– *¿Tú ta seguro que fué aquí [donde viste el cadaver], muchacho? [. . .]*
– *Sí, aquí era [donde yacía/estaba el muerto]*

The TT's shift of subject from "it" to "he" therefore offers up to the non-CE speaker a literary nuance that is not present in the ST, by having the sergeant use the neuter pronoun because he thinks of the "corpse" as an inanimate object, while Mundito personifies it to "he" because he is convinced it is a "living" corpse.

c. The boy making sport The ST's idiomatic *"son cosa de muchacho"* (more literally "it's just kids stuff") clearly calls for an equally idiomatic rendering here. As always when idioms have disparate referential elements, however, the connotative meaning may change subtly from ST to TT: here, the soldier in the ST seems to allow greater leeway to interpret Mundito's claim as merely erroneous, the product of an over-fertile imagination, whereas the TT more strongly suggests a conscious deception for the sake of entertainment. As with other features identified below, this idiom is decidedly Eastern Caribbean (*DCEU*, 525, "sport", 3.2 "make sport"). Alternatives offered by students were "the boy jus' formin' / playin' (the) fool", "the boy jus' skylarkin'" or simply "he mek that up".

d. Look, I did be coming along here with Blackie Since English does not offer separate familiar and respectful verb forms, the TT's unmarked imperative "look" risks sounding incongruously forceful, given that it issues from a child "filled with terror". One way of reproducing the more deferential tone generated by the ST's use of the *usted* form would be by **amplification** to "Look, sir", or by opting for the **communicative** "Please, Sir".

The collocation "did be" was identified as anomalous by a number of respondents to the questionnaire (see below). "Did" is identified by Allsopp as a simple or imperfective past-tense marker, but in the three examples he cites in which a continuous tense appears, "did" *replaces* the verb "to be" relative to the SE equivalent: "dey didn['t] know who dey did playin[g] wid"; "Nancy an' me did saving them up a long time now"; "I did know I did going catch wunnah" (*DCEU*, 192–93).

e. I put he to run along so The first of several examples in the TT of the pronoun "he" used with non-nominative function (that is, as an object pronoun rather than a subject pronoun), a feature of spoken English throughout the Caribbean region outside Jamaica. In literary and other examples cited by Allsopp, both "'e" and "he" appear (each having a separate entry in the *DCEU*, 211 and 287), illustrating different solutions to the question of how radical the phonemic transcription of dialogue should be in order to clearly indicate **sociolectal** marking while remaining plausible. As discussed below, Bosch's story exhibits variable degrees of deviation according to the character speaking and the tonal requirements of the utterance in question. The TT follows Bosch's variable approach to this question, but it is worthy of note that the instances of greater phonemic **adaptation** in the TT were those that Caribbean respondents to the questionnaire found least convincing.

Just as prevalent as non-nominative "he" is the adverbial use of "so" to mean "hereabouts; thereabouts; in this/that direction or area" (*DCEU*, 516).

Part B: Reception Study

As remarked above, the translator of a literary text with recognizable regional features confronts awkward choices regarding the location-specificity of the TT idiom, particularly in the case of dialogue. This difficulty is compounded when, as in the present instance, the translation is intended for a multi-regional audience. To whom, exactly, should the translation be convincing? Who is its putative reader? Is it more important that a Jamaican or a Guyanese reader should find the translation acceptable, or is it equally necessary that readers of non-Caribbean origin in Delhi, New York or London should be persuaded by it? The demand for plausibility to a diverse readership is made more acute still by the context in which the story appears: it is one of many texts in the anthology that incorporate Caribbean English in actual speech or in free indirect discourse, so that its rendering of the idiom can be compared directly to other adjacent examples. The comparison is of course cruel, since the vast majority of such examples in the anthology are not translations and are therefore not required to reconcile the conflicting vectors of plausibility in the alien context versus accuracy in the rendering of the idiom. Any implied criticism of the translation contained in the analysis below (or indeed in the commentary above) should bear in mind, then, these multiple factors militating against an unreservedly positive response to the translation on the part of any one reader.

Before studying the reception of the TT, some brief analysis of the ST is required. Bosch's tale, first published in 1962, recounts the experience of Mundito, a Dominican country boy who stumbles across what he takes to be a corpse in a cane field. In fact, Mundito has blown the cover of the fugitive Encarnación Mendoza, who is determined to see his family before Christmas Eve is over. Terrified, Mundito raises the alarm and a manhunt begins. The tale employs third-person omniscient narration, free indirect discourse and dialogue. The first two shade into each other in seamless fashion and are characterized by clear, straightforward diction that is appropriately literary without being especially elaborate. This fits the story's narrative mode, largely driven by plot and structure rather than by self-conscious literary flourishes or linguistic play. This level of discourse generally presents few problems to the translator, being closely reproducible in International Standard English. On this level, the most significant difficulty facing the translator is the rendering of lexical items relating to landscape and sugar cultivation. Here, the translator's decision to leave the word *batey* untranslated in the TT, and to provide a footnote, is the most salient feature.

Turning to the dialogue, the ST evinces a number of transcribed characteristics of Dominican speech. By way of example, the cited extract used in part A contains:

- *ta* for *está*. Example of apheresis, meaning suppression or elision of sounds at the beginning of the word.
- *son cosa de muchacho* for *cosas*. Example of apocopation or dropping of sounds at the end of the word.
- *diba corriendo asina* for *iba corriendo así*. *Diba* is an example of prosthesis, the addition of sounds to the beginning of the word (other examples would be *deplicar* for *explicar* or *pepejuelo* for *espejuelos*). *Asina* is an example of paragoge, or adding of sounds to the end of the word.
- *vide*, for *vi* is an instance of archaism.

- Finally, *de lao*, for *de lado* reflects the tendency to omit intervocalic consonants, eliding the vowels to form a diphthong (*acabao* for *acabado*) or a hiatus (*marío* for *marido*, *pedío* for *pedido*). Dominican Spanish shares this feature, called syncopation, with other variants (it is a feature in parts of Spain, for example).

Turning to the reception study itself, the sample readership was limited to a group of highly literate and educated speakers of several variants of Caribbean English. The results therefore reflect the judgements of readers with a keen sense of literary style and extensive knowledge of the TL culture and idiom. As such, the sample is emphatically not intended to be representative of the overall readership of the volume in which the TT appears; rather, a group with "privileged" knowledge has been selected in order to focus on the specifically Caribbean features of the TT. Once again, therefore, it should be borne in mind that this group is likely to be the most exacting of all possible readerships, since respondents were being asked to evaluate an attempt to reproduce a discourse they felt to be intimately their own, and which is commonly caricatured or misrepresented (most notoriously by non-Caribbean actors in films).

The questionnaire that respondents were asked to complete was divided into three sections: General Questions, Readability and Dialogue (see Appendix A). The first section was intended simply to contextualize each respondent's answers by seeking a value judgement on the quality of the story and of the translation, and a characterization of the story's style. Evaluations of Bosch's ST were uniformly positive, ranging from "quite good" to "extremely lucid, high quality" or "well structured, gripping". Such judgements can be taken to some extent as implicit praise of the translation, since these qualities of the original work could hardly be expected to be appreciable if the translation were not of a certain quality.

Assessments of the quality of the translation ranged from fairly positive with minor reservations to very positive. In the former category, a number of respondents felt the TT was "quite good", but not wholly convincing throughout: "it struggles just a bit with a keen sense that the narrative should *not* be straight standard language"; "there are a few instances where the choice of words could have been more appropriate, or certain things could have been phrased differently". Another respondent felt the finished product was "a little stagy" but supposes "this has to do with the original". In the latter category, one respondent offered an evaluation that would be music to the ears of many translators (or at least those commissioned to produce a **domesticating** translation): "One would hardly have known it was not the primary source."

Turning to section B, responses to the question on the TT's footnote explaining the meaning of the word *batey* revealed a curious ambivalence regarding the use of this time-honoured – and much abused – translator's device. A majority of respondents circled *both* the characterization "pedantic" and a positive epithet, typically "interesting" and/ or "useful". Of these, one felt that on balance it would be better to eliminate the footnote altogether, another considered it would be better placed at the end of the story because it "adds an incongruous 'scholarly' tone to the story's presentation", while a third advised no modification, apparently regarding it as a necessary evil. It seems that (some) readers welcome assistance in deciphering a **culture-bound** element, but are nonetheless aware that the footnote can ultimately be viewed as an admission of failure on the part of the translator, and that it mars the illusion that **domesticating** translations implicitly try to perpetrate, namely that the work was originally written in the TL.

Asked to identify unclear or jarring expressions in the TT (question B2 and B3), only three specific instances were identified by multiple respondents. Since any phrases identified by only one respondent can be discarded as purely subjective, these instances of common confusion are worthy of attention. The first reads as follows:

> Of course he had to see his wife and children. It was an animal impulse which drove him on, a blind force he couldn't resist. In spite of that, and being so free of regrets, Encarnación Mendoza understood that with the urge to embrace his wife and tell the children a story, there was mixed a hint of jealousy.

The final sentence of this passage and particularly the phrase "and being so free of regrets" proved perplexing for some readers. The ST reads as follows:

> *Necesariamente debía ver a su mujer y a sus hijos. Era un impulso bestial el que le empujaba a ir, una fuerza ciega a la cual no podía resistir. Con todo y ser tan limpio de sentimientos, Encarnación Mendoza comprendía que con el deseo de abrazar a su mujer y de contarles un cuento a los niños iba confundida una sombra de celos.*

Though the emotional state described here is subtle, it is hard to justify the TT's gloss of *sentimientos* as "regrets" (normally *remordimientos*). The thrust seems to be that although Mendoza's impulses are for the most part entirely sympathetic and he is basically a creature of simple and noble motives, he is aware that a somewhat less edifying sentiment, that of jealousy, is also driving him forward. The jarring effect of the TT here might have been mitigated by rendering: "Nevertheless, and in spite of the basic purity of his feelings, Encarnación Mendoza understood that mingled with his urge to embrace his wife and tell the children a story, there was also a hint of jealousy."

More than one respondent also drew attention to the following phrase in the TT: "Encarnación let himself be seen for just a moment on a distant cart-road, running as fast as a fleeing shadow". As one respondent pointed out, "it is highly unlikely that Encarnación would 'let himself be seen'; the sentence should be phrased differently, for example, 'Encarnación happened to be seen just for a moment'". The ST reads as follows: "*Encarnación se dejó ver sobre una trocha distante, sólo un momento, huyendo con la velocidad de una sombra fugaz*". The discomfort of a number of readers with this part of the TT teases out a useful piece of comparative grammar: the reflexive in English, at least in this context with "let" or "allow", appears to rule out the possibility of an involuntary action, whereas the Spanish construction with *se* is more neutral in this regard, allowing context to resolve any ambiguity. The best solution thus seems to be a gloss of the type suggested by the respondent above: "Encarnación happened to be seen just for a moment" (or "for just a moment").

The final instance that caused perplexity or discomfort in more than one reader of the TT was the second sentence of the following passage:

> Only the helper was left in the rum-shop, busy asking every blessed person who went by if "they catch him yet".

Encarnación Mendoza was not an easy man. But at three o'clock, as he was on the road which divided the canefields from the hills, crossing to go into the scrub – that is to say, more than two hours' distance from the *batey*, a well-aimed shot broke his spine.

Here, the literal rendering of the ST's idiomatic "*Encarnación Mendoza no era hombre fácil*" generates a problem of frustrated expectation in the TT: exactly what was it not easy to do to Mendoza?, the anglophone reader asks. The same respondent who provided an alternative translation in the example above suggests extending this sentence, which he finds "incomplete and not well expressed", so that it reads "Encarnación Mendoza was not the kind of man to allow himself to be easily caught" or "Encarnación Mendoza was not the kind of man that was easy to catch". These **amplifications** no doubt produce a more lucid TT, avoiding the sensation of "pulling up short" of the published version, but as always both would lose some of the possible resonances of the less specific ST, as well as being inevitably less economical. While this trade-off between semantic and syntactic clarity, on the one hand, and retained ambiguity or resonance, on the other, is determined by multiple factors in any given context, it can be argued that the readers' judgement must be the acid test here. The phrase "Encarnación Mendoza was not an easy man" might have passed unremarked had the TT generally shown a tendency to contain allusive, ambiguous phrases that seemed to serve a purpose in the overall literary design. The TT generally follows the ST, however, in being semantically and syntactically lucid throughout, causing any phrase whose meaning is not immediately apprehensible to stand out as anomalous. Erring on the side of clarity, at the risk of eliminating resonance, is therefore arguably preferable since any perceived obscurity amidst the overall lucidity inevitably leads the reader to suspect a flaw in the translation (not so if the strategy is **foreignizing** throughout).

Finally in section B, readers were asked whether St John's Day, the date of Mendoza's initial crime, had any particular association for them. This was a test of the extent to which this date, alluded to more than once, is a **culture-bound** element that might have merited a footnote in the same way that *batey* elicited this device earlier in the story. The strong associations of this day in the Catholic Hispanic world are enshrined in the *Fiestas de San Juan*, still commonly celebrated, particularly in countries such as Spain, Paraguay and Puerto Rico. The festival, symbolized by fire and water, marks both the birthday of St John and the summer solstice and has strong pagan associations with fertility, prediction of the future and good fortune. That Mendoza's crime was committed on this day therefore accentuates the irony of the tale and links thematically with the fugitive's repressed feelings of jealousy and with the suggestion that his crime was one of passion inflamed by an affront against his manhood or his proprietary rights over his spouse.

All but one of the respondents reported that the date had not triggered conscious associations for them, but some then revealed knowledge of its significance that suggested it may have had unconscious resonance: "I just passed it off as one of those Latin American Roman Catholic significant days. But, since you ask, I start thinking it might have to do with St John the Divine, the Revelations, a day of bad omen, signalling a bad future for Encarnación Mendoza." Or "might it allude to John the Baptist? If so, the Christ-like nature of suffering is a theme that might be explored in the story."

Finally, section C asked respondents to comment specifically on the effectiveness of the dialogue in the TT. Asked to characterize the dialogue generally (question C1), responses ranged from "quite convincing" to "forced", with the average evaluation falling almost exactly on the mid point, "unconvincing". Barbadian respondents, no doubt significantly, given the markedly Bajan ring of much of the ST dialogue, tended to be more convinced than speakers of other variants, though there were exceptions.

Question C2 asked respondents to comment on how consistently dialogue reflected character and situation. The question was included because the ST shows a degree of inconsistency here that the translator must decide to eliminate or reproduce. This inconsistency arises to some extent because throughout his oeuvre, Bosch's transcription of rural Dominican Spanish is not particularly radical: though he incorporates the features listed above, he chooses not to transcribe – or not to transcribe consistently – other phenomena.

A number of respondents observed that the TT fluctuated between dialect and standard forms in the dialogue, particularly in the utterances of Mundito. One example offered is Mundito's first two sentences in the story, "in perfectly standard English", as compared to his dialogue with the policeman. The reader speculates that this might be defended on the basis that the boy is "afraid and uncomfortable" in the latter scenario, but points out that he also employs standard English when first reporting the "corpse", though he is clearly also afraid at the time. Overall, readers could see no rationale for the variations they detected and felt it robbed the translation of some plausibility. As always, then, it seems that readers are less forgiving of inconsistency in a translation than they are in a primary text: all observations on the inconsistency of the dialogue assumed deficiency in the translation and no respondent suggested that the translator might simply be faithfully rendering an inconsistent feature of the ST.

II. INGLÉS > ESPAÑOL

Texto 1
"A World of Canes"[3]
By Robert Antoni (excerpt)
We begin with love? Doudou, I ain't know what we begin with. What you call that? *Bullying.* You call that bullying. We begin with bullying, meet up with little love. Maybe little bit. Una could suppose.
I could remember the first time. I did had but thirteen years then, and Berry, He did had about sixteen. Thirteen and sixteen, two children, nothing more. We wasn't nothing more than two children then. I did just finish at the elementary school. I got to look for work now. I can't go at high school, ain't got nobody to send me at high school. Buy me books and different things. I got to look for work. So my

Traducción de Jairo Sánchez
"Un mundo de cañas"
De Robert Antoni (extracto)
¿Comenzamo con amo'? [a.]**Bebé, yo no sé con qué comenzamo. ¿Cómo je llama eso?** *Acoso,* eso je llama acoso. Comenzamo con acoso, seguido e un poco de amo'. Tal bé un poquito, se podría decí.
[b.]**Me acueddo e la primera bé.** Yo tenía sólo trece año, y Berry tenía como diecisei año. Trece y diescisei año, dó niño ná má. En esentonce no eramo má que dó niño. Yo acababa e terminá la primaria. Tenía que conseguimme un trabajo. No podía ir a la secundaria. Nadie me podía dá pa ir a la secundaria. Comprá lo libro, cosa desa. Tenía que conseguime un trabajo. [c.]**Entonce mi abuela me consiguió un trabajo con una**

grandmother, she arrange for me to go by a woman does do needleworks. I go by this woman to learn the needleworks from she, Mistress Bethel. But to get from Sherman to Mistress Bethel house now, I got to pass crossroads, you know, got to pass *he* house, where he living, this Berry. Well that ain't nothing. Ain't nothing in that. I ain't fraid for the man, I ain't thinking nothing about the man. I just keeping to myself, go along my own business. My grandmother, she buy couple dresses for me, you know, to go at needleworks, I press them and I make them neat and thing. So I walking my little bag, my clasp and my earring. Looking pretty, real pretty now, and I pass this Berry sitting relaxing pon he gallery. Big wide porch front the house. Well this Berry stand up and he watch at me, you know, ogle me everytime whilst I pass. I was thinking. *What this man watching you at for? What he watching at you for like that.* But he ain't tell me nothing, and I ain't saying nothing to he neither.

mujé que hace cojtura. Voy onde ejta mujé pa aprendé el oficio e cojturera: ^d·**doña Berta.** Pero pa llegá de Cherman a la casa e doña Berta tenía que pasá pó el cruce, pó *su* casa donde bibía él, el Berry. Pue eso no é ná. No pasa ná con eso. No me daba miedo el tipo ese, no pensaba en él. Me concentraba en lo mío, sin metemme con nadie. Mi abuela me compró dó bestido pa ir a trabajá. Ló planché ló dejé limpio y tó. Así que caminaba con mi bolsito, mi broche y mi arete. Me beía bonita, muy bonita. Y pasaba pó donde el Berry que ejtaba echao en la galería. Un solar grande y amplio en el frente e la casa. Pue ejte Berry se paraba y me miraba y me miraba que me comía con la bista cada bé que yo pasaba. Yo pensaba *¿Pero qué é lo que me mira ejte tipo? ¿Po qué me mira así ejte tipo?* Pero él no me decía ná y yo tampoco le iba a decí ná.

Comentarios

Encontramos aquí un texto escrito en estilo coloquial que utiliza como herramientas la gramática y el vocabulario para ubicar a la narradora en al menos tres planos simultáneos: En primer lugar, un plano **dialectal**, en el que se la hace parte del Caribe anglófono por medio de las particularidades gramaticales del inglés caribeño como la "falta de concordancia" sujeto-verbo (*"we wasn't"*), la **omisión** del verbo *to be*, especialmente en oraciones en progresivo, y la duplicación del negativo (*"he ain't tell me nothing"*) o del pasado (*"I did had"*), entre otras. En segundo lugar, se la ubica en un plano **sociolectal** en el que se la posiciona en un estrato social bajo (**estratolecto**) como lo demuestra el contenido de la historia en sí, en combinación con la gramática y la ortografía (*fraid* por *afraid*). Finalmente, un plano **generolectal**, en el que se le da el rol de mujer. De aquí surgen varios interrogantes que han sido largamente discutidos en la historia de la traducción.

- ¿Si el **dialecto**, el **sociolecto** y el **generolecto** son tan específicos y están marcados por su historia, es válido, o aun posible, traducirlos a otro **dialecto, sociolecto, generolecto**?
- ¿Se debe traducir un **dialecto** de la LO a la llamada lengua estándar de la LM?
- ¿Qué sucede con los nombres? ¿Son traducibles?

Podríamos continuar con una larga lista de interrogantes al respecto. No se pretende aquí ser exhaustivos ni proponer *la* solución a dichos interrogantes. Simplemente diremos que nuestras respuestas están determinadas por algunas variantes entre las que se cuentan: (a) el estatus del autor; (b) la tradición literaria de la LO y la LM; (c) la proximidad geográfico-cultural-histórica de la LO y la LM; (d) los motivos que nos llevan a hacer la traducción; y sobre todo (e) el destinatario de la misma.

Situaremos la presente traducción, a modo de ejemplo, en las variantes arriba propuestas:

(a) El estatus del autor. Robert Antoni, aunque nacido en Estados Unidos, se crió en Bahamas y tiene una larga historia familiar en Trinidad y Tobago. Es hoy en día uno de los exponentes más reconocidos de la literatura caribeña. Entre sus obras se encuentran las novelas *My Grandmother's Erotic Folktales*, traducida al español, francés y finlandés; *Blessed Is the Fruit* y *Divina Trace* al igual que un gran número de cuentos.[4]

(b) En cuanto a la tradición literaria de la LO y la LM se puede decir a grandes rasgos que la escritura en lenguaje coloquial en el Caribe anglófono ha alcanzado un reconocimiento que aún no ha logrado su equivalente en español, a excepción de contados casos. Para la presente traducción se tomaron dos de los más representativos: el cubano, Nicolás Guillén, y el colombiano, Candelario Obeso. Analizando sus modos de ser fiel al habla real del español caribeño vemos que el cambio gramatical no es tan amplio como en el inglés, pero sí lo es su ortografía.

(c) La proximidad geográfica, pero sobre todo cultural, influye en nuestra decisión de traducir **dialecto** por **dialecto** o **dialecto** por lengua estándar. Hace algunos años, especialmente en la tradición de estudios literarios, para analizar una obra se le pedía al analista olvidarse de factores como el autor y el contexto en el que fue escrita, se miraba la obra como texto aislado. En las recientes teorías de la traducción, el contexto juega cada vez un papel más importante, ya que no sólo traducimos textos, sino que traducimos contextos y traducimos culturas. En nuestro caso particular, las semejanzas tanto geográficas como culturales e históricas permiten que nuestra traducción se haga en **dialecto**, pues la LO y la LM comparten varios rasgos que traspasan la barrera lingüística.

(d/e) Con respecto a los dos últimos puntos, suponemos que en una situación real traducimos este cuento para su inclusión en un libro al que tendrán acceso personas interesadas en la literatura caribeña y que conocen la LM pero no necesariamente la LO. Esto nos da libertad para la **adaptación** y la **compensación**.

Antes de iniciar la traducción es indispensable acercarse al TO, intentar comprender las partes que lo hacen un todo y también cómo ese todo se muestra en cada una de sus partes. En textos como el aquí presentado surgen infinidad de trabas a la comprensión, no sólo en el vocabulario, sino en cómo ese vocabulario se repite a través del cuento dotándolo de nuevos significados. En la larga historia de la traducción se da por sentado que el traductor debe ser bilingüe y bicultural. Esto no siempre es posible, y se hace más difícil en una región como el Caribe que abarca en una pequeña porción geográfica una inmensa variedad de hablas. Para resolver los inconvenientes que supone tal variedad se ha recurrido en esta traducción al uso de una encuesta que ayudara al traductor a acercarse a las particularidades del texto, su valor connotativo, que se escapan a cualquier diccionario, por especializado que sea. Dicha encuesta estaba dirigida a hablantes nativos de inglés caribeño y se centraba en los significados connotativos de algunos nombres y expresiones, así como en el nivel de especificidad **dialectal** del TO. Vimos arriba en la sección al inglés cómo un análisis de recepción puede servir para medir la efectividad de una traducción como producto. Se plantea aquí la utilización de un mecanismo similar como fase inicial del proceso.

a. Bebé, yo no sé con qué comenzamo El TO dictaba Doudou. Tanto en el *DCEU* de Allsopp como en las respuestas obtenidas en la encuesta diseñada se dan los siguientes sinónimos de este vocablo: *darling, sweet (little one)*. Expresión utilizada para referirse, especialmente la madre, a un pequeño, proveniente del francés *doux (sweet)* con reduplicación emotiva. Algunos de los encuestados identificaron esta forma con *though-though*, teniendo el mismo uso aunque se percibe como forma antigua. En español se escogió la forma "bebé" por presentarse en ella un uso similar y la reduplicación silábica presente en inglés.

b. Me acueddo e la primera bé Vemos aquí varias de las particularidades fonéticas que se utilizan en el resto de la traducción. En primer lugar, la neutralización de la /r/, representada aquí como duplicación de la consonante siguiente (también más adelante "consegui-mme" por "conseguirme"). En segundo lugar, la elisión de la /d/ en la preposición "de". En tercer lugar, la exageración bilabial de la /v/. La distinción entre el sonido bilabial y el labiodental se ha perdido en casi todos los **dialectos** del español, más no en su ortografía. También se representa el desgaste del sonido /s/ o /z/ final mediante su **omisión**. Finalmente, se usa la tilde no existente en la versión estándar para demostrar la supresión de uno o más sonidos al final de una palabra (sílaba apocopada), cuando en la silaba presente recaiga el acento: "bé" por "vez", "decí" por "decir", "ná" por "nada", "terminá" por "terminar", y otros.

c. Entonce mi abuela me consiguió un trabajo con una mujé que hace cojtura En algunas ocasiones el sonido /s/ intermedio pasa de ser linguoalveolar a linguovelar, representado aquí por el cambio ortográfico de la s por la j. También antes en "je" por "se" y adelante en "ejte" por "este". Este modo de representar dicho cambio aparece principalmente en Candelario Obeso, quien también sustituye algunas veces la /d/ intermedia por la /h/. Aquí preferimos no utilizarlo.

d. *doña Berta*. Surge el dilema de los nombres. Muchos traductores optan por mantener los nombres del TO, como muestra de que se trata de una traducción. Algunos opinan que los nombres son intraducibles. En la parte que compete a nuestro análisis aparecen tres nombres: *Mistress Bethel, Berry* y *Sherman*. Partimos de la base de que nada en la literatura es gratuito. El autor ha escogido ciertos nombres por determinadas razones (conscientes o inconscientes), por lo que ellos evocan. Los resultados de la encuesta muestran que el nombre *Mistress Bethel* dota al personaje de varios rasgos: una edad adulta, un estatus social superior al de la narradora, y cierto grado de seriedad, algunos dijeron que probablemente era soltera, divorciada o viuda, para algunos es un nombre casi arcaico. En cuanto a *Berry*, no lo reconocen como un nombre común, pero lo encuentran jovial. No lo cargan de estatus social, ni de una edad determinada. *Sherman* no tiene referencia explícita para los encuestados, es ambiguo pues se puede referir a una casa en particular, bien a una calle, o a un barrio.

Teniendo en cuenta los resultados de la encuesta pasamos a sopesar las opciones. *Mistress* como título es definitivamente inglés, chocaría con el lenguaje (**dialecto, sociolecto, generolecto**) que se ha venido utilizando. *Bethel* como tal no parece evocar nada de lo arriba mencionado. Se pensó en castellanizarlo a Betel (como se hizo con Cherman) pero nos remitiría a la planta trepadora. Se prosiguió a hacer un listado de posibles nombres que evocaran cualidades similares a las percibidas por los encuestados, y se escogió "Berta", que además tiene cierta proximidad fonética. "Doña" es la forma utilizada actualmente para referirse al arcaico "dueña", significado que también tiene *Mistress* en inglés. Pasamos ahora a *Berry* que se ha dejado igual, pues no tiene demasiadas **connotaciones** ni en la LO ni en la LM. Es un nombre que se percibe como inglés (sin tener el tono arcaizante de *Bethel*) pero también es posible que un caribeño hispanohablante lo tenga, especialmente por el grado de contacto que tiene la zona con turistas y tratados económicos del mundo anglófono. Lo mismo sucede con *Sherman* y su **adaptación** a "Cherman".

Los mecanismos presentados aquí no están estandarizados. El traductor debe juzgar cuáles de ellos son representativos y cuáles, más que ayudar a crear el tono del relato, crean barreras para su lectura.

III. SPANISH > ENGLISH EXERCISES

Read the full Spanish text of "La Nochebuena de Encarnación Mendoza" (http://www.literatura.us/juanbosch/mendoza.html) and answer the following questions.

1) Which of the adjectives below would you use to characterize the story? Support your choices with evidence from the text.

   a) realist   g) tragic
   b) magical realist   h) exotic
   c) ornate   i) folkloric
   d) lucid   j) epic
   e) ironical   k) poetic
   f) comic

2) Identify the features of style that anyone translating this story should bear in mind. Which of these features do you think constitute the greatest challenge to the translator of the story?

3) Give appropriate equivalents in English for the following terms describing physical features in the story:

   a) el bohío   e) la casucha
   b) el batey   f) la Cordillera
   c) la colonia Adela g) un tren del ingenio
   d) el Central

4) a) Translate the following section of the story as if for publication in a local magazine in your country:

   > El caserío donde ellos vivían – del lado de los cerros, en el camino que dividía los cañaverales de las tierras incultas – tendría catorce o quince malas viviendas, la mayor parte techadas de yaguas. Al salir de la suya, con el encargo de ir a la bodega, Mundito se detuvo un momento en medio del barro seco por donde en los días de zafra transitaban las carretas cargadas de caña. Era largo el trayecto hasta la bodega. El cielo se

veía claro, radiante de luz que se esparcía sobre el horizonte de cogollos de caña; era grata la brisa y dulcemente triste el silencio. ¿Por qué ir solo, aburriéndose de caminar por trochas siempre iguales? Durante diez segundos Mundito pensó entrar al bohío vecino, donde seis semanas antes una perra negra había parido seis cachorros. Los dueños del animal habían regalado cinco, pero quedaba uno "para amamantar a la madre", y en él había puesto Mundito todo el interés que la falta de ternura había acumulado en su pequeña alma. Con sus nueve años cargados de precoz sabiduría, el niño era consciente de que si llevaba al cachorrillo tendría que cargarlo casi todo el tiempo, porque no podría hacer tanta distancia por sí solo. Mundito sentía que esa idea casi le autorizaba a disponer del perrito. De súbito, sin pensarlo más, corrió hacia la casucha gritando:

–¡Doña Ofelia, emprésteme a Azabache, que lo voy a llevar allí!

b) Compare and contrast your translation to the published translation (http://www.caribbeantranslationmanual.com/literature.html).

IV. EJERCICIOS PRÁCTICOS INGLÉS > ESPAÑOL

1. En los comentarios se mencionó la necesidad de tener en cuenta ciertas variantes al momento de decidir cómo traducir un texto literario. Revíselas y diga bajo qué circunstancias se traduciría:
   a) De un **dialecto** en LO a un **dialecto** en LM.
   b) De un **dialecto** en LO a lengua "estándar" en LM.
   c) De lengua "estándar" en LO a un **dialecto** en LM.
2. Compare la aproximación a la traducción de los nombres propios en por lo menos cuatro obras caribeñas traducidas. Si se tradujeron, ¿qué mecanismos utilizó el traductor? Si no se tradujeron ¿qué motivos pudo tener para no hacerlo?
3. Lea "A World of Canes" en su totalidad (http://www.robertantoni.com) y traduzca este extracto de la historia en dos versiones. Una en la que se vea la variante caribeña, y otra en una versión más cercana a los estándares de escritura del español no caribeño. Compare los puntos en los que las dos versiones difieren:

> Then one time I had to go up crossroads in the night, there where he was living. I had to go up with a cousin of mine to meet with she friend. She friend uses to work at this shop, grocery shop, selling groceries. This shop close at seven o'clock, you know seven o'clock *dark*. This girl *fraid* to walk home by sheself come seven o'clock. So we gone to meet with she, you know, kepp she with company. We leave home about six, six o'clock come already you *can't* see you hand front you face. So we gone over. We making plenty noise, bunch of we walking together must be about five-six, we going over to bring my cousin friend. You know must be two-three miles from Sherman to crossroads, but all is canes. Canes canes and more canes. That place. And so dark. So we got to pass by this man house, coming *and* going.

CHAPTER 5

The Creative Arts II: Film

INTRODUCTION

In recent years, audiovisual translation (in effect, subtitling and dubbing) has steadily grown from a peripheral sub-genre of translation studies in general into a fully fledged discipline of its own. In the Greater Caribbean region specifically, subtitling activity is likely to be on the increase as production and distribution develop and diversify throughout the Americas. (Miami, for example, is a centre for subtitling US products for the Latin American market.) Even for those with no professional aspirations in the field, subtitling is an excellent linguistic exercise, demanding particularly close analysis of spoken utterances in the ST and consistent economy of language to achieve the required concision in the TT. Though subtitling exercises are still underused in language pedagogy generally, the ease of access to Spanish-subtitled material, particularly, from satellite television in the Caribbean region, facilitates increased use both in the classroom and as a self-learning tool for students.

With regard to the anglophone region, the "insular" Caribbean often seems nowhere more appropriately named than in the field of audiovisual media consumption: despite the international prestige of Latin American and francophone cinema, the aversion of most anglophone Caribbean viewers towards subtitles is extreme even by the standards of other anglophones, rarely noted for their tolerance of linguistic difference. A number of factors have contributed to this state of affairs. One is the relatively low level of diversity on local terrestrial television channels, which are generally lacking in resources and thus forced to find the most widely accessible programming possible on a shoestring budget. Somewhat out-of-date US (or sometimes British) series usually best fulfil these criteria. The aversion to subtitles on television, particularly applied to series and soaps – often "watched" while doing something else at the same time – is thus even greater than in the cinema. The head of programming for Channel 8 in Barbados, for example, reported vehement "abuse" from a significant number of viewers when confronted with even short, occasional sections of subtitled material in South African series imported in an attempt to diversify content. Another related factor is the history of audiovisual penetration of the anglophone Caribbean region by the United States, and the subsequent location of cinematic and audiovisual works as mere entertainment products, units of leisure consumption with little or no cultural or educational value.

As a result of these factors, the concept of "going to the movies" is markedly different in anglophone Caribbean territories, relative both to the non-anglophone Caribbean and to other contexts beyond the region. Colombians, Cubans and Englishmen, therefore, are equally surprised on first experiencing the raucous responses of the normally reserved Barbadians to a violent or sexually explicit scene in a film. Given the highly social and collective character of much cinema-viewing in the anglophone region, and the consequent lack of individual engagement with the film itself, it is hardly surprising that subtitled films have traditionally fared poorly. This has begun to change, however, as a consequence of several factors. One is the recent success of a number of non-English-language films that have broken through into the mainstream worldwide and proved appealing to anglophone Caribbean audiences, such as: *The Passion of the Christ*; *Crouching Tiger, Hidden Dragon*; *Hero*; and *The Blind Swordsman*. A second factor is the proliferation of satellite television platforms offering multilingual – and particularly Spanish-language – programming. The ever-increasing availability of the DVD, also, and its eventual replacement of the videotape, though happening more slowly than in many parts of the developed world as a result of economic factors and entrenched videotape piracy in the region, will also raise potential exposure to subtitled products. Some have also argued that text-messaging and Internet chat, which require assimilation of a compressed message within a physically limited space in a manner not so far removed from reading a subtitle, may cultivate greater tolerance of subtitled audiovisual products among younger viewers. Another development that may contribute in the long term to greater acceptance of subtitles in the anglophone Caribbean is the recent proliferation of film festivals showing international works, with Jamaica, Trinidad and Tobago, St Barts, Barbados, the US Virgin Islands, Belize, and the Bahamas all hosting events in recent years. Film clubs showing international cinema – much of it subtitled – are also flourishing in Trinidad and Barbados and no doubt elsewhere too, while diplomatic missions such as the Alliance Française and the embassies of Latin American countries increasingly use film to promote their cultures in anglophone territories.

The Hispanic Caribbean, meanwhile, has long boasted Latin America's largest film festival, the International Festival of New Latin American Film, known to all as the Havana Film Festival. Given the universalistic slant of the Cuban approach to culture, it is no surprise to discover that vast numbers of Cubans will make strenuous efforts to view films in languages other than Spanish. Other factors such as the importance of Portuguese-speaking Brazil as a Latin American film producer, together with the stipulation that all works must be subtitled in Spanish to be eligible for a prize at the Festival, have made subtitling and the viewing of subtitled films an integral part of Cuban cinematic culture. Consequently, the Instituto Cubano del Arte e Industria Cinematográficos (Cuban Institute of Cinematic Arts and Industry, ICAIC) has long been a centre of film-subtitling activity in the Hispanic Caribbean, while Cuban television also employs specialist subtitling translators. Puerto Rico, also, has hosted an International Film Festival since the early 1990s and now also boasts a specialist documentary and animation festival.

What does it take, then, to subtitle a film effectively? One obvious requirement is a highly assured grasp of numerous spoken styles of discourse and, particularly, colloquial **registers**, in both ST and TT. A good subtitler also has to be very aware of the norms of the craft and, particularly, its technical requirements. Since film dialogue unfolds in real time, the duration of a subtitle's appearance on the screen is preordained, a crucial determinant in the translation process. Capacity for concise expression and readiness to omit and to condense are therefore necessary qualities of the good subtitler, who must also develop resistance to inevitable criticism of the results by those who fail to understand the full implications of the temporal constraints (the common criticism that the subtitle "didn't say the same thing as the original" is very often attributable to the need to make the subtitle comfortably readable in the available time). Interest in cinema and an understanding of the dynamics of film, which simultaneously conveys meaning through image, sound and language, are also essential qualities of the expert subtitler, who must avoid carrying a subtitle across a cut to a different camera angle, for example, or prematurely revealing information that is first introduced visually in the original version. Practised professionally, film subtitling also requires a high level of computer literacy, since software packages used to subtitle audiovisual works are various and in perpetual evolution. Finally, films and television programmes can be about anything at all, so that extensive general knowledge, capacity to research quickly and access to expert collaborators are highly desirable assets.

In the transcriptions below, the double oblique stroke symbol "//" represents the end of the subtitle or subtitles on screen.

INTRODUCCIÓN

En los últimos años el área de los estudios de traducción audiovisual (es decir, subtitulación y doblaje) ha mostrado un crecimiento constante pasando de ser un subgénero de los estudios de traducción a convertirse en una disciplina en sí misma. En la región del Gran Caribe, la actividad subtituladora tiende a crecer ya que la producción y la distribución se están desarrollando y diversificando en las Américas. (Miami es uno de los centros para la subtitulación de productos estadounidenses para el mercado latinoamericano, por ejemplo.) Aun para aquellos que no aspiran a concentrarse en este campo de manera profesional, la subtitulación constituye un excelente ejercicio lingüístico que requiere un análisis detallado del lenguaje oral en el TO y una economía constante del lenguaje escrito para lograr la **concisión** deseada en el TM. Aunque en general los ejercicios que se apoyan en la subtitulación como recurso para la enseñanza de las lenguas aún no han sido utilizados al máximo de sus posibilidades, la facilidad para encontrar material subtitulado en el Caribe, especialmente en la televisión satelital, contribuye al incremento de su uso tanto por parte de los profesores en el salón de clase como por la de aquellos que lo utilizan como herramienta de autoaprendizaje.

Con respecto a la parte anglófona de la región, el nombre de Caribe "insular" parece encajar mejor en el campo del consumo audiovisual que en cualquier otro: a pesar del prestigio internacional del cine francófono y latinoamericano, la aversión de la gente del Caribe anglófono a ver películas subtituladas es extrema aun cuando se compara a la de los anglófonos en general, que no tienen fama de tolerar la diferencia lingüística.

Hay varios factores que han contribuido a esta situación. Uno de ellos es el bajo nivel relativo de diversidad en los canales de televisión locales, que en general no tienen muchos recursos y se ven forzados a encontrar, con un presupuesto muy reducido, programas para el público general: los lotes de las viejas series televisivas americanas (algunas veces británicas) por lo general cumplen estos requisitos. La aversión a los subtítulos en la televisión, particularmente cuando se usan en las series o en las telenovelas – que con frecuencia se "ven" mientras se realiza otra tarea al mismo tiempo – resulta incluso mayor que cuando aparecen en el cine. El jefe de programación del canal local de Barbados, por ejemplo, reportó una gran cantidad de quejas injuriosas por parte de un número importante de televidentes cuando se enfrentaban incluso a secciones cortas y ocasionales de subtítulos en telenovelas sudafricanas, que habían sido importadas en un esfuerzo por añadir mayor diversidad. Otro factor es la penetración histórica de Estados Unidos en el Caribe anglófono y el consecuente posicionamiento de los trabajos cinematográficos y audiovisuales como simples productos de entretenimiento, unidades de consumo y de esparcimiento con poco o ningún valor cultural o educativo.

Como resultado de estos factores el concepto de "ir a cine" es muy diferente en los países anglófonos del Caribe con respecto a los territorios no anglófonos en la zona y a otros contextos fuera de la región. Los colombianos, cubanos e ingleses se sorprenden de igual manera cuando experimentan por primera vez las respuestas estentóreas de los barbadenses, por lo general reservados, ante una escena violenta o con contenido sexual explícito en una película. Dado el carácter altamente social y colectivo de la experiencia de ir a cine en la región anglófona y la falta relativa de "meterse en la película" de manera individual, no es muy sorprendente que las películas subtituladas tengan tan poca aceptación comercial. Sin embargo, esta situación está empezando a cambiar por varios motivos. Uno de ellos es el éxito reciente de algunas películas que han entrado en el mercado mundial sin ser de habla inglesa y que han resultado llamativas para la audiencia caribeña anglófona tales como *La Pasión de Cristo, El Tigre y el Dragón, Héroe y Zatoichi.* Un segundo factor es la proliferación de plataformas de televisión por satélite que ofrecen programas en varias lenguas, especialmente en español. También la disponibilidad del DVD que con el tiempo reemplazará al videocasete, aunque sucede más despacio que en el mundo desarrollado debido a razones económicas y a la piratería sistemática de videocasetes en la región, traerá consigo el incremento potencial de la exposición a productos subtitulados. Algunos opinan que los mensajes de texto y las plataformas para chat en Internet, que requieren la asimilación de un mensaje comprimido en un espacio físicamente reducido, no difieren mucho de la lectura de subtítulos, lo que podría crear una mayor tolerancia a los productos audiovisuales subtitulados entre los espectadores jóvenes.

Otro fenómeno que podría contribuir a la aceptación a largo plazo de los subtítulos en el Caribe anglófono es la reciente proliferación de festivales de cine que exhiben trabajos audiovisuales internacionales: Jamaica, Trinidad y Tobago, San Bartolomé, Barbados, las Islas Vírgenes (EE.UU.), Belice, y las Bahamas han celebrado dichos festivales en los últimos años. También han surgido cine-clubes que presentan la mayoría de películas con subtítulos; al menos sabemos de algunos en Trinidad y Barbados, pero seguramente habrá en otros lugares. Las misiones diplomáticas como la Alianza Francesa o las embajadas de países como Colombia y Brasil usan las películas de su región cada vez más para promocionar su cultura en los territorios anglófonos.

Por otro lado, el Caribe hispano hace mucho que se precia de tener el festival de cine más grande de toda Latinoamérica: el Festival Internacional del Nuevo Cine Latinoamericano, más conocido como el Festival de Cine de La Habana. Dado el enfoque universalista cubano hacia la cultura, es normal que un gran número de cubanos hagan todo lo que esté a su alcance para ver películas en idiomas diferentes al suyo. Otros factores como la importancia de Brasil como productor cinematográfico latinoamericano, junto con las normas del Festival que estipulan que todos los trabajos deben estar subtitulados en español para poder optar a un galardón, han hecho de la subtitulación y la proyección de películas subtituladas una parte integral de la cultura cinematográfica cubana. Por consiguiente, el Instituto Cubano del Arte e Industria Cinematográficos (ICAIC) ha sido desde hace tiempo un centro de actividad subtituladora para el cine en el Caribe hispano, así como también la televisión cubana, que emplea a traductores especializados en la subtitulación. También Puerto Rico ha celebrado un Festival Internacional de Cine desde comienzos de la década de los 90 y ahora también ofrece un festival especializado para documentales y animación.

¿Qué se necesita, pues, para subtitular una película de forma efectiva? Un requisito obvio es un alto conocimiento de los diversos estilos del discurso oral y especialmente de los **registros** coloquiales de la LO y de la LM. Un buen subtitulador debe estar muy familiarizado con las normas de su profesión y de los requerimientos técnicos que ésta implica. Debido a que el diálogo se desarrolla en tiempo real, la duración del subtítulo en pantalla está altamente predeterminada, un factor crucial en el proceso de la traducción. La capacidad para expresar conceptos de forma concisa y la predisposición para omitir y condensar contenidos son por lo tanto cualidades de un buen subtitulador, que a la vez debe acostumbrarse a las inevitables críticas que harán de su trabajo las personas que no entienden la totalidad de las limitaciones temporales. La crítica más común es que el subtítulo "no dice lo mismo que el original", resultado atribuible en la mayoría de los casos a la necesidad de condensar para hacer que el subtítulo se lea de manera cómoda en el tiempo permitido. El interés por el cine y el entendimiento de la dinámica cinematográfica, que produce significados simultáneos por medio de la imagen, el sonido y el lenguaje verbal, también constituyen cualidades esenciales de un subtitulador experto que, por ejemplo, debe evitar que los subtítulos sigan pasando cuando hay un cambio de ángulo de la cámara o que se revele información antes de que se introduzca de manera visual en la versión original. Si se practica de manera profesional, la subtitulación también requiere un alto dominio de sistemas informáticos ya que los paquetes de software que se usan para subtitular documentos audiovisuales son múltiples y están en constante evolución. Para terminar debemos decir que las películas y los programas de televisión pueden tratar sobre cualquier tema, de modo que un conocimiento cultural amplio, la capacidad para investigar con rapidez y la posibilidad de comunicarse con colaboradores expertos son cualidades muy deseables en un subtitulador.

En las trascripciones que siguen, las dos líneas oblicuas "//" representan la terminación del subtítulo o subtítulos en pantalla.

I. SPANISH > ENGLISH
Text 1
This early scene from Tomás Gutiérrez Alea's *Guantanamera* opens with a shot showing the windscreen of a truck. Mariano (Jorge Perugorría) appears from behind the front seat, followed by Marilis (Louisa Pérez Nieto).[1] Mariano hurriedly puts his shirt back on, anxious to send his lover on her way. Marilis, however, has other ideas, and a heated argument ensues in which it becomes clear that Mariano has repeatedly promised to take Marilis to Havana with him in the truck, but never delivered. Ultimately, Mariano resorts again to deceit, sending Marilis to collect her things while he makes a frantic escape. The scene supplies important plot information by establishing Mariano as deceitful and exploitative towards women, characteristics he will strive to overcome through his encounters with his former teacher and true love, Gina, in the course of the film. The action is also comic, showing the sheepishness of the Latin lover when confronted with the wrath of a disrespected sexual partner, and the fearsome rhetorical resources of the Caribbean woman attempting to overcome the emotional indifference of an inveterate womanizer.

Cuban films frequently contain such confrontations, accelerating further the already rapid-fire dialogue of Caribbean Spanish – and thus making compression all the more necessary in the subtitles. In this instance, at least, the exchange is limited to two people, thereby reducing the potential for overlapping speech turns (when one character begins to speak before the other has finished), a common characteristic of conversation in many Hispanic contexts and also evident in anglophone Caribbean discourse.

1. Marilis: Puchi, ¿tú eres romántico? //	1. Marilis: Puchi, are you romantic? //
2. Mariano: ¡Con cojones! //	2. Mariano: [a.]**You bet your balls!** //
3. Mariano: Bueno, mi china . . . //	3. Mariano: [b.]**Come on, baby,** //
4. Bájate, anda, que me tengo que ir. //	4. **Off you go, I'm in a hurry.** //
5. Marilis: Estás muy raro. //	5. Marilis: You're acting strange. //
6. Marilis: Mariano, tú estás muy raro últimamente conmigo, ¿qué es lo que te pasa? //	6. Marilis: [c.]**You've been acting very strange** with me just lately. What's up? //
7. Mariano: Nada, que me tengo que ir. //	7. Mariano: Nothing. I've got to go. //
8. Marilis: Pero, ¿por qué? //	8. Marilis: Why? //
9. Pero tú me prometiste que esta vez me ibas a llevar pa' La Habana. //	9. You promised you'd take me to Havana this time. //
10. Mariano: El problema es que se me ha presentado un viaje que yo no tenía previsto. //	10. Mariano: It's just that this trip came up unexpectedly. //
11. Marilis: Ese cuento ya me lo hiciste. Yo estoy muy vieja para esto, //	11. Marilis: You already told me that one. I'm too old for stories. //
12. yo me he jugado todas las cartas por ti. //	12. I've bet all my aces on you. //
13. Mira la hora que es. A esta hora yo no puedo virar pa' mi casa. //	13. Look at the time! I can't go back home now. //
14. Mariano: Bueno, Marilis, imagínate. Marilis: Marilis, ¿qué cosa? Marilis, nada. //	14. Mariano: Well, Marilis, that's how it is. Marilis: What do I get out of it? Nothing. //
15. Tú has jugado conmigo, y ahora me tienes que llevar pa' La Habana. //	15. You've used me and now you've got to take me to Havana. //
16. Marilis: Mariano . . . //	16. Marilis: Mariano, //
17. estoy preñada. //	17. I'm pregnant. //
18. Y mi marido //	18. And my husband //
19. no va a cargar con un hijo que no es suyo, pa' que tú lo sepas. //	19. won't have a baby that's not his. Is that clear? //
20. Eso no lo va a aguantar. //	20. He won't stand for it. //
21. Mariano: Coño, Marilis. // [Marilis lanza un grito de desesperación]	21. Mariano: [d.]**Shit, Marilis!** // [Marilis lets out a despairing scream]
22. Mariano: Oye, pero, no te pongas así. Calma, cálmate, oye, //	22. Mariano: Listen, don't get all worked up. [e.]**Calm down.** //
23. ¡coño, que te calmes! Marilis: ¡Es que tú me has desgraciado, Mariano! //	23. Bloody well calm down. Marilis: It's you that's got me into trouble. //
24. Mariano: ¡Espérate! Espérate. Vamos a hablar, vamos a hablar las cosas bien. //	24. Mariano: Wait, we're going to talk things through. //
25. Mariano: Yo te prometí que te iba a llevar pa' La Habana, ¿No? Marilis: Sí. //	25. Mariano: I promised to take you to Havana. Marilis: Yes. //

26. Mariano: Bueno, cálmate, yo te voy a llevar pa' La Habana y después de lo del viaje ese lo arreglamos como sea. //

27. Marilis: ¿De verdad?
Mariano: Sí.
Marilis: ¿De verdad?
Mariano: Sí. //

28. Marilis: Entonces, espérame aquí. Recojo mis cosas y vengo volando. //

29. Y nos vamos pa' La Habana. //

26. Mariano: Okay, calm down. I'll take you. ᶠ**We'll sort things out somehow.** //

27. Amarilis: Really? Mariano: Yes. //

28. Marilis: Wait for me here then. I'll get my things and be back in a flash. //

29. And we'll set off for Havana. //

Commentary

a. You bet your balls! Both the colloquial **register** and jocular tone of the ST's highly idiomatic "*¡con cojones!*" are captured in this TT phrase, which also appositely retains the reference to the male genitalia. The ST idiom is a common colloquial intensifier in Cuban Spanish, another example from Cuban cinema being *tú eres feo con cojones* (roughly "you're one ugly son of a bitch") from Fernando Pérez's *La vida es silbar* (*Life is to Whistle*). [2]

b. Come on, baby, off you go, I'm in a hurry Use of ethnic labels such as *china/o* as terms of endearment is common in Cuban colloquial discourse, the most evident being *mi negra* or *mi mulata*, which appear very frequently in popular music. *Chino/a* is also common, reflecting the significant immigration to Cuba of Chinese workers in the nineteenth century (though, as in this instance, the evidence for actual Chinese ancestry may be scant or non-existent). However, since direct allusions to racial origin are not normally used to express affection in languages such as English, and indeed may be regarded as offensive, the TT sensibly uses a more general term of endearment.

The rest of the TT here also shows a shrewd attention to the dynamics of the scene, prioritizing the function of the language used, rather than its literal sense. Thus "off you go", as against the more literal "get out", and "I'm in a hurry" rather than "I have to go" both capture the somewhat patronizing, evasive tone of the selfish womanizer trying to dispatch his lover with the minimum of fuss once his sexual needs have been satisfied.

c. You've been acting very strange The TT **omission** of Marilis's vocative use of Mariano's name as she begins to pick a fight with him is the first instance of a number of examples of this common subtitling strategy: the name is dropped again from subtitle twenty-three, and no equivalent for the word *pero* is offered in subtitles eight, nine and twenty-two.

d. Shit, Marilis The Spanish expletive *coño* exemplifies better than any other single expression the thought that has to go into translating taboo language, and the need to avoid literalism in almost every instance of its use. Like many taboo lexical items, its function and effect are very heavily determined by context, expressing variously surprise (*¡Coño! ¿Y tú que haces por aquí?*), exasperation (*pero, coño, podías habérmelo dicho antes*), or anger (*¿qué coño quieres decirme con eso?*). Throughout the film, the subtitles reflect these shifts of intensity of function, elsewhere rendering *coño* variously as "God!", "Shit!" and "Fuck me!". Here, Mariano shrugs as he uses the word, which is barely audible, as if to say "what do you expect me to do about it?" or "how can you spring that on me now?". A more natural translation here might have been "Jesus, Marilis" or "For Christ's sake, Marilis".

The word appears again in this scene and is translated in subtitle 23 as "Bloody well calm down!" (for "*¡Coño, Marilis, que te calmes!*"). While this is a reasonable rendering, reflecting the relatively low degree of taboo status of the ST term in this context, it has a markedly non-American ring, being much more common in British, Australian and South African variants (and undoubtedly in others). Some subtitling purists would argue that this generates a dissonance with the decidedly American argot elsewhere in the dialogue (such as "you bet your balls" and "baby", above). Similarly, the very British or Australian-sounding "mate" is used elsewhere to translate *compadre*, where "man" might have offered a more Caribbean-American option that would accord better with the American tone of much of the dialogue.

e. Calm down The first of several instances in this scene where a repeated word or phrase is rendered only once in the subtitles, a common economizing strategy. Other examples are Mariano's single "wait" in subtitle 25 and the **omission** in subtitle 28 of Marilis's disbelieving second request for confirmation that Mariano will take her to Havana.

f. We'll sort things out somehow This is an example of **generalization**, where the TT is made less specific than the ST (which reads more literally "after this business with the trip, we'll sort this out somehow"). This is another common procedure for achieving greater economy of information in subtitling.

Text 2

This scene from Alejandro González Iñárritu's *Amores Perros* opens the last of the three episodes recounted in the film, entitled *El Chivo y Maru*, in which yuppie businessman Gustavo pays hitman El Chivo to wipe out his business partner, Luis (three minutes into scene 15 on the scene selection menu, or at 1:37 from the beginning of the film).[3] Gustavo is taken to meet El Chivo by Leonardo, a policeman of dubious ethics who once imprisoned El Chivo, but now uses him for "favours". Despite once being arch enemies, the two inhabit the same social space and therefore speak the same streetwise language, laced with colloquial Mexicanisms. Gustavo's diction, on the other hand, is appropriate to his much higher social status, being much blander and less obviously Mexican.

1. Leonardo: ¿Quiubo mi chivito? //	1. Leonardo: What's up, Chivito? //
2. El Chivo: Quiubo, Leonardo. //	2. El Chivo: [a]**What's up, Leonardo?** //
3. ¿Qué onda? //	3. **You all right?** //
4. Leonardo: Mira, te presento a un amigo mío, Gustavo Garfias. //	4. Leonardo: Meet my friend, Gustavo Garfias. //
5. El Chivo: ¿Quiubo, bróder? Gustavo: Mucho gusto. //	5. El Chivo: - Hello, brother. Gustavo: - Pleased to meet you. //
6. Leonardo: [Dándole la bolsa con las tortas] Te trajimos esto. //	6. Leonardo: [Giving him the bag of sandwiches] This is for you. //
7. El Chivo: ¡Hórale, cabrón! //	7. El Chivo: Great! //
8. ¡Qué chido! // [Llama a los perros y les va repartiendo las tortas]	8. Cool. // [He calls the dogs and shares the sandwiches among them]

9. El Chivo: Sin chili, sin cebolla . . . ¡qué chido! //

10. ¡Gracias! //

11. Leonardo: [A Gustavo] Siéntate allí. //

12. [A El Chivo] ¿Y tus lentes? ¿Los perdiste? //

13. El Chivo: Ya no los uso, bróder. //

14. Si Dios quiere que vea borroso, //

15. pues veo borroso, ¿verdad? //

16. Leonardo: Aquí mi amigo Gustavo quiere que le hagas un favor. //

17. [A Gustavo] La foto. //

18. El Chivo: [Sin aceptar la foto tendida por Gustavo] Ya yo no hago eso, bróder. //

19. Te lo dije desde la vez pasada. //

20. Leonardo: No mames, Chivito. //

21. ¿O es que acaso piensas vivir de la basura otra vez? //

22. El Chivo: La basura deja, Leonardo . . . //

23. [recalcando ante la incredulidad de Leonardo] ¡Me cae! //

24. Mira: es un Citizen. //

25. Me lo encontré en un bote. Y este otro [enseñando una sortija que lleva en la mano derecha] también me lo encontré. //

26. Leonardo: ¡No me vengas con chingaderas! //

27. Te lo has de haber robado, cabrón. //

28. El Chivo: [Riéndose mientras niega con la cabeza] Venía en la basura. //

29. Gustavo: El Comandante me dijo que usted era muy bueno. //

30. El Chivo: ¿Bueno para qué? //

31. Leonardo: Éntrale, Chivito. No mames. //

32. El Chivo: [Cogiendo la foto] ¿Quién es? //

33. Gustavo: Mi socio. //

34. El Chivo: ¿Qué te hizo? //

35. Gustavo: Me está transando. //

36. El Chivo: Pero, ¿cómo va a ser el negocio? //

9. El Chivo: No chili, no onion. Perfect! //

10. Thanks. //

11. Leonardo: [To Gustavo] Sit there. //

12. [To El Chivo] Did you lose your glasses? //

13. El Chivo: I stopped using them. //

14. If God wants me to see blurry, //

15. I'll see blurry. //

16. Leonardo: My friend Gustavo needs a favour. //

17. [To Gustavo] The photograph. //

18. El Chivo: [Not taking the photo held out by Gustavo] I don't do that anymore. //

19. I told you last time. //

20. Leonardo: [b.]Come on. //

21. How are you going to live? On trash? //

22. El Chivo: Trash provides, Leonardo. //

23. [responding to the evident incredulity of Leonardo] Really. //

24. Look, a Citizen. //

25. I found it in the dumpster. [Showing a ring on his right hand] This, too. //

26. Leonardo: [c.]Don't bullshit me. //

27. You stole it. //

28. [Laughing as he shakes his head] [d.]No, I found it. //

29. Gustavo: [e.]The Commander says you are very good. //

30. El Chivo: Good at what? //

31. Leonardo: Come on, take it. Don't fuck around. //

32. El Chivo: [Taking the photo] Who is he? //

33. Gustavo: My partner. //

34. El Chivo: What did he do? //

35. Gustavo: He's cheating me. //

36. El Chivo: How much are you paying? //

37. Leonardo: cincuenta mil ahorita, cincuenta mil después. //	37. Leonardo: ᶠ·**50,000 now, 50,000 after.** //
38. El Chivo: Cien ahorita, cincuenta después. //	38. El Chivo: 100 now, 50 after. //
39. Leonardo: [A Gustavo] ¿Va? //	39. Leonardo: [To Gustavo] Done? //
40. Gustavo: Está bien, pero ahorita sólo traigo cincuenta. //	40. Gustavo: Okay, but I only have 50 on me. //
41. El Chivo: ¿Cómo se llama? Gustavo: Luis Miranda Solares. //	41. El Chivo: - His name? Gustavo: - Luis Miranda Solares. //
42. Leonardo: Vive en Cerro de Maika mil cuatrocientos sesenta. //	42. Leonardo: ᵍ·**He lives at 1460 Sierra de Maika.** //
43. Sus oficinas están en Montes Urales. //	43. **He works on Montes Urales Street.** //
44. El Chivo: [A Leonardo, riéndose] ¡Todo un proletario! ¿Verdad? //	44. El Chivo: [Laughing] ʰ·**Real blue collar, huh!** //
45. Leonardo: [Levantándose] Está bueno, pues. //	45. Leonardo: [Getting up] All right. //
46. Gustavo: Que parezca que fue un robo, ¿okey? //	46. Gustavo: Make it look like a robbery. //
47. Sin gente, sin líos . . . //	47. No people, no trouble . . . //
48. El Chivo: Seguro, bróder: //	48. El Chivo: Of course, brother. //
49. sin gente, sin líos, sin bronca . . . //	49. No people, no trouble, no shit. //

Commentary

a. What's up, Leonardo? You all right? The distinctly colloquial tone of the ST's *quiubo* is conveyed aptly enough by the common, informal greeting "What's up", but the same ST item is inexplicably translated as the much more neutral "hello" in subtitle five. This is unfortunate, since, as discussed above, much of the scene's dramatic force stems from the clash of class markers between Gustavo and his interlocutors. El Chivo's greeting contrasts very markedly with Gustavo's guarded, blandly international *mucho gusto*, a point made by Paul Julian Smith in his critical study of the film, in which he renders El Chivo's greeting – much more tellingly – as "Whassup, bro"?'. While excessive deviation from standard spellings is discouraged in subtitling because it tends to obstruct easy comprehension, "What's up, bro?" would have been more in keeping with the dynamics of the scene here.

Omission of the verb in El Chivo's second greeting to Leonard, "You all right?", both supplies colloquial tone and reduces the word count.

b. Come on Another example of how context determines the degree of obscenity to be used when translating a taboo item: exactly the same ST item, *"no mames"*, is rendered as "don't fuck around" in subtitle thirty-one.

c. Don't bullshit me In the circumstances, this is a perfectly reasonable translation of the archetypal Mexicanism used in the ST. However, the inevitable loss of resonance and association incurred when translating an item as polysemic as *chingar* and its derivatives is indicated by Octavio Paz's evocation of this term, which though used in many parts of Latin America, is intimately associated with the Mexican character:

[C]hingar implies the idea of failure . . . businesses that fail, fiestas that are rained out, actions that are not completed, *se chingan*. In Colombia *chingarse* means to be disappointed. Almost everywhere *chingarse* means to be made a fool of, to be involved in a fiasco. In some parts of South America *chingar* means to molest, to censure, to ridicule. It is always an aggressive verb, as can be seen in these further meanings: to dock an animal, to incite or prod a fighting-cock, to make merry, to crack a whip, to endanger, to neglect, to frustrate.

In Mexico the word has innumerable meanings. It is a magical word: a change of tone, a change of inflection, is enough to change its meaning. It has as many shadings as it has intonations, as many meanings as it has emotions. One may be a *chingón*, a *gran chingón* (in business, in politics, in crime or with women), or a *chingaquedito* (silent, deceptive, fashioning plots in the shadows, advancing cautiously and then striking with a club), or a *chingoncito*. But in this plurality of meanings the ultimate meaning always contains the idea of aggression, whether it is the simple act of molesting, pricking or censuring, or the violent act of wounding or killing. The verb denotes violence, an emergence from oneself to penetrate another by force. It also means to injure, to lacerate, to violate – bodies, souls, objects – and to destroy. When something breaks, we say *se chingó*. When someone behaves rashly, in defiance of the rules, we say *hizo una chingadera*.[4]

There is a barely perceptible irony, then, in Leonardo's imprecation to El Chivo that he should leave off his *chingaderas* about finding the ring in the trash: he spends the rest of the scene cajoling him to perform a *chingadera* of far greater magnitude, namely murdering Gustavo's partner. It is this kind of subliminal glance at another sense of a word that is so often inevitably lost in translation, robbing the TT of the richness of associations present in the ST.

d. No, I found it The subtitler has opted for an **explicitation** here: the ST merely has El Chivo saying "it was in the trash". Beyond its isolated meaning, however, the function of El Chivo's remark is as a protestation, a rebuttal of Leonardo's accusation.

e. The Commander says you are very good The word "Commander" here seems misplaced, since in the anglophone world it is always associated with the armed forces of national defence, not with the police force. The ST's *Comandante* is used in Mexico instead of *Comisario*, more common elsewhere in the Hispanic world, meaning Chief of Police or Superintendent. Given the North American ring of the rest of the subtitles, "Chief" would probably have been most appropriate here.

f. 50,000 now, 50,000 after As in all areas of translation, the rendering of numbers in subtitles has to be handled with care, as different clients and media have distinct norms regarding which numbers should be spelt out in letters and which should be given in figures. Generally speaking, the norm is that low numbers (typically from one to ten, twelve or twenty) should be spelt out in letters, while anything higher should be given as a figure. For ease of comprehension by the reader, however, most audiovisual subtitlers use a combination of words and numbers where millions or billions are involved, the feeling being that it is easier to process "56 million" than "56,000,000". Another exception is the appearance of numbers in idioms such as "not in a thousand years", where using words is the norm.

Care also has to be taken to respect the regional TL orthographic norms regarding figures, though Spanish seems to show more variation than English in this regard (thus for English ten thousand, Spain prefers "10.000", Mexico "10,000" and Cuba "10 000"). The rendering of metric into imperial measurements, however, does require attention to regional norms in English, as British still prefers "16 stone" to the "224 pounds" that is more common in most of the anglophone world, while in some areas metric weights or distances in kilometres are now conventionally used and will not require conversion. As always, the translator should consult the client if in doubt. If this is not possible, ensuring that the translation is at least internally consistent is the minimum requirement.

g. He lives at 1460 Sierra de Maika. 43. He works on Montes Urales Street The incorrect inclusion of the word *Sierra* in the address is a strange error on the part of the subtitler, since the words "*1460 Cerro de Maika*" are clearly visible on screen at this point, as we see the back of the photo from El Chivo's point of view. Clearly this type of dissonance between the subtitles and the visual evidence of the film image is distracting for the viewer and should be avoided.

The **amplification** by addition of the word "Street" in the TT address is important here, since failure to include it would leave readers of the subtitles without a mental image of the location in question and possibly confuse them into thinking that Luis works somewhere in the hills (*Montes* triggering associations to "mount", "mountains").

h. Real blue collar, huh! This gruffly sarcastic remark by El Chivo – in response to learning Luis's places of residence and of work, which are clearly well known as upper class areas – is economically conveyed by this TT idiom, which, though distinctly American, has sufficiently common currency worldwide. The inclusion of the "huh" and the exclamation mark are important cues to the viewer/reader that El Chivo's remark is ironical, and are considerably more effective for this purpose than the more literal "right?" would have been.

Texto 1
La siguiente es una escena extraída de la película *The Perez Family* (1995) de Mira Nair.[5] La película cuenta la historia de Juan Raúl Pérez (Alfred Molina) un preso político cubano que llega a la Florida en busca de su esposa, Carmela Pérez (Angélica Huston) a quién no ha visto en veinte años. En la entrevista al llegar a territorio norteamericano, el agente de inmigración estadounidense confunde a Dorita Evita Pérez (Marisa Tomei) por la esposa de Juan Raúl. Dorita convence a Juan Raúl de que siga el juego ya que será más fácil para ellos encontrar patrocinadores que los ayuden a incorporarse a la vida civil. Ella sigue buscando maneras de agrandar su improvisada familia. Aquí entra Felipe, un adolescente que camina por las calles vendiendo de todo un poco en un carro de mercado.

A pesar de que la película se desarrolla en inglés, los personajes muestran su origen tanto mediante el uso de palabras en español intercaladas en sus frases como en su acento evidentemente latino. La gramática utilizada por los hablantes difiere de la llamada estándar.

1. Felipe: Rolex watches, aquí.
(Looking at Dorita who is buying
something from a street vendor)
2. Oh, mama. Come o'er here, I like the
way you walk.
3. Street Vendor: Hey Perez, that's my
customer.
4. Dorita: You Perez?

5. Me too. Dottie Perez
6. Felipe: Felipe, glad to know you.
[Kissing her hand]
7. Dorita: You're from Mariel.
Felipe: Yeah.
8. Dorita: Oye mijo, My husband and I
can use another Perez.
9. The bigger the family the quicker we
get the job.
10. Felipe: Thanks m'am but I did the
sponsor, you know.
11. I'm finished with that,
I'm out.
12. Besides, I'm el Lobo, the wolf.
13. I'm better alone.
14. Dorita: You're smart to have your
own business, mijo. [Looking at the
cart Felipe is carrying]
15. How much for the nail polish?
16. Felipe: 50 cents, and . . . no family
discounts, mama.
17. Did I ask you for a discount?

1. Felipe: [a.]**Vendo relojes Rolex aquí. //**
(Mirando a Dorita que compra en
otra caseta)
2. [b.]**Ven acá, me gusta como caminas. //**
3. Vendedor: Oye, Pérez, ella es mi cliente. //
4. Dorita: ¿Te apellidas Pérez?
Yo también. //
5. Soy Dottie Pérez //
6. Felipe: [c.]**Soy Felipe, encantado de
conocerte. [Besa la mano de Dorita] //**
7. Dorita: [d.]**¿Eres de Mariel?**
Felipe: Sí //
8. Dorita: [e.]**A mi esposo y yo nos caería
bien otro Pérez. //**
9. [f.]**Las familias grandes hallan empleos
con más rapidez. //**
10. Felipe: Gracias pero ya hablé con el
patrocinador. //
11. Terminé ese asunto.
Salí de ahí. //
12. Además, yo soy el Lobo. //
13. Me va mejor solo. //
14. Dorita: Eres inteligente por tener tu
propio negocio. [Mirando el carro de
Felipe] //
15. ¿Cuánto cuesta el barniz de uñas? //
16. Felipe: [g.]**50cts, y no hay descuentos
familiares, mamá. //**
17. Dorita ¿Acaso te pedí un descuento? //

Comentarios

a. Felipe: Vendo relojes Rolex aquí En esta primera intervención de la escena se presenta
el fenómeno de **explicitación**. Es un recurso poco utilizado en la subtitulación debido a
que por lo general el idioma hablado muestra mayor velocidad que el escrito. Se utiliza
cuando hay elementos culturales que no se entienden fácilmente en la cultura de llegada,
o cuando el significado de un enunciado es ambiguo. En este caso no parece existir la
necesidad de ampliar pero el subtitulador ha optado por hacerlo quizás porque también
es cierto que la lectura de una frase completa (con sujeto opcional, verbo y predicado)
muchas veces se procesa más rápido que una incompleta. Esto se debe a que la frase completa cumple uno de los requisitos fundamentales de los subtítulos: no llamar demasiado
la atención sobre el subtítulo en sí, sino en su contenido semántico.

b. Ven acá, me gusta como caminas Aparece en el enunciado anterior del TO una palabra en español ("aquí") que se ha trascrito en el subtítulo. En este subtítulo encontramos un ejemplo de **omisión**. El "*Oh, mama*" se ha omitido en el subtítulo porque es ya fácilmente reconocible en español, lo que ocurre también en el subtítulo 14 con "mijo" y con la muletilla "*you know*" del 10. Este fenómeno se extiende al uso de los vocativos y muletillas tanto en la LO como en la LM. Se suele omitir también la información redundante, los apellidos y nombres propios, elementos que redundan con la imagen e interjecciones. La **omisión** es una de las herramientas de las que puede hacer uso el subtitulador, pero no es la única ni la más importante. Más importante incluso es la capacidad de síntesis, ya que los subtítulos interlingüísticos no pueden nunca trasvasar todo el contenido del texto hablado.

c. Soy Felipe, encantado / de conocerte. [Besa la mano de Dorita] Felipe se muestra desde el comienzo de la escena como un chico conquistador, un pequeño *Latin lover*. Aquí se ha escogido una fórmula de presentación que está de acuerdo con esta característica. Se dice que el subtitulador debe intentar condensar lo mejor posible el contenido tanto lingüístico como situacional de los enunciados del TO. Otra opción que viene a la mente para presentarse es "mucho gusto", pero aunque es más corta, es muy neutra y dejaría de lado la faceta conquistadora de Felipe.

d. ¿Eres de Mariel? El enunciado del TO tiene la forma gramatical de una afirmación, pero su función pragmática es la de una pregunta, dicha función es captada en los subtítulos. En muchas ocasiones el subtitulador debe alejarse de forma más radical de lo que se dice, cambiando por ejemplo referencias culturales de la LO por otras de la LM, o cambiando una pregunta por una interjección. Le interesa pues más la intención comunicativa del TO que su estructura gramatical.

e. A mi esposo y yo / nos caería bien otro Pérez En esta intervención de Dorita se produce una falta gramatical que puede tener dos funciones. Por un lado hace más breve el enunciado al cambiar "a mí" por "yo"; por otro, nos acerca al modo de hablar de Dorita y de casi todos los personajes de la historia como se mencionó antes.

"Caer bien" puede tener el significado de "sentar bien" cuando se refiere a una prenda, pero al referirse a una persona toma generalmente el significado de "resultar simpático". Una frase más común y que se ajusta más al propósito comunicativo de la intervención es "venir bien".

f. Las familias grandes hallan / empleos con más rapidez Se presenta un cambio entre la manera en que se formula el enunciado en la LO y aquella de la LM. Una vez más es la necesidad de ser breve la que lleva al subtitulador a realizar dicho cambio. Se podría haber reducido incluso más el número de palabras de haberse sustituido "con más rapidez" por "más rápido".

g. 50cts, y no hay descuentos / familiares, mamá Se ha optado por reducir "centavos" por cts. Refiérase a los comentarios del texto 2 español > inglés, especialmente el del subtítulo 37(f.).

Se puede anotar aquí también el hecho de que se mencione la palabra *mamá* tanto en el primer enunciado de la escena como en éste. Sin embargo, en cada una de sus apariciones tiene unas **connotaciones** diferentes: en el primer caso funciona como un piropo, en el segundo se refiere a un miembro de la familia, el subtitulador optó por omitir la primera referencia y subtitular la segunda.

Texto 2

Los subtítulos que estudiaremos a continuación provienen de una escena de la primera temporada de la serie televisiva de acción *24 Horas* de 20th Century Fox.[6] En esta escena aparece Kimberly, que había sido secuestrada y ha logrado escapar en parte gracias a la ayuda de Rick, uno de los secuestradores, quien por ayudarla ahora está herido. Kimberly es la hija del protagonista de la serie que trabaja en la unidad antiterrorista. Rick por su parte es un joven que se mueve en el bajo mundo, aunque en el fondo no hace las veces de un tipo malo. La escena introduce a Frank, que busca a su hermano Dan. Dan ha muerto pero Rick teme decírselo.

En la traducción para la subtitulación se tienen en cuenta dos factores importantes. El primero de ellos es el código (la lengua que se utiliza) y el segundo el canal lingüístico (oral o escrito). Tendiendo en cuenta estos factores podríamos definir la **traducción vertical** o **intralingüística** como la traducción que se realiza de un canal a otro, (del lenguaje oral al escrito) y la **traducción horizontal** o **interlingüística** aquella que se realiza de un código a otro (de una lengua a otra). Un tercer tipo de traducción específica para la subtitulación es la **traducción diagonal** que como su nombre lo indica consiste en traducir directamente del lenguaje oral de la LO al escrito de la LM.

Antes de entrar a estudiar los subtítulos que siguen vale la pena mencionar que los guiones de la cadena 20th Century Fox que se preparan para la subtitulación en otro idioma pasan primero por una **traducción intralingüística**. Este tipo de traducción es común y se utiliza por diversos motivos entre los que se cuentan la ayuda destinada a personas con discapacidad auditiva, estudiantes de la LO y, en algunos casos, como medio de entretenimiento del tipo karaoke. Los subtituladores reciben un guión con los diálogos y uno con la subtitulación propuesta en la LO. Además de esto reciben comentarios contextuales que facilitarán su labor y que ayudarán a asegurar la calidad de los subtítulos en la LM. Otra aproximación al proceso de subtitulación consiste primero en hacer la **traducción interlingüística** sin tener en cuenta las limitaciones de espacio y paso seguido realizar la **intralingüística** teniendo el límite de dos líneas con un máximo de 35 caracteres cada una.

En la trascripción que sigue se ha optado por numerar las participaciones de los hablantes tanto en el TO como en el TM. Algunas de ellas tienen un numeral "a" que corresponde a la **traducción vertical** que se realizó previamente y que como se verá sirvió de base para la **traducción horizontal**.

1. Frank: Hey, Rick //	1. Frank: [a]**Oye, Rick.** //
2. Rick: Hey. //	2. Rick: Oye. //
3. Frank: So, how did it go last night? //	3. Frank: ¿Cómo te fue anoche?//
3a. How did it go last night?	
4. Rick: Went fine. //	4. Rick: Bien. //
5. Frank: Yeah? //	5. Frank: ¿Sí? //
6. Doesn't look fine. What happened to you? //	6. No parece. ¿Qué te pasó?//

7. Rick: Nothing, I'm okay//	7. Rick: Nada estoy bien. //
8. Frank: Hey, Dan! //	8. Frank: ¡Oye, Dan! //
9. Dan! //	9. ¡Dan! //
10. Rick: Go, just get out of here. [Whispers to Kimberly] //	10. Rick: [b.]**Vete, ya vete. [A Kimberly, susurrando]** //
10a. Go, just leave. [Whispers to Kimberly] //	
11. Grab a cab on 4th.	11. Toma un taxi en la cuarta.
12. Kimberly: I know. //	12. Kimberly: Lo sé. //
13. Frank: Where is my brother?	13. Frank: ¿Dónde está mi hermano?
14. Rick: He's out. //	14. Rick: [c.]**Salió** //
15. Frank: Out where?	15. Frank: ¿Adónde?
16. Rick: We got separated. //	16. Rick: Nos separamos. //
17. Frank: Aha, so where is the money?	17. Frank: [d.]**¿Dónde está el dinero?**
17a. Frank: So where is the money?	
18. Rick: He's got it. //	18. Rick: Lo tiene él. //
19. Kimberly: I'm sorry, I should get going.	19. Kimberly: [e.]**Mejor me voy.**
19a. Kimberly: I should get going.	
20. Frank: Where are you going? //	20. Frank: ¿Adónde vas? //
21. Kimberly: What do you mean?	21. Kimberly: ¿Qué quieres decir?
22. Frank: I don't know you. //	22. Frank: [f.]**No lo sé.** //
23. Kimberly: My name is Kim.	23. Kimberly: Me llamo Kim.
24. Frank: Hi Kim, how do you know Rick? //	24. Frank: [g.]**Hola, ¿cómo conoces a Rick?** //
24a. Frank: Hi, how do you know Rick? //	
25. Rick: She's a friend of mine from San Diego.	25. Rick: Es una amiga de San Diego.
26. She's got to get back home. //	26. Tiene que volver a su casa. //
27. Frank: She's not going anywhere	27. Frank: [h.]**No irá a ninguna parte.**
27a. Frank: She's not going.	
28. Rick: What's that supposed to mean? //	28. Rick: ¿Cómo es eso? //
28a. Rick: What's that mean? //	
29. Frank: My brother is not here, my money is not here.	29. Frank: [i.]**Mi hermano y mi dinero no están,**
29a. My brother and my money aren't here.	
30. and I don't know her.	30. Y yo no la conozco. //
30a. and I don't know her. //	
31. Rick: I told you she's a friend of mine . . .	31. Rick: [j.]**Es una amiga . . .**
31a. Rick: She's a friend.	
32. Frank: Yeah, I understand . . . //	32. Frank: Entiendo, pero . . . //
32a. Frank: I understand //	

33.	But I got business going down here	33.	. . . tengo un negocio en media hora.
33a.	But I got business here in half an hour. //		//
34.	Until Dan gets back	34.	k.**Nadie se irá hasta que Dan regrese**
35.	with the money, nobody leaves.	35.	**con el dinero.**

Comentarios

a. Oye, Rick Si se compara la expresión "oye" de este subtítulo con la del numeral ocho veremos que el TO utiliza la expresión *hey* en ambos casos. Sin embargo, su función es diferente y al traspasarla de una lengua a otra estas diferencias salen a relucir. En el caso del subtítulo 1, se trata de un saludo informal entre jóvenes; en el segundo caso es un vocativo que sirve para llamar a alguien. En español la traducción "oye" funciona perfectamente para cumplir la segunda función, pero no la primera ya que como saludo no es muy natural. Esto nos recuerda que el contexto en que se produce una palabra o expresión modifica el significado de la misma. Las expresiones de saludo en cualquier lengua son muy variadas ya que demuestran el tipo de relación que hay entre dos personas, la formalidad de la situación e incluso su estrato social. El subtitulador requiere una gran cantidad de factores contextuales para tomar su decisión en éste y otros casos pues su labor le pide sincronizar el plano lingüístico con el tiempo en que el subtítulo aparece en pantalla, con las imágenes, música y ruidos de modo que no redunden ni los contradigan. Para el subtítulo que nos ocupa veremos que algunas de las opciones de saludo pueden ser "hola", "¿qué tal?" e incluso "quiubo". Ver ejercicio 3 inglés > español.

b. Vete, ya vete. [A Kimberly, susurrando] Dos cosas valen mención en este subtítulo. La primera de ellas se refiere a uno de los puntos que más ha despertado críticas acerca de los subtítulos en las películas: la falta de **equivalencia** entre lo que se dice y lo que el espectador lee. Esta falta de **equivalencia** puede explicarse por las limitaciones de espacio por una parte y por otra en que la **equivalencia** que se busca no es meramente formal sino que hace más énfasis en la parte funcional. Sin embargo, los defensores de esta postura se dan cuenta de que muchas veces al perder en la forma se pierden rasgos de la función: una frase que es una orden acompañada de un ruego, puede pasar a convertirse en una simple orden. En algunos casos la forma en que un personaje articula sus frases nos ayuda a hacernos una idea de su personalidad. Si esto cambia el espectador puede hacerse una idea totalmente diferente de éste.

La segunda se refiere a los comentarios contextuales que aparecen entre corchetes. Estos comentarios le ayudan al subtitulador a entender mejor la escena y a proponer el subtítulo que más natural parezca dentro del contexto.

c. Salió La **traducción literal** de esta intervención sería "está afuera" o "no está". Estas dos opciones son lo bastantemente cortas para poder ser consideradas como traducciones apropiadas para la subtitulación. Sin embargo, en la intervención siguiente Frank pregunta "*out where?*". Si bien se hubiera podido encontrar una solución para las alternativas propuestas, el subtítulo 15, siendo sencillo, encaja perfectamente con éste. Esto nos recuerda que la unidad básica de la traducción para subtítulos no puede reducirse a la frase. En casos como éste, cuando además tenemos un ritmo de habla apresurado, debemos tener en cuenta la totalidad del diálogo.

d. ¿Dónde está el dinero? Éste, como muchos otros, es un caso en el que se omiten las interjecciones. En la traducción intralingüística se omite una de ellas (*aha*) por ser un elemento que corresponde principalmente al lenguaje oral. En la traducción interlingüística se omite un segundo elemento (*so*) que, si bien está cargado de **connotaciones** en la LO, puede omitirse en la LM ya que también funciona en este caso como simple interjección siendo más enfática que portadora de información. La razón por la cual se omiten las interjecciones es debido a que en la subtitulación se produce un cambio de código y de canal lingüístico. Cada canal tiene sus propias características y particularidades. En el caso que nos compete se puede decir que el canal oral permite las interjecciones y las repeticiones mucho más que el escrito.

e. Mejor me voy Vemos aquí un caso de **omisión** de una frase entera (*"I'm sorry"*). La frase tiene una función social, pero de ser tan común ha perdido mucha de su fuerza (lo mismo sucede con *"excuse me"*), motivo por el cual se ha decidido omitir en este contexto tanto en la LO como en la LM.

f. No lo sé Si bien la calidad de los subtítulos de esta serie televisiva es alta se encuentra en esta instancia un error. Éste le quita toda **coherencia** a los diálogos que componen esta parte de la escena. El subtitulador ha cambiado *I don't know you* por *"I don't know"*. Si bien en inglés se omite tan sólo una palabra, ésta cambia por completo el significado de la frase resultando en un cambio en español de "no te conozco" a "no lo sé". La primera opción encaja perfectamente con el subtítulo anterior y con el siguiente en el que Kim se presenta. La segunda parece una respuesta extraña al subtítulo anterior que se puede entender como "no sé lo que quiero decir", dándole un toque gracioso que corta el ritmo seco, rápido y nervioso de la escena.

g. Hola, ¿cómo conoces a Rick? Se omite aquí el nombre del personaje (Kim) pues el espectador ya lo conoce y lo puede haber escuchado. A la vez que se reduce el número de caracteres utilizados se evita la redundancia.

h. No irá a ninguna parte Vemos aquí que debido a la naturalidad de la frase y al no presentar mayores problemas de espacio el subtitulador ha optado por traducir no desde la **traducción intralingüística** sino del diálogo en el TO.

i. Mi hermano y mi dinero no están En el diálogo se usa un recurso repetitivo en el que se crean dos oraciones paralelas en singular; el subtitulador en su afán por sintetizar logra unir los dos sujetos y someterlos a un sólo verbo en plural.

j. Es una amiga . . . Aquí se encuentran otros casos de **omisión**. En primer lugar se omite *"I told you"* ya que implica repetición; además, es redundante en el lenguaje escrito para este tipo de traducción incluir *"of mine"* o su equivalente "mía".

k. Nadie se irá hasta que Dan regrese // con el dinero Vemos aquí un cambio en la organización de los elementos del TO al TM. En este caso no hay grandes problemas ya que no se espera un elemento sorpresa. Sin embargo, muchos espectadores se ven frustrados cuando en una película, aunque sea un segundo antes, se les anticipa algún detalle que debían conocer sólo hasta más tarde o cuando leen los subtítulos antes o después de una intervención ya que algunas veces puede dar lugar a confusiones sobre quién dice qué a quién. De allí la importancia de la sincronización entre el dialogo del TO y el de los subtítulos.

III. SPANISH > ENGLISH EXERCISES

Film Titles

Either individually or together, research these films on the Internet (the Internet Movie Database at http://www.imdb.com is a good starting point), noting country of origin, genre and plot outline. Also note the specific country of distribution of the English title(s). Then, in class, analyse and discuss the English titles, speculating on their effectiveness in the country of distribution and commenting on how well the title would work in your own country. Based on the content of the films, conjecture as to how the translators or distributors of each film may have arrived at the chosen English title and, where relevant, discuss alternative titles.

> i. *Amores perros* – Love's a Bitch
> ii. *La Virgen de los sicarios* – Our Lady of the Assassins
> iii. *La boca del lobo* – The Lion's Den
> iv. *Pantaleón y las visitadoras* – Captain Pantoja and the Special Services
> v. *Golpe de estadio* – Time Out

Subtitling

i) Write English subtitles for the following scene from *Guantanamera*. (Research the plot of the film on the Internet Movie Database if you are able.) As a rough guide, the numbering shows how the subtitles are divided in the distributed version of the film, subtitled by the ICAIC, while the bracketed number after each unit of dialogue shows how many characters, including spaces, each published subtitle contains. Retain the same divisions as the published version and try to stay roughly within the number of characters used, condensing or omitting where necessary.

ii) Having watched the subtitled scene on tape or DVD, compare the published subtitles with your own, then answer the following questions:

a) Observe how the imperative *mira* is translated in subtitles 8 and 14. Do you think this is an acceptable translation? Suggest any alternatives that would be equally or more acceptable.

b) Why does subtitle 16 include the speech turns of two different characters? How is this subtitle punctuated in order to show that it refers to two different speakers?

c) In the second speech turn in subtitle 16, "*¿a ti quién te dio vela en este entierro?*", what **translation loss** has been incurred?

d) Identify sections of the ST below that have no equivalent in the subtitles (that is, examples of **omission**).

e) Subtitles 19 to 21 together, though they correspond to the speech of a single actor, contain fewer characters in total than subtitle 23 on its own. Why do you think subtitles 19 to 21 have been divided in this manner?

f) What translation strategy has been used in subtitle 17 to translate "*Compañeros, para hablar, hay que pedir la palabra*"?

The scene opens 3 minutes, 13 seconds from the beginning of the opening credits (and the same time from the beginning of chapter 1 of the DVD menu). A meeting room, with civil servants sitting round a table, except for Adolfo, who stands looking through the window at Havana rooftops. They are arguing . . .

Rivero: 1. ¡Por favor, compañeros, por favor! (23) 2. Que lo que estamos dando es demasiadas vueltas a este asunto. (59)

Paula: 3. Lo merece. (15)

Rivero: 4. No, no, no, yo tengo que regresar lo antes possible a Camagüey. (57) 5. Para mí el asunto es bien sencillo: (25) 6. si el hombre se muere en Baracoa, pues que lo entierren en Baracoa, (52) 7. porque en definitiva compañeros, la patria es una sola . . . (41)

Paula: 8. Mira, Rivero, si yo me muero en Baracoa, (39) 9. no hay quien me obligue a quedarme allí enterrada, no me fastidies. (54) 10. Yo soy de Santa Clara, mi hermano, y toda mi familia y toda mi gente (51) 11. está allí. (11)

Benito: 12. Suavito, suavito, suavito, compañeros, suavito . . . . (32)

Hombre: 13. Con permiso, Benito. (18) 14. Mira, Rivero, yo estoy de acuerdo con Paula. (38) 15. ¿Qué culpa tengo yo de haberme muerto en Baracoa? (38) 16. A lo mejor fui allí a visitar a unas amistades . . .

Otro Hombre: [Inaudible] ¿a ti quién te dio vela en este entierro? (56)

Presidente: 17. Compañeros, para hablar, hay que pedir la palabra. (33) 18. A ver, Adolfo. (17)

Adolfo: 19. ¿Y si . . . (8) 20. nos repartimos el muerto . . . (21) 21. entre todos? (16)

Presidente: 22. Concreta tu idea. (17)

Adolfo: 23. Si cada empresa provincial asume su responsabilidad territorial, (71) 24. si cada uno de nosotros se compromete al traslado del difunto por su provincia, (59) 25. entonces todos tocamos a menos, (28) 26. lo cual quiere decir que entonces sí alcanza (32) 27. la cuota de gasolina que se le asigna a cada funeraria. (48) 28. Mira, Justo, (12) 29. yo pienso que si se hace un estudio sobre la marcha, casuístico, (45) 30. aplicando la metodología, (34) 31. ese plan no puede fallar. (21)

(See http://caribbeantranslationmanual.com/film.html for published subtitles.)

IV. EJERCICIOS PRÁCTICOS INGLÉS > ESPAÑOL

1. La traducción de los títulos de las películas generalmente sorprende a la audiencia que habla el idioma origen y el de la traducción. Es después de un detenido análisis que encontramos los motivos por los que un título fue traducido de determinada manera, aunque no estemos de acuerdo con el resultado. Intente analizar por qué los siguientes títulos originalmente en inglés han resultado en la versión española que se presenta al frente. Para hacer este análisis es importante haber visto la película o al menos haber buscado información sobre ella. La sinopsis, el país de origen, el género y el año son algunos de los elementos que le ayudarán a entender el porqué de la traducción.
   i. *White Chicks* – ¿Y dónde están las rubias? (Latinoamérica); Dos rubias de pelo en pecho. (España)

ii. *Not Another Teen Movie* – Esta no es otra tonta película americana
iii. *The Forgotten* – Misteriosa obsesión
iv. *Sideways* – Entre copas

2. Antes de subtitular una película es importante hacer un análisis de los elementos que pueden presentar problemas (elementos culturales, léxico local, variación de **registros**, y otros). Este análisis en condiciones óptimas lo debe realizar un hablante nativo. A continuación encontrará una ficha modelo en donde se analiza una película que se va a subtitular al inglés. Léalo y luego escoja una película y realice su propio análisis.

FICHA MODELO:

<table>
<tr><td>

1. Ficha técnica:
   Título original: *Bolívar soy yo*[7]   Otros nombres: Bolivar Is Me / I Am Bolivar.
   País: Colombia / Francia, 2002.   Dirección: Jorge Alí Triana.
   Intérpretes: Amparo Grisales, Robinson Díaz, Jairo Camargo.

</td></tr>
<tr><td>

2. Sinopsis: Un actor (Robinson Díaz) personifica a Simón Bolívar en una telenovela. El actor se mete tanto en su papel que, para sus compañeros de trabajo, se ha enloquecido. Gracias a su popularidad en la telenovela logra llegar a varias esferas de la vida nacional de Colombia y va por el país intentando conseguir el sueño bolivariano. Tiene elementos cómicos pero también refleja los problemas políticos y de violencia que aquejan a Colombia.

</td></tr>
<tr><td>

3. Elementos culturales (costumbres, actividades). Es importante saber sobre la situación social y política del país pues aparecen grupos guerrilleros (de nombre ficticio) y otros actores del conflicto. También es esencial conocer la historia nacional de Colombia y sus personajes (héroes de la independencia y sus conflictos y amistades) para poder entender algunos comentarios y juegos de palabras.
   La importancia de las telenovelas para un país como Colombia y su poder para mover las masas.

</td></tr>
<tr><td>

4. Elementos lingüísticos
   a. **Registros** y estilos de habla.
      - Español siglo XVIII y XIX bogotano.
      - **Registro** usado por la prostituta.
      - El **registro** usado por los componentes del grupo guerrillero (con vocabulario que hace alusión al marxismo, leninismo e izquierdas).
      - La forma en que se dirige la madre del protagonista a él.
      - El español de Bogotá.
   b. Elementos léxicos propios de la cultura. Aguardiente, y en general el lenguaje soez.

</td></tr>
</table>

3. Se mencionó en el segundo texto que los saludos muestran la relación que hay entre dos personas, su grado de familiaridad y su situación social. Intente llenar el siguiente cuadro con dicha información recordando que una misma expresión puede usarse en diversos contextos y por diferentes tipos de personas y que las mismas personas pueden saludarse de distinta manera dependiendo del grado de formalidad de la situación:

SALUDO	TIPO DE RELACIÓN	GRADO DE FORMALIDAD / SITUACIÓN SOCIAL
Hola		
¿Qué tal?		
¿Quiubo?		
¿Qué más?		
¿'Tos qué?		
¿Cómo andas?		
Buenas tardes		
¿Qué pasó?		

CHAPTER 6

Law

INTRODUCTION

The translation of legal texts raises the same issues in the Caribbean as it does elsewhere. In order to understand these issues, we must first consider the nature of the legal text and its implications. Legal documents are specialized texts, with their own structures, conventions and terminology that differentiate them from other types of texts (though the classification of texts into different types of discourse is far from clear-cut or mutually exclusive). Linguistically, legal texts tend to be far more explicit than the majority of other text types, as a result of the need to eliminate any trace of ambiguity that might lead to misunderstandings between the interested parties. The legal document thus tends to be lengthy, complex and repetitive. A legal text also does more than merely transmit information; rather it also implies an action of some kind: a contract, as well as being a piece of paper bearing information, also serves to bind the parties in an agreement; a sentence serves to sentence; a marriage certificate ratifies the union between two people, and so on. Thus, when such texts are produced and signed, there is an implied action that will have consequences in the lives of persons, companies and social institutions in general. A legal document also has validity within the specific legal system in which it is produced.

Various factors make such texts particularly difficult to translate, so that translators wishing to work in this area require specialized training. One of these factors is the disparity between the legal systems of different countries, which for historical reasons tends to be greater when a different language is spoken: the legal systems in the countries of the anglophone Caribbean derive from British law, while those of the Hispanic territories are based on the Spanish model. Some Caribbean territories, on the other hand, still form part of France, the United Kingdom or the United States, or are dependent territories, and their local administrations are governed by the laws of those countries.

The implications of a badly translated legal document constitute a further complicating factor. On the one hand, a deficient translation may partially or completely invalidate the contract, treaty, agreement or other text being translated. In such cases, the translator may be culpable and thus suffer professionally or personally as a result. On the other hand, the translation or mistranslation of a legal text may change the life of an innocent person or result in a criminal being freed, in the case of court translating or interpreting. Ideally, this latter task is carried out by specialist interpreters who are expert in the language of the court room and who take an oath that they will translate or interpret **faithfully** when called upon to do so.

In the case of written translation, legal translators are obliged to pay great attention to detail as they attempt to transfer the text as literally as possible from SL to TL. This does not mean, however, that legal translators use only dictionaries, however specialized, to produce their versions of texts. They must also be highly expert in analysis and comparison, keeping up to date with legal matters in both languages and cultivating familiarity with the differences and similarities between the legal systems of the countries or regions from which and into which they are translating. Furthermore, as well as being voracious readers of legal texts and extremely well versed in their language, they must consult regularly with legal experts. Finally, like all translators, they cannot work solely at the linguistic level; rather, they must view legal texts and procedures as features of a culture that must be understood by members of a different culture. **Culture-bound elements**, therefore, are a crucial factor in the decision-making process. A now classic example relates to a case that arose in Australia in 1990, after a woman had been accused of murdering her daughter on a campsite. An aboriginal woman, an expert tracker, appeared as a witness and testified that the tracks at the scene were those of a dingo carrying a baby. However, under cross-examination she was asked to consider whether the dingo might have been carrying a rabbit or a kangaroo instead of a baby. The woman refused to entertain the lawyers' hypothesis on the basis that the moral tradition of her culture prohibited discussion of false hypotheses. The translator was obliged to transmit all of this information and serve as a cultural liaison. Eventually the tracker responded to the question by asking, "Was a kangaroo living in the tent?"

While this may be a more extreme instance, there is always cultural content that the translator must be aware of, since it is precisely this awareness of cultural and linguistic implication that will allow the resulting translation to meet the requirements of **fidelity** of form and content that are uppermost in legal translation.

Finally, the degree of visibility of the translator is a matter that has generated considerable debate among theorists. Many advocate a posture of invisibility on the part of the translator, meaning that the TT should read like an original text; in this view, footnotes constitute an admission of the translator's incapacity to transfer the nuances of the ST into the TL. In legal translation, however, the approach is almost always rather different, since such annotations are often required to explain terms whose meaning is divergent in the source and target cultures. The translator may thus use this device in order to bridge the gap between the two cultures and systems. The texts in this chapter are intended to give some idea – though a necessarily restricted one – of the variety and complexity of legal documentation.

INTRODUCCIÓN

La traducción de textos legales en el Caribe presenta los mismos problemas que la traducción de este **tipo textual** en otros contextos. Para entender cuáles son estos problemas es necesario hacer una descripción de lo que es un texto legal y de sus implicaciones.

Un texto legal pertenece al ámbito de los textos especializados, es decir que tiene sus propias estructuras, convenciones y terminología que lo distinguen de otro **tipo de textos,** aunque las líneas divisorias entre los tipos textuales distan mucho de ser claras y excluyentes. Se caracterizan lingüísticamente por recurrir a la **explicitación** mucho más que la mayoría de los otros tipos textuales. Esto se debe a la necesidad de eliminar cualquier rastro de ambigüedad que pueda dar lugar a malentendidos entre las personas o entidades interesadas. Por ello son casi siempre extensos, complejos y tienden a repetir la información. Los textos legales son textos que no se limitan a dar información sino que llevan en sí un acto: un contrato, además de ser un papel con información, sirve como base para el acto de contratar, una sentencia, para sentenciar; un acta de matrimonio para demostrar la unión de dos personas. En el momento en que se producen y se firman los textos se puede dar por hecha una acción que tiene repercusiones directas en la vida de las personas, las empresas y las instituciones sociales en general. Además, un texto legal tiene validez dentro de un sistema judicial determinado.

Hay varios aspectos que los hacen especialmente difíciles de traducir y que han llevado a que los traductores que se interesan por esta rama de la traducción requieran un entrenamiento especial. Uno de estos aspectos es la disparidad entre los sistemas legales de un país y otro, que tiende a acrecentarse entre una lengua y otra por razones generalmente históricas: en el Caribe los países anglófonos tienen una tradición jurídica basada en las leyes británicas, mientras que los sistemas de los países hispanohablantes tienen sus raíces en el modelo español. Algunas islas caribeñas, por su parte, todavía pertenecen a países como Francia, Inglaterra o Estados Unidos, o son dependencias de ellos, lo que hace que sus gobiernos locales se rijan bajo las normas de dichos países.

Otro aspecto tiene que ver con las implicaciones de una mala traducción del texto legal. Por un lado, puede dar lugar a la invalidez parcial o total de contratos, tratados, acuerdos, y otros documentos. Cuando este caso se presenta se culpa al traductor y puede tener graves repercusiones en su carrera o en su persona. Por otro lado, la traducción o la mala traducción de un texto legal puede cambiar la vida de una persona inocente o dejar en libertad a un criminal, en el caso de la traducción para la corte. Esta labor la realizan en la medida de lo posible intérpretes especializados en el lenguaje de la corte, quienes deben hacer un juramento de que interpretarán o traducirán con **fidelidad** lo que se les pida.

En casos de traducción escrita, el traductor se ve forzado a realizar un trabajo minucioso, intentando transvasar casi siempre literalmente el texto de la LO a la LM. Pero esto no quiere decir que un traductor de textos legales se limite a utilizar un diccionario (aunque sea especializado) para lograr su versión del texto. Debe, ante todo, mantenerse al día en cuestiones legales en las dos lenguas, conociendo los sistemas judiciales de los países o regiones desde los cuales y hacia los cuales traduce, entendiendo sus semejanzas y diferencias: debe ser un gran analista y comparador. Además, debe conocer muy bien el lenguaje legal, ser un ávido lector del tema y asesorarse constantemente. Una última cualidad que queremos mencionar es que, como todo traductor, no puede quedarse al nivel del sistema lingüístico sino que debe comprender los textos y procedimientos como entidades inmersas y provenientes de una cultura que requieren ser entendidas por los miembros de otra cultura: los **elementos culturales específicos** tienen gran importancia a la hora de la toma de decisiones. Para ilustrar este aspecto podemos citar el ya clásico ejemplo en traducción legal de un hecho que ocurrió en Australia en 1990. Una mujer fue acusada de asesinar a su hija mientras acampaba. Se llamó al juicio a una mujer aborigen experta en huellas quien declaró, con la ayuda de un traductor, que las marcas en el suelo indicaban la presencia de un dingo, o perro salvaje, cargando a un bebé. Sin embargo, durante el juicio se le pidió que supusiera que el dingo llevara un conejo o un canguro en lugar del bebé. La mujer se negó a contestar a la petición de los abogados ya que en la tradición moral de su cultura no es permitido hablar de hipótesis falsas. El traductor tuvo que verter toda esta información sirviendo de enlace cultural. Al final, la mujer aborigen contestó: ¿acaso vivía algún canguro en la tienda de campaña?

Aunque el anterior puede ser un caso extremo, hay siempre un contenido cultural que el traductor no puede pasar por alto ya que es precisamente la comprensión del contenido cultural y de las implicaciones lingüísticas la que hará que su traducción cumpla con los requisitos de **fidelidad** de contenido y forma que priman en la traducción de textos legales.

Por último, la visibilidad del traductor es un tema que siempre ha generado gran debate entre los teóricos. Muchos abogan por la invisibilidad del traductor, es decir que piden que el TM sea leído como si fuera un texto original, evitando en lo posible las anotaciones marginales pues para algunos de ellos las notas de pie de página no muestran más que la falta de habilidad del traductor para verter los matices del mensaje del TO en la lengua de llegada. Sin embargo, en la traducción legal el acercamiento es casi siempre distinto. Las traducciones de los textos legales piden notas explicativas de términos que divergen entre las dos lenguas o sistemas legales. El traductor de textos legales puede por tanto hacer uso de este recurso para salvar las diferencias entre las dos culturas y sistemas. Veremos a continuación una serie de textos, que aunque restringida, pretende dar una idea de la variedad de lo que llamamos textos legales y de su complejidad.

Text 1

CONCLUSIONES Y RECOMENDACIONES ADOPTADAS EN LA IV REUNIÓN DE MINISTROS DE JUSTICIA O DE MINISTROS O PROCURADORES GENERALES DE LAS AMÉRICAS SOBRE DELITO CIBERNÉTICO (Puerto España, Trinidad y Tobago 10 al 13 de marzo de 2002)[1]

Al finalizar los debates sobre los diferentes puntos comprendidos en su agenda, la Cuarta Reunión de Ministros de Justicia o de Ministros o Procuradores Generales de las Américas, convocada en el marco de la OEA, mediante la resolución AG/RES.1781 (XXXI-O/01), adoptó las siguientes recomendaciones para ser elevadas, a través del Consejo Permanente de la OEA al trigésimo segundo período ordinario de sesiones de la Asamblea General:

IV. DELITO CIBERNÉTICO

La REMJA-IV recomienda:

1. Que los Estados respondan al cuestionario elaborado por la Secretaría General de la OEA con el fin de evaluar los avances y de implementar, lo antes posible, las recomendaciones, formuladas en relación con el combate contra el delito cibernético por la REMJA-III.

2. Que, en el marco de las labores del Grupo de Trabajo de la OEA encargado de dar cumplimiento a las recomendaciones de las REMJA, se convoque de nuevo al Grupo de Expertos Gubernamentales en materia de Delito Cibernético, con el siguiente mandato:

a) Dar seguimiento al cumplimiento de las recomendaciones formuladas por dicho Grupo y adoptadas por la REMJA III, y

b) Considerar la elaboración de los instrumentos jurídicos interamericanos pertinentes y de legislación modelo con el fin de fortalecer la cooperación hemisférica en el

FINAL REPORT OF THE FOURTH MEETING OF MINISTERS OF JUSTICE OR OF MINISTERS OR ATTORNEYS GENERAL OF THE AMERICAS ON CYBER CRIME March 10–13, 2002. Port-Of-Spain, Trinidad And Tobago CONCLUSIONS AND RECOMMENDATIONS[2]

After concluding [a·]**the discussion of its different agenda items,** the Fourth Meeting of [b·]**Ministers of Justice or of Ministers or Attorneys General** of the Americas, convened under the aegis of the OAS by means of resolution AG/RES.1781 (XXXI-O/01), adopted the following recommendations, to be brought before the Permanent Council of the OAS for submission at the [c·]**thirtieth regular session of the General Assembly.**

IV. [d·]CYBER-CRIME

REMJA-IV recommends:

1. [e·]**That the states complete the questionnaire prepared by the OAS General Secretariat** in order to assess the progress made and with a view to implementing as soon as possible the recommendations drawn up by REMJA-III on the fight against cyber-crime.

2. That, in the framework of the activities of the OAS working group to follow up on the REMJA recommendations, the Group of Governmental Experts on Cyber-Crime be reconvened and given the following mandate:

a) To follow up on implementation of the recommendations prepared by that Group and adopted by REMJA-III, and

b) To consider the preparation of pertinent inter-American legal instruments and model legislation for the purpose of strengthening hemispheric cooperation in

combate contra el delito cibernético, considerando normas relativas a la privacidad, la protección de la información, los aspectos procesales y la prevención del delito. Puerto España, Trinidad y Tobago, 13 de marzo de 2002.

combating cyber-crime, considering standards relating to privacy, the protection of information, procedural aspects, and crime prevention. March 10–13, 2002. [f]Port-Of-Spain, **Trinidad And Tobago.**

Commentary

a. the discussion of its different agenda items As with the Spanish > English legal translation discussed in chapter 2 (Commerce, Text 1), the TT reflects the tendency towards somewhat greater concision and directness in anglophone legal discourse. A more literal approach to this phrase might easily have rendered a more laborious version such as "the discussion of the different items appearing on its agenda". Other examples of this tendency towards greater economy can be found in the phrase "the activities of the OAS working group to follow up on the REMJA recommendations", in which the ST's *encargado de* becomes simply "to", or in the designation "Group of Governmental Experts on Cyber-Crime", where *en materia de* is condensed to "on".

b. Ministers of Justice or of Ministers or Attorneys General This formulation is tortuous in both ST and TT. It reflects the need to encompass all representatives at the gathering, whose titles clearly differ according to the political structure in each country. The apparent pedantry of the wording here is of course a diplomatic necessity and translators should resist the temptation to shorten such wordings in the interests of **acceptability**. Mercifully for the drafter of the document and the translator, there was no involvement in this case from the United Kingdom, where an attorney-general exists, but where the lord chancellor and home secretary wield the powers now normally associated with the term in the New World. Note also the plural "Attorneys General" (hyphenation appears to be optional), a rare example of post-position of the adjective in English. Other examples of this archaic feature of English, which as here require the plural inflection to be attached to the pre-posed noun, are the compounds princes regent, presidents elect and courts-martial.

c. the thirtieth regular session of the General Assembly This appears to be an error, as the ST clearly indicates the thirty-second session.

d. CYBER-CRIME English is generally more economical than Spanish in its denomination of areas of criminal activity, often because it allows nouns to be used adjectivally, as in:

- credit-card fraud/crime – *el fraude/el delito por/con/de (las) tarjeta(s) de crédito* or more broadly *el fraude crediticio*;
- road crime – *el delito/los delitos en las carreteras/autovías*;
- drug crime – *los delitos relacionados con la droga* (the formulation *delitos de droga* appears in some texts, but sounds inelegant to most native speakers and is likely to be a direct calque from the English term).

The word *delito(s)* itself also requires some thought on the part of translator, since context may determine that it be translated as "offence(s)" rather than "crime" (as in "drug offences"), while the English "crime" may elicit *delito* or *crimen* depending on degree of seriousness (with "misdemeanour" equating approximately to *falta* or *delito menor*).

e. That the states complete the questionnaire prepared by the OAS General Secretariat
This is the first of two subordinate clauses stemming from the main clause "REMJA-IV recommends that". Note that no modal verb, such as "shall" or "should" is used to reflect the Spanish subjunctive in this instance. While in the first clause this vestigial English subjunctive is indistinguishable from the normal indicative form, "be" is required in the second clause as opposed to the indicative "is". Since this solution is somewhat archaic in English, other formulations are perhaps more common, as in the following example:

> In light of the foregoing considerations, and with a view to pursuing the process initiated at this meeting, we make the following recommendations: [...]

> - To promote the exchange of national experience and technical cooperation in prison and penitentiary policy matters, within the framework of the OAS.
> - To promote the sharing of experience and technical cooperation in matters related to criminal prosecution systems, access to justice and judicial administration.
> - To reinforce the fight against corruption, organized crime and transnational criminal activity, and to adopt new legislation, procedures and mechanisms as necessary to combat these scourges. [3]

f. Port-Of-Spain, Trinidad And Tobago In the vast majority of occurrences, neither the "Of" nor the "And" carries an initial capital here. However, hyphenation of Trinidad and Tobago's capital appears to be optional, with the official government web site using both forms (though the non-hyphenated version is markedly more frequent). In general, care must be taken to remember to translate names of countries and cities, particularly when translating directly onto a source text received as a computer file; it is very easy unconsciously to categorize these elements as invariable and therefore not requiring translation. Most Hispanic countries of the Caribbean region have identical names in both languages: Costa Rica, Cuba, Honduras, Nicaragua, Puerto Rico, Venezuela (the exceptions are México and Panamá, which must lose their accents in English, and República Dominicana, which becomes Dominican Republic). A number of the officially anglophone territories, however, together with some islands of the French and Netherlands Antilles, are normally adapted in Spanish: Belice (Belize), Curazao (Curaçao; also often found unadapted in Spanish), Granada (Grenada), Guadalupe (Guadeloupe), las Islas Caimán (the Cayman Islands), Martinica (Martinique), San Bartolomé (St Barts), San Cristóbal y Nieves (St Kitts and Nevis), Santa Lucía (St Lucia), San Martín (St Martin), San Vicente y las Granadinas (St Vincent and the Grenadines). The Republic of Haiti of course acquires an accent in Spanish: República de Haití. With regard to other Greater Caribbean toponyms, the following should be borne in mind (into English): La Habana > Havana; Ciudad de México / México Distrito Federal (colloquially "D.F.") > Mexico City; Ciudad de Guatemala > Guatemala City; Ciudad de Panamá > Panama City; Puerto Príncipe > Port-au-Prince. And into Spanish: Florida > La Florida (though now often used without the article); Port of Spain > Puerto España (many of these are of course a kind of "retranslation" or recuperation of the initial Hispanic colonial designations for these places).

Text 2

ESTADO LIBRE ASOCIADO DE PUERTO RICO DEPARTAMENTO DE TRANSPORTACIÓN Y OBRAS PÚBLICAS DIRECTORÍA DE SERVICIOS AL CONDUCTOR SOLICITUD PARA CERTIFICADO DE LICENCIA PARA CONDUCIR VEHÍCULOS DE MOTOR[4]

REQUISITOS BASICOS
[. . .]
Conteste las siguientes preguntas
Nombre y apellidos del padre y la madre:

Lugar de Nacimiento del solicitante:
¿Entiende el español? Sí □ No □
¿Posee alguna licencia de conducir? Sí □ No □
¿De dónde procede?
¿Ha sido suspendida o cancelada su licencia en Puerto Rico? Sí □ No □
Judicial □ Sistema de Puntos □ Incapacidad □ Revocación del Secretario □ Ley ASUME □
[. . .]
Indique si tiene obligación alimentaria
Sí □ No □
De contestar sí, presente certificación de ASUME, de que está cumpliendo con la misma. (No más de 30 días de emitida). De no cumplir con esta disposición de ley, su privilegio de Licencia de Conducir, podrá ser suspendido.
[. . .]
CERTIFICADO DE PATRIA POTESTAD
Solicitantes menores de 18 años y mayores de 16 deben venir acompañados de su padre o madre debidamente identificado o tutor legal quién deberá presentar la resolución del Tribunal asignándole Patria Potestad, para firmar la Patria Potestad. Esta será firmada frente a un funcionario autorizado por el Departamento de Transportación y Obras Públicas o Notario Público Autorizado. La persona con la Patria Potestad bajo la cual se encuentre el menor se

[a.]COMMONWEALTH OF PUERTO RICO DEPARTMENT OF TRANSPORTATION AND PUBLIC WORKS DRIVER'S SERVICES DIRECTORATE APPLICATION FOR DRIVER LICENSE[5]

BASIC REQUIREMENTS
[. . .]
Answer the following questions:
[b.]**Father's first and last name:**
Mother's maiden name:
Applicant's place of birth:
[c.]**Do you understand Spanish? Yes □ No □**
Do you have a driver license? Yes □ No □
If yes, from where? _______________
Has your license been suspended in Puerto Rico? Yes □ No □ If yes, why?

____

____

[. . .]
[d.]**State if you have any child support obligation (ASUME)? Yes □ No □**
[e.]**If yes, explain:**

____

____

Non-compliance with this question may result in suspension of driver license.

[. . .]
PATRIA POTESTAS
[f.]**The applicants between sixteen (16) years old but less than eighteen (18) years old** must be with their mother, [g.]**father or legal tutor with the Court authority to sign in the law parental authority certificate.** This will be signed in front of an authorized employee or a Notary Public. The person signing the law parental authority will be responsible for every fine, infraction, and [h.]**lesions to persons and public and private property.**

hará responsable de todas las multas que
le impusieran a dicho menor por cualquier
infracción a la Ley Número 22 de 7 de
enero de 2000, según enmendada, cono-
cida como "Ley de Vehículos y Tránsito de
Puerto Rico" y al pago de los daños y per-
juicios que dicho menor cause.

Commentary

a. Commonwealth of Puerto Rico . . . Application for Driver License Though it presents
no translation difficulties, it is interesting to note the ST's use of *conducir*, which bilingual dictionaries tend to label as an exclusively European Spanish equivalent to the more
common Latin American term *manejar*. In fact, a number of Latin American countries
use both terms for "to drive", with *conducir* predominating in higher **registers**. In Latin
America, one thus also hears *licencia/permiso de/para manejar* or *de manejo* for *licencia
de conducir*, while Spain tends to prefer *carné de conducir*. In Puerto Rico, the verb *guiar*
is also used in more colloquial **registers**, so that *conducir – manejar – guiar* all represent
alternatives for "to drive", moving from high to low on the **register** scale.

Usage in the United States allows both the apostrophized and non-apostrophized
forms of "driver['s] license", whereas European and Caribbean English still insist on the
apostrophe.

b. Father's first and last name: Mother's maiden name: The translator has **amplified** here
in order to accommodate the divergent conventions governing matrimonial name changes
in the Hispanic and anglophone worlds. Traditionally the convention in the Hispanic
world is for the female spouse to retain her first surname (that of the father), but to lose
the second, maternal surname, substituting *de + surname of husband*. Thus Laura Sánchez García, on marrying Aurelio Zapata Rodríguez, becomes Laura Sánchez de Zapata.
In the anglophone world the norm has traditionally been for the female spouse to lose her
family name and acquire that of her husband. However, it is increasingly common – certainly in the anglophone Caribbean and the United States – for women to exercise the
option of either retaining their maiden name after marriage, or hyphenating it together
with their husband's surname. Equally, in the Hispanic world it has become increasingly
common for women to leave their full name unchanged on marrying.

c. Do you understand Spanish? It may seem odd to include this question at all, but most
particularly in the case of the ST: how could anyone answer "no" to it if the text they are
reading is in Spanish? It seems likely that this question reflects the linguistic complexity
of Puerto Rico and its fluid relationship with the United States, which generate a spectrum of competence in Spanish among residents, particularly the descendents of migrants
to the mainland, or simply visitors, residents or migrants of non-Puerto Rican origin. It
is possible, therefore, that a form such as this might be filled out by a party competent
in Spanish on behalf of one who is less so. It may thus be bureaucratically useful to have
a record of which applicants understand Spanish and which do not (for the purposes of
assigning an examiner for the road test, for example).

d. State if you have any child support obligation (ASUME)? A **modulation** is required here, as English specifies the party being supported, but not the explicit type of support, while the Spanish wording has an inverse emphasis. In the case of the **explicitation** entailed by the inclusion of the word "child", this arguably generates a legal difficulty, since the *obligación alimentaria* in Puerto Rico also refers to the legal duty of adults to support relatives over sixty years old, if the need arises.[6]

e. If yes, explain This blatant **generalization** may have been motivated by the probability that the specific obligations of those who have chosen to use the English version of the document – and are therefore likely not to be native Puerto Ricans – may be those laid down in other states, not those stipulated in the local legislation under the purview of the *Administración para el Sustento de Menores (ASUME)*. Against this interpretation, however, is the inclusion of the *ASUME* acronym in the previous line.

f. The applicants between sixteen (16) years old but less than eighteen (18) years old The use of the article as the first word of this sentence strikes an unnatural note in the TT here. Equally, the rest of the sentence seems to juxtapose elements of two mutually exclusive options: either, "between sixteen and eighteen years old" (which remains ambiguous as to whether the upper figure is inclusive); or "over sixteen but under eighteen", which seems the clearest solution.

g. or legal tutor with the Court authority to sign in the law parental authority certificate The term "tutor" is generally limited to educational contexts in English, while "guardian" covers the legal sense of the SL term. The wording "law parental authority certificate" is not found elsewhere, and is either an accepted local equivalent or simply a formula invented by the translator. Other US states variously use formulae such as "Affidavit of Liability and Guardianship" (Colorado), "Affidavit of Parental Authorization" (Washington) or simply "Affidavit for Minor to be Licensed" (Nevada). An alternative version of this phrase thus might be: "or legal guardian with documents attesting guardianship, in order to sign the Affidavit of Parental Authorization".

h. lesions to persons and public and private property Though standard bilingual dictionaries offer *lesión* for lesion, they are in fact false cognates in contexts such as this. The English word has a decidedly technical ring and is far more likely to be heard in a casualty department (or "emergency room" in the US) or seen in a coroner's report, while the Spanish term perhaps occurs most frequently in sports commentary. In this latter context, as here, the appropriate English equivalent is "injury", so that an alternative version would be: "The person . . . will be responsible for all fines resulting from traffic offences committed by the minor, and any injury or damage said minor may cause to persons or property".

Text 3

ACTA DE DECLARACIÓN
JURAMENTADA
YO:

___________________, mayor de edad,
de estado civil SOLTERO, de ocupación
DOCENTE, identificado con cédula de
ciudadanía número ___________________
expedida en Bogotá D.C., domiciliado y
residente de Bogotá D.C, Colombia, en la
CARRERA ___ no. _______ con teléfono
___________.

Bajo la gravedad del juramento, de mi
libre y espontánea voluntad, de acuerdo
con la verdad y para FINES
EXTRAPROCESALES.

DECLARO

Que mis generales de ley son los anotados
anteriormente.

Que no he contraído matrimonio por lo
civil ni por lo católico ni por ningún otro
rito o credo en Colombia por cuanto mi
estado civil es el de soltero, y en la actualidad no hago vida marital con personal
alguna ni he procreado hijos.

Que no tengo ninguna clase de impedi-
mento para contraer matrimonio ni dentro
ni fuera de este país.

OBJETO: La presente declaración es con
el objeto de presentarla ante: GOBIERNO
DE BARBADOS.

[...]

1. Art. 299 C.P.C. TESTIMONIO ANTE
NOTARIO Y ALCALDES. Los testimo-
nios para fines no judiciales se rendirán
exclusivamente ante Notario y Alcaldes.
Igualmente los que tengan fines judiciales y
no se pida la citación de la parte contraria;
en este caso el peticionario afirmará bajo
juramento, que se considera presentado con
la presentación del escrito, que sólo están
destinados a servir de prueba sumaria en
determinado asunto para el cual la ley
autoriza esta clase de prueba, y sólo tendrán valor para dicho fin.

CERTIFICATE OF SWORN
DECLARATION[7]
I:

___________________, [a.]an adult,
**BACHELOR and EDUCATOR by
profession,** bearer of the national I.D.
card ___________________ issued in
Bogotá D.C., domiciled and resident in
Bogotá D.C, Colombia, at CARRERA
___ No. _______, telephone ___________.

[b.]**Under oath and of my own free will, do
hereby truthfully and to whatever end –**

DECLARE

That my personal circumstances and interests are as set out above.

That I have never contracted matrimony
whether in a civil ceremony, Catholic nor
any other rite or creed in Colombia and
therefore my marital status is that of
Bachelor, and that presently [c.]**I am not co-
habiting with anyone** nor have I fathered
children.

That I have no impediment whatsoever to
my contracting matrimony be it within or
outside of this country.

PURPOSE: The present Declaration is made
for the purpose of presenting it before:
THE GOVERNMENT OF BARBADOS.

[. . .]

1. Art. 299 C.P.C. TESTIMONY BEFORE
NOTARY AND MAYOR. Testimony for
non-judicial purposes will be given only
before Notaries and Mayors. Likewise those
that may be for judicial purposes and where
[d.]**the citation of the opposing party** is not
requested; in this case the petitioner will state
under oath that [e.]**(s)he considers her/himself
served** with the filing of the written document, that is only destined to serve as sum-
mary evidence in certain matters for which
the law authorizes this kind of evidence, and
they will only be used to this end.

Commentary

a. an adult, BACHELOR and EDUCATOR by profession Though English has more legalistic, somewhat archaic-sounding expressions such as "having attained his majority" or "full (legal) age", "adult" is also a conventional counterpart of "minor" in contemporary legal contexts in English. *Soltero* may frequently elicit the English "single" in other contexts (in which "bachelor" may be laden with unwanted **connotations**), but the common term used to designate unmarried status for men in legal discourse remains "bachelor". Finally, the term *docente*, here rendered with the suitably general "educator", can be used as a noun or as an adjective to mean "pertaining to teaching or instruction". The adjectival use may elicit various translations depending on context: "educational institution" (*centro docente*), "teaching experience/staff" (*experiencia/personal docente*) or "teacher training" (*formación docente*).

b. Under oath and of my own free will, do hereby truthfully and to whatever end The TT comes out significantly shorter here by **omitting** equivalents for *la gravedad del* and *espontánea*. This reflects the greater tendency of contemporary legal discourse in Spanish, relative to its equivalent in English, to retain archaic flourishes that supply solemnity. As in other contexts (such as tourist advertising and academic essays), contemporary legal English in many contexts now tends to suppress such adornment, acquiring a more pragmatic, less esoteric tone.

c. I am not co-habiting with anyone This **explicitation** arguably volunteers specific information that the ST does not: the expression *"no hago vida marital"* can be interpreted as simply reinforcing the statement *"mi estado civil es el de soltero"*, possibly extending it to cover common-law arrangements, beyond official systems of registration. An alternative rendering that retains this ambiguity might thus be "I do not have conjugal ties with any person". Unlike the commissioned TT, this would technically allow the applicant to sign the declaration in English even if they were living with a partner.

d. the citation of the opposing party The ST term *citación* offers an illustration of the advantages of access to specialized resources when working in a technical area such as legal discourse. A standard bilingual dictionary offers only "subpoena, summons". A specialized legal dictionary, on the other hand, gives "notice, notification, summons, subpoena, writ, process, call" and then a series of specific idioms such as *citación para aportar pruebas (subpoena duces tecum)*. Interestingly, neither dictionary offers the cognate used in the TT here as an equivalent, though back-checking of the English term reveals that they are equivalents, with the specialized dictionary offering *citación de comparecencia ante un tribunal*.

e. (s)he considers her/himself served The tendency to allude explicitly to both genders, once condemned as a "politically correct" excess, is now common throughout the anglophone world. The use of the masculine as the default gender, though still more common than in English, has also been challenged in the Hispanic world. Usage of femenine forms may vary in acceptability according to country (thus *jueza* continues to sound somewhat forced in Spain, but is normal in Colombia).

Texto 1

Cuban Adjustment Act Public Law 89-732, November 2, 1966, as Amended[8] SEC. 1. That, notwithstanding the provisions of section 245(c) of the Immigration and Nationality Act the status of any alien who is a native or citizen of Cuba and who has been inspected and admitted or paroled into the United States subsequent to January 1, 1959 and has been physically present in the United States for at least one year, may be adjusted by the Attorney General, in his discretion and under such regulations as he may prescribe, to that of an alien lawfully admitted for permanent residence if the alien makes an application for such adjustment, and the alien is eligible to receive an immigrant visa and is admissible to the United States for permanent residence. Upon approval of such an application for adjustment of status, the Attorney General shall create a record of the alien's admission for permanent residence as of a date thirty months prior to the filing of such an application or the date of his last arrival into the United States, whichever date is later. The provisions of this Act shall be applicable to the spouse and child of any alien described in this subsection, regardless of their citizenship and place of birth, who are residing with such alien in the United States.	[a.]**Ley de Ajuste Cubano** Ley Pública 98-732.[9] Sin prejuicio de lo establecido en la sección 245(c) del Acta de Inmigración y Nacionalidad, [b.]**el status de cualquier extranjero nativo o ciudadano cubano o** [c.]**que haya sido inspeccionado y admitido o puesto bajo palabra (parolee) en Estados Unidos después del 1ro. de enero de 1959 y que haya estado presente físicamente en Estados Unidos al menos durante un año, puede ser ajustado por el Fiscal General,** a su discreción y conforme a las regulaciones que pueda prescribir, a la de extranjero admitido legalmente para residir permanentemente, si el extranjero hace una solicitud de dicho ajuste, y el extranjero es elegible para recibir una visa de inmigrante y es admisible en Estados Unidos para residir permanentemente. Al aprobarse dicha solicitud de ajuste del status, el Fiscal General creará un registro de la admisión del extranjero para residir permanente con una fecha treinta meses anterior a la presentación de dicha solicitud o [d.]**la fecha de su último arribo a Estados Unidos, cual sea la fecha posterior.** [e.]**Las disposiciones de esta Acta serán aplicables al cónyuge** e hijo de cualquier extranjero descrito en esta subsección, independientemente de su ciudadanía y lugar de nacimiento, que residan con dicho extranjero en Estados Unidos.

Comentarios

a. **Ley de Ajuste Cubano** El nombre original en inglés es *Act* y no *Law*. El sistema legal norteamericano distingue entre estos dos términos. El primero es más amplío e incluye al segundo. Estos *acts* que pueden ser *public bills* pasan a ser *public laws* cuando son firmados por el congreso. Ya que ésta es una ley ya aprobada se ha traducido como tal al español. El traductor debe ser consciente de la terminología jurídica y de cómo esta cambia de lengua a lengua y aun entre diferentes países de la misma lengua.

b. el status de cualquier extranjero nativo o ciudadano cubano . . . puede ser ajustado por el Fiscal General Este es un claro ejemplo de las dificultades que presuponen estos textos en lo referente a la concordancia. Debido a que el lenguaje jurídico tiene como premisa la univocidad, éste requiere frases nominales largas que no den pie a malentendidos y en el que por lo tanto no se deje nada implícito. El traductor debe tener siempre presente la estructura gramatical con la que se está enfrentando y mantenerla. En este caso la estructura de la frase es "el estatus de X puede ser ajustado" en donde X representa una serie de explicitaciones sobre quiénes son los beneficiarios de la ley.

c. que haya sido inspeccionado y admitido o puesto bajo palabra (parolee) en Estados Unidos En algunas ocasiones incluso para añadir univocidad es preciso incluir la palabra en el idioma origen con su traducción. El traductor en este caso ha optado por traducir *paroled* como "puesto bajo palabra" y ha añadido *parolee*, que no aparece en el TO. Bien podría tratarse de un error tipográfico, pero dado el **tipo textual** con el que trabajamos estos errores podrían repercutir seriamente en lo expresado.

d. la fecha de su último arribo a Estados Unidos, cual sea la fecha posterior. Ya que es esencial para este **tipo de texto** trasvasar con la mayor **fidelidad** posible lo expresado en el documento origen nos encontramos en ocasiones con este tipo de frases en las que la selección del léxico tiende a imitar la selección que se hizo en el TO. Algunas veces esta selección resta naturalidad al texto. Compárese "arribo" con "llegada" y "cual sea la fecha posterior" con "la que sea posterior".

e. Las disposiciones de esta Acta serán aplicables al cónyuge Se le llama aquí por primera vez "acta" aunque el título fue traducido y es reconocido como "ley". Se pierde pues la referencia interna entre esta parte y el título del texto, restándole la **coherencia** que se produce en el documento origen.

<table>
<tr><td>

Texto 2
RENTAL CONTRACT [10]
All agreements are between the Caribbean
Centre for Sports, Education, Training
Corporation and the renting parties.
Contact Date: Date of Agreement:
Rental Date: (day only)   Time:
Contact Person: Title:
Emergency:
Organization: Email:
Note: Check in time is after 3:00 pm on the
day of arrival. Check out is 3:00 pm on the
day of departure.

Number of Persons:
Cost Per Day:
($40.00)
Number of Days:

</td><td>

Traducción de Jairo Sánchez
CONTRATO DE ARRENDAMIENTO
Todos los acuerdos se establecen entre
[a]**Caribbean Centre for Sports, Education,
Training Corporation y los arrendatarios.**
Fecha de Contacto: Fecha del Acuerdo:
[b]**Fecha del Arriendo:** (día) Hora:
Persona de Contacto: [c]**Título:**
[d]**Emergencia:**
[e]**Compañía:**   Correo-e:
Nota: La hora de registro es después de las
3 de la tarde del día de llegada. La hora
de salida es a las 3 de la tarde del día de
partida.
Número de personas:
Costo Por Día:
($40.00)
Número de Días:

</td></tr>
</table>

Total Residency Cost:
Subtotal:
Extra Fees:
Meals:
B or L-$10
D-$12
Discount:
($5 per person/full day)
Total:

i. The total fee according to the agreed upon time will be for $EC / US dollars. CCSET Corporation will only provide lodging for the rental party as outlined above. Check in is at 3:00 pm and check out is 3:00 pm unless separate arrangements are made.

ii. The deposit is also your only guarantee towards the rental time booked. If you do not use the camp as scheduled, the deposit fee will be forfeited.

Damages include but are not limited to excessive wear and tear, damage to screens, excessive garbage around the property, loss of kitchen equipment, tearing of curtains or shower curtains, etc.

iii. All improvements to the land and buildings from the renting party will be considered a donation of good will to CCSET.

iv. Sheets, towels, and pillows must be supplied by the rental party. Water may be turned off by the government, and is not the responsibility of CSET.

v. CSET and HERO take no legal responsibilities for any accidents or injuries that occur on the property or off the property by the rental party or any of its affiliates or partners.

Name of Contact:
Signature: Date:
For Office Use Only
Name:
Deposit:
Date:

Costo Total de Estadía:
Subtotal:
Cargos Extra:
[f]**Comida:**
D o A-$10
C-$12
Descuento:
($5 por persona/día completo)
Total:

i. [g]**El cargo total de acuerdo a la duración acordada será en dólares americanos (US) o del Caribe del Este (EC).** La Corporación CCSET sólo hospedará al arrendatario ciñéndose a lo expuesto arriba. [h]**La hora de registro es después de las 3 de la tarde del día de llegada** y la salida a las 3 de la tarde a menos que se hagan acuerdos diferentes.

ii. El depósito es la única garantía sobre el tiempo de alquiler reservado. Si no utiliza las instalaciones según el programa acordado, el dinero del depósito será retenido.

Los daños incluyen, pero no se limitan al desgaste excesivo, [i]**daño a los mosquiteros,** basura en exceso alrededor de la propiedad, pérdida de utensilios de cocina, rasgado de cortinas o de cortinas de baño, etc.

iii. Toda mejora que se le haga a la tierra o construcciones por parte del arrendatario se considerará una donación de buena fe a CCSET.

iv. Las sábanas, toallas y almohadas deben ser provistas por el arrendatario. El gobierno puede cortar el agua y CSET no se hace responsable.

v. CSET y HERO [j]**no incurren en responsabilidad legal** por accidentes o lesiones que ocurran en la propiedad o fuera de ella al arrendatario o cualquiera de sus afiliados o acompañantes.

Nombre de Contacto:
Firma: Fecha:
Para Uso Interno
Nombre:
Depósito:
Fecha:

Comments re History:		Comentarios Historia:	
Total Cost:		Costo Total:	
Payment:		Pago:	
Approv:		Aprob:	
Approval:	Signature:	Aprobado:	Firma:
Date:		Fecha:	

Comentarios

a. Caribbean Centrer for Sports, Education, Training Corporation y los arrendatarios
Para efectos legales el nombre de las partes debe mantenerse en el idioma origen a menos
que tenga un nombre registrado en la LM. En el resto del documento el nombre se refiere
mediante las siglas. Una fórmula muy común es dar el nombre en la LO seguido por
dichas siglas para aclarar este aspecto al lector. En cuanto a "renting parties" se ha
preferido "arrendatarios" sobre "las partes que arriendan" ya que aunque la **traducción
literal** en este **tipo de textos** es común, la construcción es un **calco** del inglés y le quita
naturalidad al texto.

b. Fecha del arriendo En español la palabra "arriendo" generalmente se refiere a estadías
largas o incluso a un lugar en el que se planea vivir. Cuando se refiere a periodos limitados se prefiere "estadía". Sin embargo, "fecha de estadía" tampoco cumple la función que
propone el TO. Sugerimos "fecha inicial de estadía" ya que es esto a lo que se refiere la
fórmula. Siguiendo esta opción se combina *"rental date"* y *"day only"*.

c. Título: En inglés es muy común poner la forma de dirigirse a una persona bajo *title*. En
español esta no es una práctica tan común. De ser necesario se puede **explicitar** mediante la opción: Sr., Sra. Es muy común en algunos países latinoamericanos, entre ellos
Colombia, referirse al cliente a nivel oral mediante la fórmula "doctor" o "doctora", sin
importar si éste es realmente el título de la persona.

d. Emergencia: En español haría falta una expresión **equivalente** más que la sola palabra.
Se diría "número de emergencia" o "en caso de emergencia contactar"

e. Compañía: Esta palabra es preferible en este contexto a su cognado "organización" ya
que ésta tiene una referencia más reducida refiriéndose principalmente a grupos gubernamentales regionales o internacionales: Organización de Estados del Caribe, Organización
de las Naciones Unidas; Compañía Nacional de Tabaco.

f. Comida D o A-$10, C-$12 El traductor suele encontrarse con siglas, abreviaciones y
letras de las que debe encontrar su significado y traducirlas cuando así convenga. El contexto en el que se encuentran es esencial para comprender el hecho o proceso al que se
refieren. Más adelante en el texto nos encontramos con "aprob.". Aquí "D o A" significa
"desayuno o "almuerzo"; "C", cena. Hay discrepancias entre los nombres dados a las
comidas del día principalmente entre el español americano y el de la península ibérica.
El caso que más confusión causa es el de la "comida" que en España es equivalente a "almuerzo" y en Latinoamérica es sinónimo de "cena".

g. El cargo total de acuerdo a la duración acordada será en dólares americanos (US) o del Caribe del Este (EC) Tenemos en primer lugar un problema de estilo en el que las palabras "acuerdo" y "acordada" aparecen en la misma frase. En inglés, aunque aquí no sucede, hay por lo general mayor libertad para repetir palabras en un texto. El español en cuanto al estilo prefiere bien buscar sinónimos o condensar las frases que comparten, por ejemplo, un mismo sustantivo o adjetivo. En segundo lugar parece haber una errata en el TO donde en lugar de *for* debería ser *in* ya que no se menciona ni hay espacio para colocar un precio, sino que se dice simplemente en qué moneda se realizarán las transacciones. En la traducción, además, se le da más relevancia a los dólares americanos que a los del Caribe del Este, al cambiar su posición en la frase. Hay aquí una fórmula oculta de modificación basada en la ideología donde el traductor cree que las personas que leerán el contrato en la LM tienen mayor conocimiento de la moneda americana. Un traductor puede hacer estos cambios a nivel consciente o subconsciente, pero debería estar atento a cómo su ideología influye en las decisiones que toma.

h. La hora de registro es después de las 3 de la tarde del día de llegada En la cultura turística caribeña *check in* y *check out* tienen tanto vigor que se llegan a utilizar como **préstamos** en la LM. El equivalente de la primera es "registro"; de la segunda "salida". En cuanto a la hora de salida también sería una buena idea **explicitar** que "la hora de salida es *antes* de las 3 de la tarde". Si hubiese un problema de espacio "de la tarde" se puede reemplazar perfectamente por "p.m.".

i. daño a los mosquiteros Se ha dicho que el significado de las palabras y expresiones va ligado no sólo a su esencia en el idioma en general sino a su posición y contexto en el uso real. Si nos encontramos con una palabra tan polisémica como *screen* podremos probar este punto: es el contexto, más que la palabra en sí, el que nos va a ayudar a tomar la decisión sobre la acepción que tiene una palabra en su uso real y puntual y por tanto a encontrar el equivalente más aproximado. La capacidad para hacer una búsqueda que dé resultados relevantes, tanto en diccionarios como mediante recursos y herramientas electrónicas, es básica, pero raramente tratada en cursos de traducción. En algunas variantes del español se prefiere "mosquitera".

j. no incurren en responsabilidad legal Este es un ejemplo de cómo la **colocación** ayuda a dar naturalidad a todo **tipo de textos**. La combinación más **aceptable** de palabras está ligada íntimamente con el **tipo textual**. En otros contextos, "responsabilidad" puede tener mayor **frecuencia de coocurrencia** con verbos como "tener".

Texto 3
SAINT LUCIA[11]
THE EASTERN CARIBBEAN
SUPREME COURT
IN THE HIGH COURT OF JUSTICE

[CRIMINAL]
CASE NO. 63 of 2003
THE QUEEN
V
EJ
Appearances:
Mrs. V C-C for the Prosecution.
Accused in person
2004: February 03
February 11

DECISION
1. **H-C J:** This is another case involving the proliferation of unlicensed firearms in Saint Lucia by youngsters. It concerns what seems like the uncaring shooting of MW, a young man, aged 18 of Leslie Land, Castries.

The Facts
2. Briefly, the facts are that on Sunday, 14th July 2002 at about 8.55 p.m. MW was at a drink up at Wilton's Yard, Castries with his girlfriend. A group of young men stopped by them. One R searched M while the Accused, EJ used a gun and lashed him on the left side of the face near his eye. Mitch fell to the ground, turned away and began to run. He heard a loud bang which sounded like a gun shot. The group of young men ran after him as he ran to the home of his girlfriend at Leslie Land. On arrival there, he felt his right leg weakening. He saw a small hole to the back of his thigh and it was then that he realized that he had sustained a gunshot wound to the back of his right thigh. He proceeded to Victoria Hospital for medical treatment where he was detained for 2 days. He was discharged on 16th July 2002.

Traducción Encargada
[a]SANTA LUCÍA[12]
TRIBUNAL SUPREMO DEL CARIBE
ORIENTAL
ANTE EL [b]ALTO TRIBUNAL
DE JUSTICIA
[SALA DE LO PENAL]
[c]PROCESO N° 63 de 2003
S.M. LA REINA
contra
E.J.
Comparecencias:
Sra. V C-C en la Acusación.
[d]**El Acusado en persona**
03 de febrero de 2004
11 de febrero de 2004

---

[e]RESOLUCIÓN
1. **M.A.T.:** Se trata de otra causa que denota la proliferación de armas de fuego sin licencia [f]**entre los jóvenes santalucenses [g]y que concierne al presunto disparo imprudente efectuado a M.W., un joven de 18 años de Leslie Land, Castries.**
[h]***Antecedentes de hecho***
2. En resumen, los antecedentes de hecho consisten en que el domingo, 14 julio de 2002, a las 8:55 p.m. aproximadamente, M.W. [i]**se encontraba con su novia en un bar de copas** a punto de cerrar en Wilton's Yard, Castries, cuando un grupo de hombres jóvenes se detuvo a su lado. Uno de ellos, R., inspeccionó a M. en tanto que el Acusado, E.J., [j]**empleó un arma para golpearle en el lado izquierdo** de la cara cerca del ojo. Mitch cayó al suelo, se apartó y comenzó a correr. Entonces escuchó un estrepitoso sonido que le pareció el de un disparo. El grupo de jóvenes le persiguió mientras él corría hacia la casa de su novia en Leslie Land, lugar donde, al llegar, sintió que su pierna derecha se debilitaba. Observó que tenía un pequeño orificio en la parte anterior del muslo derecho y se dio cuenta en ese momento de que había

3. Police Constable 000 FM investigated this matter. He subsequently formally arrested and charged the Accused for using a firearm with intent to cause a wound to MW contrary to Section 151 (b) of the Criminal Code.

4. The Accused has pleaded guilty to the charge and he is before the court for sentencing.

Section 151 (b)
5. Section 151 (b) of the Criminal Code in effect states that whoever uses a firearm with intent to cause harm to any person is liable indictably to imprisonment for ten (10) years, and to flogging. Of course, I do not need to repeat that flogging is inhumane and degrading and unconstitutional.

6. In order to determine the appropriateness of the sentence, I have to look at all of the surrounding circumstances including the mitigating as well as the aggravating factors.

Mitigating Factors
7. The Accused has pleaded guilty to the offence and has saved the court a considerable lot of time. He is a young unemployed man about 22 years old with a clean record. He aimed for M's leg and not for his head or a vital organ of the body. I know of no other factors which may enable me to mitigate the sentence as the Accused remained silent before this court.

---

sufrido una herida de bala en el mismo. A continuación, se dirigió al Hospital Victoria para recibir asistencia médica, ᵏ·**donde tuvo que permanecer 2 días. El 16 de julio de 2002 fue dado de alta.**

3. El agente de policía 000, F.M., llevó a cabo la investigación del caso y, posteriormente, detuvo y procesó al Acusado por utilización de un arma de fuego con voluntad de herir a M.W. en contra de lo dispuesto en el artículo 151 (b) del Código Penal.

4. El Acusado se ha reconocido culpable del delito imputado y comparece ante el tribunal a la espera de la pronunciación de la sentencia.

Artículo 151 (b)
5. El artículo 151 (b) del Código Penal establece en efecto que al que haga uso de un arma de fuego con voluntad de herir a otro se le considerará criminalmente responsable por lo que se le impondrá una pena de diez (10) años de prisión, y la pena de flagelación. Por supuesto, no es necesario reiterar que la pena de flagelación es inhumana, degradante e inconstitucional.
6. Con el fin de determinar la adecuación de la pena, debo considerar todos los hechos circunstanciales, incluidos tanto los factores atenuantes como los agravantes.

Circunstancias atenuantes
7. El Acusado se ha reconocido culpable del delito, gracias a lo cual el tribunal se ha ahorrado un tiempo considerable. El Acusado es un hombre joven de aproximadamente 22 años, desempleado y sin antecedentes penales. Apuntó a la pierna de M. y no a su cabeza o cualquier otro órgano vital del cuerpo. No conozco otros factores que pudiesen atenuar la sentencia ya que el Acusado ha permanecido en silencio ante el presente tribunal.

Aggravating Factors

8. M is a young man. At the time of the offence some 18 months ago, he was a student. It appeared from the evidence that there was no justifiable reason for this uncaring incident.

In fact, there appeared to be no sensible reason at all except that M's brother and two cousins may have had some problems with the said group of youngsters.

9. A medical report duly signed by Dr R. indicates that M received a bullet wound to his right thigh. The entry wound was on the lateral aspect of the thigh and it was located in the muscle mass on the medial side. The bullet was removed.

10. I pause to observe that there is an upward surge in the number of firearm offences in Saint Lucia making this once peaceful society a dangerous place to live in. The perpetrators are notably young persons like the Accused. The court must send out a strong signal to potential perpetrators of violent crimes that they will receive the full force of the law.

11. Having taken into consideration all the circumstances of the case the sentence of this Court is that the Accused, EJ, be incarcerated for a period of three (3) years.

I H-C
High Court Judge

Circunstancias agravantes

8. M es un hombre joven. En el momento de la comisión del delito, hace aproximadamente 18 meses, era estudiante. De acuerdo con las pruebas aportadas, parece ser que no había un motivo justificable para que este imprudente incidente se produjera.
De hecho, no había al parecer ningún motivo razonable en absoluto, excepto que el hermano y dos primos de M. pudieron haber tenido algún problema con el anteriormente mencionado grupo de jóvenes.
9. Un informe médico debidamente firmado por el Dr. R. indica que M. sufrió una herida de bala en su muslo derecho. El orificio de entrada se hallaba en el lateral del muslo y la bala se localizó en la masa muscular del plano medial. La bala fue extraída.
10. Haré un inciso con ánimo de advertir del fuerte incremento del número de delitos cometidos con armas de fuego en Santa Lucía, lo cual convierte a esta sociedad antes tranquila en un lugar peligroso para vivir. Los autores son mayormente personas jóvenes como el Acusado, por lo que el tribunal debe emitir el mensaje de advertencia a los autores en potencia de delitos violentos de que se les aplicará todo el peso de la ley.
11. Habiendo considerado todas las circunstancias relativas a la causa, el presente Tribunal resuelve que el Acusado, E.J., permanecerá en prisión durante un periodo de tres (3) años.
I. H.C.
[1.]**Magistrado del Alto Tribunal de Justicia**

Comentarios

La traducción de este texto fue realizada en España. La traductora nos ha proporcionado una serie de relevantes comentarios sobre los aspectos que resaltaron al momento de traducir y que incluimos aquí. Por nuestra parte también mencionaremos aquellas instancias en las que la traducción posee elementos culturales propios de España y presentaremos las opciones para remplazarlo con elementos más cercanos al Caribe.

a. SANTA LUCÍA Sobre los nombres de los países caribeños ver comentarios del Texto 1, español > inglés.

b. ALTO TRIBUNAL DE JUSTICIA En España, como en Latinoamérica, existe el término Tribunal Superior de Justicia como equivalente a *High Court of Justice* (recomendado por Alcaraz Varó).[13] Sin embargo, la traductora ha optado por el Alto Tribunal de Justicia por dos motivos. El primero es que los términos de la LO y la LM no se corresponden exactamente. El segundo es que al utilizar un término que no es común en la LM se recalca el hecho de que es una traducción, que lo que en ella se relata sucede en un contexto diferente al del lector del TM, que por ende tiene elementos extranjeros y que se debe leer como tal. Además de estos motivos, la **traducción literal** ayudará al lector a vislumbrar cuál es el término origen.

c. PROCESO N° 63 de 2003 En los programas televisivos y películas de tema jurídico estamos habituados a escuchar el término "caso". Se sugiere que se evite en la traducción legal y que se emplee en cambio "proceso" o "causa".[14]

d. El Acusado en persona El presunto delincuente recibirá distintos nombres en las diversas fases del procedimiento penal: imputado (el que se cree responsable de un delito), procesado (persona contra la que se sigue un proceso judicial), acusado (persona al que se le atribuye un delito), reo (persona acusada de un delito y declarada culpable). En este caso, "procesado" sería igualmente válido.

e. RESOLUCIÓN En caso de duda entre "sentencia", "fallo" y "veredicto", puede emplearse el término "resolución", más general y por lo tanto menos susceptible de ser incorrecto.

f. entre los jóvenes santalucenses Muy probablemente en este contexto "los jóvenes santalucenses", "los jóvenes de Santa Lucía" y "los jóvenes en Santa Lucía" corresponden al mismo grupo. Sin embargo, en otros contextos es necesario tener cuidado porque "los jóvenes en Santa Lucía" no incluye solamente a los santalucenses. Por otro lado, muchos estudiantes de traducción tienen problemas con los nombres de los países y sus gentilicios. Los más importantes para el Caribe son: antiguano, bahameño o bahamés, barbadense, beliceño, colombiano, costarricense, cubano, dominiqués (Dominica), granadino, guatemalteco, guyanés, haitiano, hondureño, jamaicano, mexicano o mejicano, nicaragüense, panameño, puertorriqueño, dominicano, sancristobaleño, santalucense, sanvicentino, trinitense, venezolano.[15]

g. y que concierne al presunto disparo imprudente efectuado a M.W., un joven de 18 años de Leslie Land, Castries Una de las particularidades del inglés es la construcción corta de sus oraciones que hay que unir en español empleando nexos según la relación (no siempre obvia) establecida entre unas y otras. En los textos legales en Latinoamérica se tiende a referirse al lugar de proveniencia o de residencia mediante estas opciones: un joven de 18 años natural de, vecino de, o residente en.

h. *Antecedentes de hecho* Los "antecedentes de hecho" son un "relato pormenorizado de los hechos juzgados, organizados cronológicamente y enlazados entre sí de forma coherente", mientras que los "hechos probados" son "la resolución del tribunal sobre la verdad de los hechos controvertidos, y sobre cada una de las circunstancias fácticas alegadas por las dos partes que, de resultar demostradas a satisfacción del tribunal, puedan afectar a la apreciación exacta del delito, determinar la inexistencia del mismo o tener consecuencias para la imposición eventual de la pena".[16] En Latinoamérica también podríamos decir simplemente "Los hechos".

i. se encontraba con su novia en un bar de copas *Drinking up time* es el reducido tiempo que deja un *pub* inglés a los consumidores para terminar las bebidas antes del cierre. Aunque *drink up* como sustantivo no aparece en el diccionario, puede deducirse el significado. Quizás podría traducirse por "estaba tomando unas copas" o "terminando su copa", pero el hecho de estar en un bar no implica necesariamente que dicha persona esté consumiendo y el sentido general es más vago. El vocabulario es característico de la península; para acercarlo más a la región caribe se puede optar por "se encontraba con su novia en un bar". Cuando nos encontramos con una palabra que está cargada de referencias locales podemos dejarlas si aclaran el texto y no lo contradicen o buscar alguna que sea más neutra y funcione en más contextos. La neutralidad será siempre relativa. Analícense por ejemplo los siguientes sinónimos de bar: café, cantina, cervecería, club, discoteca, mesón, pub, taberna, tasca.

j. empleó un arma para golpearle en el lado izquierdo En este caso la traductora ha preferido utilizar la preposición de finalidad "para" en lugar del nexo copulativo "y" debido a la obviedad de la interrelación de ambas acciones, ya que no se expresa que disparase en ese momento y, por tanto, "emplear el arma" significa sin duda "golpear con ella".

k. donde tuvo que permanecer 2 días. El 16 de julio de 2002 fue dado de alta Podría haber confusión porque se mezcla un caso judicial con uno médico. Según se trate de uno u otro, *detain* y *discharge* significan "retener/detener" y "poner en libertad" o "retener/hacer quedar" y "dar de alta", respectivamente.

l. Magistrado del Alto Tribunal de Justicia "Magistrado" se corresponde con el término jurídico británico de *judge*, y "juez" se corresponde con *magistrate*, por lo que hay que tener cuidado.

III. SPANISH > ENGLISH EXERCISES

1. In Text 1, above, the following words or their derivates appear more than once in the TT, but each time they translate different terms in the ST. Find the words in the TT and transcribe the phrase in which they appear alongside the corresponding ST phrase, compiling a table like the one below. Discuss how these words or cognates came to translate different items in the ST and offer alternatives to avoid the repetition where possible.

TT word	TT phrase	ST phrase	Alternative translation
Implement	1. 2.	1. 2.	
Prepare	1. 2.	1. 2.	
Follow up	1. 2.	1. 2.	

2. Also in Text 1, above, the following words or their derivatives appear more than once in the ST, but two of the three elicit different translations in the TT. Compile a similar table and where relevant discuss why the translator may have chosen to avoid repeating the same translation. Finally, try to think of any other possible translations for the words given, whether in a legal context or not, and suggest a phrase illustrating the use of each translation.

ST word	ST phrase	TT phrase	Alternative translations
Marco	1. 2.	1. 2.	
Formular	1. 2.	1. 2.	
Elaborar	1. 2.	1. 2.	

3. Translate into English the following extract of the *Convención de Belém Do Pará* on the protection of the rights of women in the Americas.[17] Discuss your respective translations in the classroom, focusing particularly on: how you have rendered the subjunctive; the terms *tener lugar* (paragraphs a. and b.), *maltrato* (paragraph a.) and *establecimientos de salud* (paragraph b.). Consult the official English version and make any relevant observations.[18]

CONVENCIÓN INTERAMERICANA PARA PREVENIR, SANCIONAR Y ERRADICAR LA VIOLENCIA CONTRA LA MUJER "CONVENCIÓN DE BELÉM DO PARÁ"

<u>Artículo 2</u>

Se entenderá que violencia contra la mujer incluye la violencia física, sexual y psicológica:
    a. que tenga lugar dentro de la familia o unidad doméstica o en cualquier otra relación interpersonal, ya sea que el agresor comparta o haya compartido el mismo domicilio que la mujer, y que comprenda, entre otros, violación, maltrato y abuso sexual;
    b. que tenga lugar en la comunidad y sea perpetrada por cualquier persona y que comprenda, entre otros, violación, abuso sexual, tortura, trata de personas, prostitución forzada, secuestro y acoso sexual en el lugar de trabajo, así como en instituciones educativas, establecimientos de salud o cualquier otro lugar; y
    c. que sea perpetrada o tolerada por el Estado o sus agentes, dondequiera que ocurra.

IV. EJERCICIOS PRÁCTICOS INGLÉS > ESPAÑOL

Trabajen en parejas. Escoja uno de los dos textos que se proponen a continuación y haga su traducción al español. Luego intercambie textos con su compañero/a y traduzca su texto de nuevo al inglés (re-traducción). Cuando hayan terminado comparen los textos meta con los textos origen.

Texto A: Extracto de la Constitución de Barbados

Protection from discrimination on ground of race, etc.[19]

23. 1. Subject to the provisions of this section
    a. no law shall make any provision that is discriminatory either of itself or in its effect; and
    b. no person shall be treated in a discriminatory manner by any person acting by virtue of any written law or in the performance of the functions of any public office or any public authority.

   2. In this section the expression "discriminatory" means affording different treatment to different persons attributable wholly or mainly to their respective descriptions by race, place of origin, political opinions, colour or creed whereby persons of one such description are subjected to disabilities or restrictions to which persons of another such description are not made subject or are accorded privileges or advantages which are not afforded to persons of another such description.

Texto B: Extracto de la Constitución de Bahamas

Protection of freedom of assembly and association.[20]

24. 1. Except with his consent, no person shall be hindered in the enjoyment of his freedom of peaceful assembly and association, that is to say, his right to assemble freely and associate with other persons and in particular to form or belong to political parties, or to form or belong to trade unions or other association for the protection of his interests.

   2. Nothing contained in or done under the authority of any law shall be held to be inconsistent with or in contravention of this Article to the extent that the law in question makes provision:
    a. which is reasonably required: (i) in the interest of defence, public safety, public order, public morality or public health; or (ii) for the purpose of protecting the rights and freedoms of other persons; or
    b. which imposes restriction upon persons holding office under the Crown or upon members of a discipline force.

CHAPTER 7

Environment

INTRODUCTION

The environment and its preservation has become a topic of such pressing concern world-wide that a danger of pedagogical over-saturation has arisen in some contexts, with schoolchildren being subjected to a sustained barrage of information that can end up eroding an initial interest in the subject. The extent to which acquisition of formal knowledge in this manner leads to changes in behavior and the "environmental culture" of the inhabitants of the Caribbean is also open to question: many of us are familiar with the mantra of "reduce, reuse and recycle", but do not necessarily relate this to the inordinate quantity of plastic bags used to wrap our groceries at the supermarket checkout, or the lack of recycling deposits for materials such as paper in many Caribbean territories.

With respect to translation specifically, the technical nature of many texts relating to the environment can also prove off-putting, as environmental phenomena may relate to a vast range of contingent or sub-areas that involve specialized knowledge and terminology: geography, meteorology, biology and zoology; land use, agriculture and urban planning; industry and social planning; tourism. It is precisely the all-encompassing nature of the term "environment", however, and the relatively recent awareness that every human activity has an impact on it and is affected by it, that makes it such fertile ground for the trainee translator, who will be enriched by intense exposure to a holistic discourse of conservation that can only become ever more prevalent as the world's environmental predicament intensifies.

Despite the increase in social and political awareness of environmental issues, it is not usual for it to be set apart as a distinct type of discourse in textual taxonomies or works in translation studies. In the case of the Caribbean, however, a discrete focus on this area is amply justified by both the history and the contemporary reality of the region. An understandable preoccupation with the massive human cost of colonialism and slavery has, until relatively recently, tended to obscure the fact that environmental degradation has also been a constant of the Caribbean experience from the earliest days of European intervention to the present. The aggressive monoculture of sugar cane and other export crops and the subsequent impoverishment of soils directly explain today's lack of food security and the excessive urbanization of the great majority of Caribbean nations. In turn, these and other related phenomena have contributed to the deterioration of the marine and coastal zone environments, self-evidently crucial resources for the tourist industry that now keeps many territories in the region economically afloat. As if these difficulties were not enough of a concern, supra-regional factors such as global warming are rendering the Caribbean steadily more vulnerable to damage from natural hazards such as hurricanes and tsunamis.

The region has undoubtedly begun to take note, as attested by the proliferation of bodies, projects, conferences and publications advocating and implementing more sustainable alternatives to present practices. Translation activity in the area has thus increased, as there can hardly be a more comprehensively pan-Caribbean topic than this one: natural phenomena and processes of environmental change are no respecters of cultural, political or linguistic divides, so that the problems of Belize will be those of Guatemala, those of Guadeloupe are likely to be shared by Antigua, and so on. The production of quality translations in this area is therefore a vital necessity for the region, in order to overcome the short-sighted and unscientific tendency to view environmental issues from a merely national perspective. By learning to produce such translations, translators not only raise their own awareness of the issues, but also become advocates of responsible social change and awareness.

The challenges facing the translator of an environmental text are inferable from the considerations outlined above: the need to be familiar with specialized vocabulary in specific areas; the vast range of text types that address environmental issues (treaties and agreements, scientific or academic papers, reports and impact studies, educational descriptions, news reports) each with its own conventions; and the importance of rendering proper names of bodies and projects correctly (Internet search engines are of great assistance here). In this chapter, we have tried to reflect the diversity of text types to some extent, while generally avoiding excessively technical material that would require exclusive specialization on the part of the translator. Nonetheless, we hope that by foregrounding the environment as an arena of translation activity in the Caribbean, at least some translation students will be encouraged to cultivate further their knowledge and skills in this growth area and, if they become professional translators, to bear it in mind as a socially beneficial area of specialization in the future.

INTRODUCCIÓN

El medio ambiente y su conservación se han convertido en temas de tal importancia en todo el mundo que en algunos contextos se corre el riesgo de una saturación pedagógica. Los niños en edad escolar son bombardeados constantemente con información que puede resultar en la reducción de cualquier interés inicial que tuvieran en el tema. También se puede cuestionar la medida en que la adquisición del conocimiento formal por estos medios lleva a cambios del comportamiento y a una "cultura medioambiental" en los habitantes del Caribe: la mayoría de nosotros estamos familiarizados con la fórmula "reducir, reusar, reciclar", pero no lo relacionamos con la cantidad ingente de bolsas plásticas que se usan para empacar nuestros víveres en los supermercados, ni con la falta de depósitos de reciclaje de materiales como el papel en muchos países caribeños.

En cuanto a la traducción, la naturaleza técnica de los textos relacionados con el medioambiente puede resultar desmotivante pues los fenómenos ambientales se relacionan con una gran cantidad de áreas de las que dependen o subáreas que requieren terminología y conocimientos especializados: geografía, meteorología, biología y zoología, uso de suelos, agricultura y planeamiento urbano, industria y planeación social, turismo. Es precisamente la capacidad del término "medioambiente" de abarcar todos los ámbitos y la conciencia relativamente reciente de que toda actividad humana afecta el medioambiente y se ve afectada por él, lo que lo convierte en un terreno fértil para el traductor en preparación, quien se enriquecerá con el contacto intenso con el discurso holístico de la conservación, que no puede sino prevalecer más a medida que los problemas ambientales del mundo se intensifican.

A pesar del crecimiento en la conciencia política y social en los temas ambientales, no es común que se distinga como un tipo de discurso en las taxonomías textuales, ni en los trabajos de los estudios de traducción. Sin embargo, en el caso del Caribe la atención dedicada a esta área se justifica enormemente tanto por la historia como por la realidad actual de la región. La merecida importancia dada al gran costo humano del colonialismo y la esclavitud ha tendido a poner en segundo plano, hasta hace relativamente poco, el hecho de que la degradación ambiental también ha sido una constante en la experiencia caribeña desde los primeros días de la intervención europea hasta el presente. El agresivo monocultivo de caña de azúcar y otras cosechas para la exportación, y sus efectos en el empobrecimiento del suelo, explican la falta de seguridad alimenticia de hoy y la urbanización excesiva de la mayoría de los territorios caribeños. A la vez, éstos y otros fenómenos similares han contribuido al deterioro de los hábitats marinos y costeros – recursos obvios para la industria turística que ahora mantiene a flote a muchos países del Caribe. Como si estas dificultades no fueran suficientes, factores supraregionales como el calentamiento global hacen cada vez más del Caribe una zona vulnerable a peligros como huracanes y tsunamis.

Sin lugar a dudas el Caribe ha empezado a tomar cartas en el asunto, como lo demuestra la proliferación de entidades, proyectos y publicaciones que piden e implementan alternativas más sostenibles a las prácticas actuales. Por lo tanto, la traducción en esta área se ha incrementado, ya que éste es uno de los temas que más afectan al Caribe en su totalidad: los fenómenos naturales no respetan las barreras idiomáticas, culturales ni políticas; así que los problemas de Belice son los mismos que los de Guatemala, los de Guadalupe probablemente sean los mismos que los de Antigua y así sucesivamente. La producción de traducciones de calidad en esta área, por lo tanto, son de vital necesidad para la región, para eliminar la tendencia poco científica y con poca visión de atender los asuntos ambientales desde una perspectiva exclusivamente nacional. Al aprender a producir este tipo de traducciones, los traductores no sólo aumentan la propia conciencia sobre estos asuntos, sino que se convierten en voceros de un cambio social y de conciencia responsables.

Los retos que afronta el traductor del texto ambiental se pueden inferir de lo dicho hasta ahora: la necesidad de familiarizarse con vocabulario especializado, la gran variedad de tipos textuales que tratan de asuntos relacionados con el medio ambiente (tratados y acuerdos, artículos científicos y académicos, informes y estudios de impacto medioambiental, descripciones pedagógicas, reportes de noticias), cada uno con sus propias convenciones; y la importancia de dar correctamente los nombres de organizaciones y proyectos (los buscadores de Internet son de gran utilidad en este punto). En este capítulo hemos intentado reflejar la diversidad de los tipos textuales hasta cierto punto, si bien generalmente evitamos el uso de materiales excesivamente técnicos que requerirían especialización exclusiva por parte del traductor. No obstante, esperamos que al fundar el medioambiente como un campo de la actividad traductora en el Caribe, al menos ciertos estudiantes se sientan motivados a cultivar más a fondo su conocimiento y habilidades en esta área en constante crecimiento y, si se convierten en traductores profesionales, que lo tengan presente en el futuro como un área de especialización con beneficios sociales.

I. SPANISH > ENGLISH

Text 1

EcoBreves	Eco-Briefs
1. COSTA RICA: Escolares estudiarán murciélagos[1]	1. COSTA RICA: [a]Kids Take a Closer Look at Bats[2]
SAN JOSÉ. Más de 550 estudiantes de educación primaria de la capital costarricense y las zonas de Sarapiquí, en el norte, y Guanacaste, en el noroeste, estudiarán los murciélagos en el ciclo escolar que se iniciará en febrero.	SAN JOSE. More than 550 primary school children from the Costa Rican capital, from Sarapiquí, in the north, and from [b]**Guanacaste, in the northeast,** will study [c]**the lives of bats** through a program to begin in February.
Un curso sobre estos mamíferos forma parte de la educación ambiental y biológica que reciben los escolares, por iniciativa del Museo Nacional, la Reserva Biológica La Tirimbina, el Parque Zoológico Simón Bolívar y el Área de Conservación Guanacaste.	A course on [d]**these flying mammals** [e]**is part of the environmental and biological education the schoolchildren receive as part of** an initiative of the National Museum, La Tirimbina Biological Preserve, the Simón Bolívar Zoological Park, and the Guanacaste Conservation Area.
El curso busca introducir políticas de conservación de un animal benéfico que	The class on bats promotes policies for protecting a beneficial species that people

se elimina por ignorancia, afirmó a Tierramérica la bióloga Karla Barquero, de la Reserva Biológica La Tirimbina.

Más de la mitad de los mamíferos costarricenses son murciélagos, de los que se cuentan 110 especies. Sus beneficios incluyen el control de plagas, la dispersión de semillas y la polinización de plantas y árboles valiosos como el marañón (Ocotea endresiana), importante en la dieta de las comunidades rurales.

kill out of ignorance, biologist Karla Barquero, of La Tirimbina Preserve, told Tierramérica.

[f]**There are 110 species of bats in Costa Rica.** These mammals control pests, distribute seed, and pollinate plants and trees, such as the valuable marañón (Ocotea endresiana), important in the diet of rural communities.

Commentary

a. Kids Take a Closer Look at Bats This title adapts significantly from the more obvious "Schoolchildren to Study Bats", containing both an example of **omission** or **generalization** (*escolares* > *kids*) and of **amplification** (*estudiarán* > *take a closer look at*). This degree of **adaptation** is not evident elsewhere in the TT and perhaps exemplifies the relatively greater tendency towards the use of set phrases or idioms and of colloquial **register** in English titles. The **adaptation**, coupled with the shift from future to present tense, has the effect of making the participants' engagement in the activity seem greater, thus making the project seem less "dry". This may also reflect a perceived difference in educational norms between the source and target cultures, the translator reasoning that a more interactive and less formal-sounding wording was appropriate to the anglophone world, where "student-centred" learning has perhaps been given greater prominence than in the Hispanic world.

b. Guanacaste, in the northeast This is evidently an oversight on the part of the translator or an editor, since the area in question is clearly located in the North West of Costa Rica, as the ST states. The small typographical difference between *este* and *oeste* makes this pitfall one to guard against when translating material with geographical content.

c. the lives of bats The first of a series of **explicitations** judiciously used in the body text of the TT in order to avoid an excessively vague rendering. The ST has simply "will study bats", but journalistic style in English seems to prefer the more specific formula of the TT.

d. these flying mammals Another **explicitation** (the ST has no equivalent for "flying") that functions merely as a stylistic embellishment, accentuating the unique character of the object of study.

e. is part of . . . receive as part of This infelicitous repetition is likely to be the result of haste on the part of the translator. It might be avoided by rendering simply: "A course on these flying mammals is part of the environmental and biological education initiative for schoolchildren undertaken by the National Museum."

f. There are 110 species of bats in Costa Rica The evident **omission** of the first clause of this sentence may be the result of uncertainty as to the precise meaning of the ST here.

Does it mean that of the total number of *individual* mammals in the territory, half are bats, or that of the total number of *species* of mammal, half of these are bat species? Clearly, clarification would ideally be sought from the original author, but haste may have determined the recourse to **omission**.

Text 2

EcoBreves

2. GLOBAL: Anuncian simposio sobre tortugas marinas

SAN JOSÉ. Más de mil investigadores de setenta países debatirán entre el 22 y el 29 de febrero en Costa Rica sobre el estado actual de las tortugas marinas y las medidas necesarias para evitar su extinción.

El XXIV Simposio Internacional de Tortugas Marinas es organizado por el Ministerio de Ambiente y Energía de Costa Rica (MINAE), la Sociedad Internacional de Tortugas Marinas (ISTS, por sus siglas en inglés) y el Centro de Ciencia Aplicada de Conservación Internacional (CI).

"Analizaremos cómo las tortugas marinas pueden brindar a las poblaciones locales más ingresos como recursos turísticos vivos que como bienes de consumo cada vez más escasos", señaló a Tierrámerica Marco Solano, Secretario General de la Convención Interamericana para la Protección y Conservación de las Tortugas Marinas.

Algunas especies amenazadas que anidan en playas arenosas del continente americano son la tortuga verde (Chelonia mydas), la tortuga cabezona o caguama (Caretta caretta) y la tortuga carey (Eretmochelys imbricata), muy apetecida por su caparazón usado en la fabricación de artesanías.

Eco-Briefs

2. GLOBAL: Sea Turtle Symposium

SAN JOSE. More than one thousand researchers from seventy countries will gather in Costa Rica from Feb 22 to 29 to debate the current state of sea turtles and the measures necessary to prevent their extinction.

[a.]**The 24th International Sea Turtle Symposium is being organized by the Costa Rican Ministry of Environment and Energy, the International Sea Turtle Society, and Conservation International's Center for Applied Science.**

"We will analyse how sea turtles can provide local populations [b.]**with more income, such as living tourism resources, rather than consumer goods that are becoming increasingly scarce,**" Marco Solano, head of the [c.]**Inter-American Convention on the Protection and Conservation of Sea Turtles**, told Tierramérica.

Some endangered turtle species that nest on the sandy beaches of the Americas include [d.]**the green sea turtle (Chelonia mydas), the "caguama", or loggerhead (Caretta caretta) and the carey, or hawksbill (Eretmochelys imbricata)**, prized for its shell, which is used in handicrafts.

Commentary

a. The 24th International Sea Turtle Symposium . . . and Conservation International's Center for Applied Science This paragraph illustrates effectively the attention to detail in the area of proper nouns required by the translator of texts relating to a geopolitical issue such as the environment. First, the TT's use of Arabic as opposed to Roman numerals for the ordinal number of an international gathering exemplifies this common difference of usage between the source and target cultures. The change of order in the name of the ministry, placing the country adjectivally at the beginning, and the judicious **omission** of the acronym (which would have caused confusion because of its failure to tally with the translated proper name) further demonstrate an attention to the slightly different norms that govern the naming of institutions in the source and target cultures. Lastly, use of the Anglo-Saxon genitive (apostrophized form) in the final proper name helps to keep down the word count and avoid accumulation of prepositions.

b. with more income, such as living tourism resources, rather than consumer goods that are becoming increasingly scarce The TT is somewhat unclear here, resulting from a mistranslation of the word *como*, taking it to mean "such as/for example" rather than "as". The TT should read "how sea turtles can provide local populations with more income as living tourism resources, rather than as increasingly scarce consumer goods".

c. Inter-American Convention on the Protection and Conservation of Sea Turtles The official web site uses the preposition "for", rather than "on". Where time permits, translators, editors and proofreaders should endeavour to check proper names in order to maintain consistency.

d. the green sea turtle (Chelonia mydas), the "caguama", or loggerhead (Caretta caretta) and the carey, or hawksbill (Eretmochelys imbricata) The *Caribbean Multilingual Dictionary of Flora, Fauna and Foods* is a recent and valuable resource for translators in the field of the environment, among other areas.[3] In this instance, finding the appropriate equivalents would have presented no difficulty since items are indexed across four languages (English, French, French Creole and Spanish) as well as by the taxonomic (Latin) name.

Texto 3

Programa TRAMIL[4]	TRAMIL Program[5]
TRAMIL, proyecto de investigación aplicada sobre la medicina tradicional popular de Haití, de República Dominicana y de las demás islas, nació de un esfuerzo común de enda-caribe, del Laboratorio de las Substancias Naturales de la Facultad de Medicina y Farmacia, Puerto Príncipe, de la Federación de Asociaciones Campesinas de Zambrana-Chacuey, República Dominicana, y del dispensario SOE de Thomonde, en la planicie Central de Haití, con miras al mejoramiento y la racionalización de las prácticas medicinales populares fundadas en el uso de las plantas medicinales. [. . .]	**TRAMIL is ⁿ·an investigation project applied to the popular traditional medicine of Haiti, Dominican Republic and of other islands. It was born out of a common effort from enda-caribe, the Laboratory of the Natural Substances of the University of Medicine and Pharmacy, Port-au-Prince, the Federation of Rural Associations of Zambrana-Chacuey, Dominican Republic, and the clinic SOE of Thomonde, in the Central plain of Haiti. It aims to improve and rationalize the popular medical practices based on the use of medicinal plants.** [. . .]

Estamos particularmente ligados al aspecto de la investigación aplicada, y uno de los objetivos importantes es la disminución del costo de la terapéutica medicamentosa, al poner a la disposición de los pueblos y del personal paramédico de base, conocimientos prácticos para el tratamiento con plantas – por ende, a un costo mínimo y en armonía con la tradición popular – de ciertas afecciones corrientes.

TRAMIL quiere ser así mismo una investigación-acción que podrá ser una herramienta de formación para los médicos, farmacéuticos y el personal de salud en general, en los programas de salud de base.

[. . .]

Es por esta misma razón que hemos juzgado como indispensable el reforzar los intercambios de experiencias y la colaboración intercaribe, concretizada por la presencia en los seminarios TRAMIL de numerosos participantes provenientes de dicha zona geográfica, y por la formación de una red de colaboradores que toman a su cargo las investigaciones científicas programadas durante esos seminarios.

[b.]We are particularly focused on the applied aspect of our research, as one of the important objectives is decreasing the costs of medical treatment. [c.]We want to obtain this goal by making available to the locals, and the basic paramedical personnel, practical knowledge for the treatment with plants of some current affections. [d.]As well, this represents the minimum cost. Moreover, it respects the popular tradition.

[e.]TRAMIL also tries to become an investigation-action project that will be a formation tool for doctors, pharmacists, and health personnel in general that are enrolled in the programs of basic health.

[. . .]

It is for this reason that we considered necessary [f.]a thickening of experience exchanges and of the intercaribbean collaboration. This expansion of collaboration has taken place through the growing number of participants coming to the TRAMIL seminars from this geographical area, and through the formation of a network of collaborators responsible for the scientific research scheduled during these seminars.

Commentary

a. an investigation project . . . based on the use of medicinal plants In common with much of the TT, this first paragraph shows partition of long sentences in the ST into shorter ones. Though the opening sentence of the TT benefits from this strategy, other problems arise within it. The translator has interpreted the ST's *aplicada*, for example, as a participle used alongside the preposition *sobre* to link the project with its subject matter. However, in English it functions more naturally as an adjective qualifying *investigación*: "TRAMIL is an applied research project designed to study popular traditional medicine in Haiti". (Note also the modification of "investigation" to "research".) The repetition of "it" as the first word and subject pronoun of the second and third sentences of the TT might have been avoided by using a synonym of "project", such as "this initiative", in one of the instances.

b. We are particularly focused on . . . decreasing the costs of medical treatment Various features show sound judgement here: the apposite gloss "focused on" for *ligados a*; the added clarity achieved by shifting the adjective "applied" onto "aspect", rather than leaving it on "research" (note *investigación* is correctly rendered here); the interpretative use of "as", rather than merely "and", after the comma, serving to tighten up the logic of the sentence; and the normalization or flattening out of the rather pretentious-sounding *terapéutica medicamentosa* to plain "medical treatment".

c. We want to obtain this goal . . . some current affections The noun "goal" collocates more naturally with "achieve" than with "obtain", which in turn is seen more frequently with "results". An idiomatic alternative for *de base*, particularly in an environmental or developmental context, is the adjective "grassroots", though given the specific subject matter of herbal remedies, its use here arguably generates a distracting pun. Finally, the false cognate "affections" should be modified to "ailments", "afflictions" or "complaints".

d. As well . . . the popular tradition The urge to partition the ST's long periods has been taken too far here, as conversion of the parenthetical clause *"por ende . . . la tradición popular"* into two sentences tagged on to the end of the paragraph both interrupts flow and causes a sense of anticlimax. Partition could in fact be avoided entirely without sacrificing clarity in this instance: "Since one of the primary objectives is to reduce the cost of medical treatment, the applied aspect of our work is paramount: by offering locals and grassroots paramedical workers practical information on how to treat commonplace ailments with plants, costs are kept to a minimum while popular traditions are maintained."

e. TRAMIL also tries to become an investigation-action project . . . the programs of basic health The structure of the TT, embedding one relative clause inside another ("[a] project that will be a formation tool for doctors [. . .] that are enrolled"), is stylistically inadvisable in English. The reappearance of the false friend "investigation", together with a new one ("formation"), also detracts from the **acceptability** of the TT here. Equally, while the main verb "tries" may be an improvement on the more literal "wants to" for *querer*, it still fails to sound natural in this context. An alternative rendering might be: "As well as research, the TRAMIL project is ultimately intended to promote actual development by becoming a practical training tool for doctors, pharmacists and primary healthcare personnel in general" (note also a second alternative rendering of the ST's *de base*).

f. a thickening of experience exchanges A literal, physical meaning is confused with a figurative one here, as *reforzar* is translated as if it applied to a wall or cement mixture. The subtleties governing the use of nouns as adjectives in English also elude the translator here, as "experience exchanges" would not be spontaneously produced by a native speaker. The sentence might be modified to read: "We have therefore considered it vital to promote the exchange of experiences and inter-Caribbean cooperation through our TRAMIL seminars, which have been attended by many participants from throughout the region."

Texto 1

DOMINICA'S FIRST NATIONAL REPORT TO THE CONFERENCE OF PARTIES – CONVENTION ON BIOLOGICAL DIVERSITY

(Prepared Pursuant to the Guidelines for National Reporting on the Implementation of Article 6 Contained in COP Decision II/23)
SECTION 1 – INTRODUCTION
(Excerpt) [6]

In Dominica the conservation and protection of natural ecosystems and species is deeply entrenched in national values. Indeed, the country has accepted the importance of conserving national biodiversity as the basis for sustainable national development. In recognition of the need to conserve and protect these vulnerable resources Dominica established from 1975 a system of national parks and protected areas that presently cover in excess of 20% of land area. Dominica's system of national parks includes two marine protected areas and the Morne Trois Piton National Park, which in 2000 was declared a World Heritage Site by UNESCO.

The *Convention on Biological Diversity*, signed by the Commonwealth of Dominica on the 6th July 1994, represents a shared commitment to the conservation of biological diversity, the sustainable use of biological resources, and the fair and equitable sharing of the benefits arising out of the use of genetic resources. *Dominica's Biodiversity Strategy and Action Plan* is intended to implement the country's obligations under the Convention.

Dominica's Biodiversity Strategy and Action Plan establishes for the first time a strategic framework to guide the continued

Traducción de Jairo Sánchez

PRIMER INFORME DE DOMINICA AL CONGRESO DE LAS PARTES – CONVENIO DE DIVERSIDAD BIOLÓGICA

(ª·**Redactado de conformidad con los lineamientos para Informes Nacionales** *sobre la Implementación del Artículo 6 contenido en la Decisión II/23 del CDP)*
SECCIÓN 1 – INTRODUCCIÓN
(Extracto)

En Dominica, la conservación y protección de los ecosistemas naturales y las especies están muy arraigadas en los valores nacionales. En efecto, ᵇ·**el país ha admitido la importancia de conservar la biodiversidad** como base para el desarrollo sostenible de la nación. En reconocimiento a la necesidad de conservar y proteger estos recursos vulnerables, Dominica estableció en 1975 un sistema de parques nacionales y áreas protegidas que en la actualidad cubren más de un 20% del territorio nacional. El sistema nacional de parques incluye dos áreas marinas protegidas y ᶜ·**el Parque Nacional Morne Trois Piton, que la UNESCO declaró Patrimonio de la Humanidad en el año 2000.**

El *Convenio de Diversidad Biológica*, firmado por ᵈ·**la Mancomunidad de Dominica** el 6 de julio de 1994, representa un compromiso conjunto para la conservación de la biodiversidad, el uso sostenible de los recursos biológicos, y la distribución justa y equitativa de los beneficios percibidos por el uso de recursos genéticos. *El Plan de Acción y Estrategias de Dominica para la Biodiversidad* ha sido diseñado para cumplir las obligaciones del país según el Convenio.

El Plan de Acción y Estrategias de Dominica para la Biodiversidad establece por primera vez un marco estratégico para

conservation and protection of Dominica's vulnerable natural resources. It also outlines strategies and actions to address newly emerging concerns relating to the control of biotechnology, the impacts of climate change on biodiversity, and the protection and enhancement of traditional knowledge, values and culture.

guiar la continua conservación y protección de los recursos naturales vulnerables de Dominica. También esboza las estrategias y acciones a seguir a la hora de enfrentar los nuevos asuntos emergentes relativos al control de la biotecnología, el impacto del cambio climático en la biodiversidad, y la protección y mejoramiento del conocimiento, de los valores y de la cultura tradicionales.

Comentarios

El tono de este **tipo de textos** es marcadamente formal al tratarse de informes sobre tratados internacionales. Es un texto mixto que por un lado presenta expresiones típicas de informes legales y de textos diplomáticos; por otro, aquellas referentes al tema tratado: el medio ambiente.

a. Redactado de conformidad con los lineamientos para Informes Nacionales Este es un ejemplo de la formulación mediante expresiones legales ("de conformidad con", "lineamientos", "informe"). Nótese la escogencia de "redactar" y no de "preparar". Si bien un informe puede ser redactado o preparado, preferimos el primer verbo por ser más conciso y tener mayor **frecuencia de coocurrencia**. Por otro lado, en algunos países se utiliza el sustantivo "reporte" (especialmente en México), pero en la mayoría de los países se prefiere "informe". Estos dos casos nos muestran una de las dificultades más frecuentes con las que se encuentra el traductor: la precisión en la selección léxica. ¿Cómo saber qué palabra escoger entre dos lexemas con aparente **equivalencia** funcional? No hay una respuesta única a este interrogante pero plantearemos aquí algunos de los aspectos a tener en cuenta a la hora de realizar nuestra elección: en primer lugar debemos ser conscientes del **tipo o tipos de texto** que traducimos (ver discusión sobre este aspecto en la introducción del capítulo de La Creación Artistica I: La Literatura). Esto nos ayudará a escoger el grado de formalidad y el grado de especialización que se requiere. En segundo lugar, debemos tener en cuenta el grado de **concisión** de nuestras alternativas, es decir, cuál de las opciones que tenemos refleja más exactamente el significado que se intentó expresar en el TO. En el ejemplo que nos compete, "preparar" posee un significado mucho más amplio que redactar. En el *Oxford Spanish Dictionary* aparece en la segunda acepción que *prepare* significa preparar una comida, o un discurso, y que si se refiere a un informe su equivalente es redactar. El tercer punto a tener en cuenta es la **frecuencia de coocurrencia o colocación**, que se refiere al número de veces en que dos palabras aparecen juntas en un corpus lingüístico. Se diría, basándonos en este aspecto, que "redactar" tiene una mayor **frecuencia de coocurrencia** con "informe" que "preparar". Otro punto se refiere a las asociaciones que tienen las palabras. Por último, debemos tener cautela a la hora de enfrentarnos con los **falsos amigos**, como puede ser el caso de "reporte" por *report*.

b. el país ha admitido la importancia de conservar la biodiversidad Siguiendo con los aspectos a tener en cuenta a la hora de decidirnos por una palabra o la otra, encontramos en esta frase otro ejemplo. La palabra *accept* del TO presenta por lo menos tres posibles traducciones: aceptar, admitir, reconocer. Si bien esta última es la que mejor se adapta a la frase en cuestión, fue necesario escoger "admitir" ya que la oración siguiente comienza con "En reconocimiento . . .". Vemos pues que el contexto lingüístico inmediato también influye en nuestra elección de palabras, en este caso para evitar la redundancia léxica.

c. el Parque Nacional Morne Trois Piton, que la UNESCO declaró Patrimonio de la Humanidad en el año 2000 En el TO esta frase está expresada en su forma pasiva. Ya que el agente de esta acción aparece explícitamente, el español prefiere la forma activa.

d. la Mancomunidad de Dominica Ya que en el TO se decide dar el nombre completo del país se debe buscar su equivalente. *Commonwealth* para algunos países se traduce como "República de", "Mancomunidad", "Confederación", "Estado" o "Estado Asociado". En ocasiones también se hace **préstamo** lingüístico ("la Commonwealth").

Texto 2

LAND-BASED POLLUTION AS A SOURCE OF THREAT[7]

It is generally agreed that within the Wider Caribbean Region, the land-based sources of pollution (point and non-point sources) form the most significant threat to the marine environment. The main sources have generally been identified as the following:

1. Point sources (industrial, sewage and solid waste);
2. Urban non-point runoff (stormwater runoff and combined overflow discharges);
3. Non-urban non-point runoff (cropland, pastureland, and forestland runoff);
4. Upstream sources (pollutants carried into the coastal zone as part of a river's streamflow); and
5. Irrigation return flows (irrigation water return to lake, stream or canal).

Though the pollution inputs from land-based sources have not been fully quantified, the impacts on the nearshore and marine environment are well known;

LA CONTAMINACIÓN DE ORIGEN TERRESTRE COMO FUENTE DE AMENAZAS[8]

Generalmente se reconoce que, en la región del Gran Caribe, las fuentes de contaminación de origen terrestre (las puntuales y no puntuales) constituyen la amenaza más notable para el medio ambiente marino. De forma general, las fuentes principales se han identificado de la siguiente manera:

1. [a.]**Fuentes puntuales (industriales, aguas albañales y desechos sólidos);**
2. Escorrentías no puntuales (escorrentías del agua de tormentas y descargas combinadas de desbordamientos);
3. [b.]**Escorrentías no puntuales no urbanas** (terrenos de cultivos, terrenos de pastos y escorrentías de terrenos boscosos);
4. Fuentes aguas arriba (contaminantes llevados a la zona costera como parte del flujo de la corriente de los ríos); y
5. Flujos de retorno de la irrigación (el agua utilizada para irrigar regresa al lago, corriente o canal).

Aunque no se han cuantificado por completo los aportes de contaminantes de las fuentes de origen terrestre, se conocen bien los impactos producidos en el medio

encompassing degradation and destruction of the nearshore habitats, reducing bathing water quality (sometimes resulting in the temporary or permanent closure of bathing beaches) and generally creating public health hazards (UNEP 1987).

ambiente marino y la costa: la degradación y destrucción de hábitats litorales, [c.]**la reducción de la calidad del agua para bañarse** (que a veces trae como resultado [d.]**el cierre temporal o permanente de las playas**) y la creación en general de peligros para la salud pública [e.](**PNUMA 1987**).

Comentarios

a. Fuentes puntuales (industriales, aguas albañales y desechos sólidos) Esta frase nominal muestra el uso de la terminología específica del área. El traductor debe estar al día en estos términos para poder hacer un trabajo que refleje los avances lingüísticos que se manejan en un área específica. Una manera de hacer esto es tener **fichas terminológicas** bilingües. Para recopilar las palabras relevantes se debe hacer un **vaciado terminológico** del texto o textos con los que trabajemos.

b. Escorrentías no puntuales no urbanas En algunas ocasiones el traductor se encuentra con este tipo de frases que a primera vista resultan poco naturales. Sin embargo, la falta de naturalidad aparente se debe a que éstas son **calcos** de las construcciones inglesas. El inglés muestra mayor flexibilidad a la hora de acuñar nuevos términos y puede formarlos añadiendo varios adjetivos a un solo nombre, creando así conceptos que son precisos y unívocos. Actualmente, mediante el **calco**, el español tiende a sacar provecho de esa característica del inglés, como lo demuestra nuestro ejemplo: se crea una extensa frase nominal en donde se omiten preposiciones y conjunciones y que funciona como un solo término, es decir, equivale a un concepto único y, en este caso, gramaticalmente funciona como un sustantivo.

c. la reducción de la calidad del agua para bañarse Este parece ser un contraejemplo del anterior. No obstante, el carácter de *bathing water quality* no es el de un término, es simplemente una frase nominal. Cuando una palabra o frase se puede usar en multitud de contextos y es fácilmente entendible, parafraseable además de **equívoca,** no es necesario considerarla cómo término.

d. el cierre temporal o permanente de las playas El texto origen presenta el sustantivo con función adjetival *bathing*. El traductor ha decidido omitirlo por no agregar información relevante en español. De haberse incluido se necesitaría la formulación "para bañistas", "para bañarse" u otra expresión similar.

e. PNUMA, 1987 En este **tipo textual** nos encontramos a menudo con siglas. El traductor debe estar bien informado sobre los nombres de los organismos y si ellos tienen su representación tanto en el mundo anglófono como en el hispano. En algunos casos las siglas de los organismos se adecúan a la lengua (UN-ONU); en otros la sigla original se mantiene en la lengua de llegada (UNICEF).

<table>
<tr><td>

Texto 3
NEXT LAUNCH, NEGRIL
(11–11–2003)[9]
The Negril area, one of Jamaica's premier tourism destinations, will have some added activities on November 11 and 12 as the Caribbean Regional Environmental Programme (CREP) launches the Amenity Area Demonstration Project.

CREP is providing 500,000 Euros to be used for further development of some tourism facilities and for conservation in the selected site – the Negril Environmental Protection Area and Negril Marine Protection Area, including the Negril Morass and Royal Palm Reserve.

Among the activities included under the CREP project will be the development of a Benthic habitat map of the protected area, which uses a combination of aerial photography and satellite imagery.
There will also be feasibility studies on effluent disposal including consultations with the public and with the National Water Commission on possible ways to replenish areas of the Morass that are noticeably drier.
The first activity of the launch is a day-long stakeholder workshop on Tuesday November 11, and this will be followed by the public ceremony on Wednesday November 12 at the Negril Community centre from one o'clock in the afternoon.

The CREP Demonstration Project is geared at strengthening collaboration between government and civil society in the management of sensitive natural areas in the region in ways that make them economically viable while ensuring their sustainability.
The National Environmental Planning Agency (NEPA) will represent the Jamaican

</td><td>

Traducción de Jairo Sánchez
PRÓXIMO LANZAMIENTO: NEGRIL
(11–11–2003)
El área de Negril, [a]**una de las zonas turísticas más destacadas** de Jamaica [b]**contará con nuevas actividades** el 11 y 12 de noviembre cuando el Programa Ambiental Regional del Caribe ([c]**CREP, por sus siglas en inglés**) lance el Proyecto de Prueba del Área de Servicios.
CREP proporciona 500.000 euros utilizables para el mejoramiento de [d]**algunas instalaciones destinadas al turismo** y para la conservación del área seleccionada: el Área de Protección Ambiental de Negril y el Área de Protección Marina de Negril que incluye [e]**La Reserva Royal Palm y el Pantano de Negril.**
[f]**Una de las actividades incluidas en el proyecto** será el desarrollo de [g]**un mapa, que combina fotografía aérea e imágenes satelitales**, del hábitat del fondo marino del área protegida.
Habrá igualmente estudios de [h]**viabilidad de aguas residuales** que incluirán consultas con el público y con la Comisión Nacional para el Agua sobre las posibles formas de recuperar áreas del Pantano que están evidentemente más secas.
La primera actividad del lanzamiento es un taller para los interesados que se llevará a cabo el martes 11 de noviembre durante todo el día, al que le seguirá una ceremonia pública [i]**el miércoles 12** en el centro comunitario de Negril a partir de la una de la tarde.
El proyecto de prueba CREP se enfoca al fortalecimiento de la colaboración entre el gobierno y la sociedad civil para el manejo de [j]**áreas naturales delicadas** de la región con métodos económicamente viables y que a la vez aseguren su sostenibilidad.
[k]**La Agencia Nacional de Planeamiento Ambiental (NEPA)** representará al

</td></tr>
</table>

government in the running of the project while the Negril Environmental Protection Trust and the Negril Coral Reef Preservation Society are the two NGOs chosen to act as stewards of the Demonstration Site.

The purpose of CREP is to strengthen regional cooperation in conservation management and sustainable development of the Areas.

The Demonstration Project facilitates collaboration between Government Agencies and NGOs to demonstrate management processes that empower communities to undertake economic activities, which integrate social benefits and environmental conservation as the basis for their value.

CREP is implemented by the CCA through a Programme Management Unit (PMU) established at the Secretariat in Barbados. Current Programme financing comes from the European Commission with a commitment of 9.1 million Euros.

For more information on CREP visit the CCA web site: www.ccanet.net or contact Collin Cunningham at crepinformation@ccanet.net or Cathal Healy-Singh at crepmanager@ccanet.net

---

gobierno de Jamaica en lo concerniente al desarrollo del proyecto y El Fondo para la Protección Ambiental de Negril y la Sociedad de Conservación de los Arrecifes de Coral de Negril [l.]**son las dos ONG escogidas** para actuar como supervisoras del área de prueba.

El propósito de CREP es fortalecer la cooperación regional en el manejo de la conservación y en [m.]**el desarrollo sostenible de las áreas en cuestión.**

El proyecto facilita la colaboración entre Agencias del Gobierno y las ONG para demostrar procesos administrativos que alienten a las comunidades a llevar a cabo actividades económicas cuya base valorativa integre los beneficios sociales y la conservación ambiental.

CREP se implementa mediante la [n.]**Asociación Caribeña para la Conservación (CCA)** a través de una Unidad de Administración de Programas (PMU) establecida en la Secretariat en Barbados. El financiamiento actual para el programa viene de la Comisión Europea con una asignación de 9,1 millones de euros.

Para mayor información acerca de CREP visite la página de CCA: www.ccanet.net o contacte a Collin Cunningham en crepinformation@ccanet.net o Cathal Healy-Singh en crepmanager@ccanet.net.

Comentarios

a. una de las zonas turísticas más destacadas El traductor ha hecho una **modulación** al cambiar "destinos" por "zonas", sin un motivo realmente válido, pues "destino" es una palabra que se conjuga (**colocación**) generalmente con "turístico", lo que haría que el texto ganara en naturalidad.

b. contará con nuevas actividades Nos encontramos con un caso de **omisión** muy común. Aquí se ha omitido *added*, ya que en español "nuevas" incluye "las que se han añadido" en este contexto. Así, cuando los significados de dos o más palabras de la LO se pueden condensar en una sola de la LM, es usual utilizar sólo ésta, a menos que por razones estilísticas se precise explicitar los significados de ambas mediante unidades léxicas en la LM.

c. CREP, por sus siglas en inglés Esta es una estrategia común cuando aparecen siglas de una organización o evento que no tienen su correspondiente en la LM. Se utiliza la primera vez que aparecen las siglas en el texto para dejarle la referencia clara al lector.

d. algunas instalaciones destinadas al turismo Es común este tipo de **ampliación** debido a que el inglés es más conciso en la forma de utilizar los adjetivos. En español se reemplaza en estos casos el adjetivo por una frase adjetiva o una relativa adjetiva precedida por "que".

e. La Reserva Royal Palm y el Pantano de Negril Un caso problemático para los traductores es la forma de verter los nombres de la LO a la LM. Aunque se han dado pautas para la traducción de los nombres propios, éstas no cubren todos los casos. Se ha dicho por ejemplo que los nombres se deben conservar en el idioma origen a menos que haya un equivalente reconocido en la LM. En el caso que nos ocupa la descripción del lugar hace parte del nombre: *Reserve* y *Morass*. Se ha optado por traducir esta parte del nombre y dejar el restante en la LO pues su traducción es esencial para la comprensión por parte del lector del TM.

f. Entre las actividades incluidas en el proyecto Se omite aquí el nombre del proyecto que sí aparece en el TO ya que en el contexto se puede deducir de qué proyecto se habla. Esta es una **omisión** que pide implicitación por parte del lector del TM.

g. un mapa, que combina fotografía aérea e imágenes satelitales Fue necesario aquí cambiar la posición de la relativa adjetiva acercándola más al sustantivo al que modifica. Al ser tan larga se prefiere escribirla entre comas y no dejarla para el final pues puede dar lugar a confusiones en la lectura por venir después de dos sustantivos ("mapa" y "área").

h. viabilidad de aguas residuales Este es un ejemplo de cómo la terminología aparece en muchos tipos y subtipos textuales. Aunque está pensado para la lectura por parte del público general es vital la inclusión de términos relevantes. Es decir que la terminología, contrario a lo que se puede pensar, no es de uso exclusivo en textos densos y especializados sino que es parte activa del lenguaje.

i. el miércoles 12 Se **omite** aquí la repetición de "noviembre" por ser ampliamente deducible en el contexto y por ceñirse a la norma natural de la LM.

j. áreas naturales delicadas El gran número de palabras que se parecen en inglés y en español muchas veces son obstáculos para la traducción, pues causan interferencias, *sensitive* por "sensitivo" aquí. De este modo, en el Spanglish por ejemplo, el rango de significación del elemento léxico de la LM se amplía para asemejarse al que tiene la LO. Es esta, pues, una de las maneras en que las lenguas extranjeras influyen en la propia, dándole vitalidad a través de la invasión. Sin embargo, esta influencia es frecuente cuando entre las lenguas se establece una relación de poder, en la que la lengua dominante modifica la dominada y no al revés. El traductor debe ser cauteloso con estos **falsos amigos**.

k. La Agencia Nacional de Planeamiento Ambiental (NEPA) En este caso el traductor ha optado por no utilizar la fórmula sugerida en el tercer comentario de este texto dejando simplemente las siglas en inglés, dando por hecho que el lector lo deducirá, al haber ejemplos en ocasiones anteriores como CREP. Esto sucede más adelante con PMU.

l. son las dos ONG escogidas ONG es un término relativamente reciente en español y por lo tanto no se ha unificado su forma de uso, especialmente en el plural. En ocasiones nos encontramos con "ONGs". Como se ha dicho en capítulos anteriores, mediante el uso de un buscador en Internet se puede comprobar la frecuencia de uso. Tendemos a utilizar en las traducciones aquellas maneras de formulación que aparecen más veces en textos creados en la lengua a la que traducimos. Se ha reconocido que en ocasiones algunas fórmulas se utilizan más en traducciones a la LM que en textos creados en la LM. Es decir que se encuentran expresiones que son características de las traducciones a una LM pero no muy frecuente en la redacción en esta lengua.

m. el desarrollo sostenible de las áreas en cuestión El traductor se ve forzado a hacer una **explicitación** debido a las normas que rigen la **coherencia** y **cohesión** en español. Al inglés le basta con añadir el artículo definido; el español debe utilizar una fórmula que remita al lector al concepto al cual se refiere el sustantivo. Otro modo de resolver esto sería explicitar añadiendo el nombre completo de las áreas a las que se refiere. Otras fórmulas comunes son "arriba mencionadas" o "anteriormente mencionadas".

n. Asociación Caribeña para la Conservación (CCA) Aquí el traductor decidió ampliar la información proveyendo el nombre completo de la asociación que se omite en el TO. Esto se hace por lo general cuando las siglas son de conocimiento común en la cultura origen pero no en la meta.

III. SPANISH > ENGLISH EXERCISES

Read carefully the following text and answer the questions below:

FIDEICOMISO DE CONSERVACIÓN DE PUERTO RICO[10]

Cuidado con lo nuestro

Programas educativos

Salvar nuestras tierras es tan sólo uno de los muchos objetivos del Fideicomiso. También está comprometido con la educación del pueblo respecto a los asuntos ambientales y con la importancia de preservar nuestros recursos naturales. El Fideicomiso aspira a promover grupos que auspicien y perpetúen la causa conservacionista, marcando así el paso de su desarrollo futuro. Los innovadores programas educativos e interpretativos desarrollados por el Fideicomiso están diseñados para llenar las necesidades particulares de cada una de las propiedades.

Conservación en la Cuenca del Caribe

El Fideicomiso y el *Nature Conservancy* han emprendido una innovadora estrategia para proveer alternativas técnicas y financieras que ayuden a los países del Caribe a desarrollar planes de protección ambiental para hábitats amenazados.

Ambas instituciones auspician una serie de proyectos financiados mediante el canje de "deuda por naturaleza", que consiste en la adquisición de parte de la deuda externa de un país en manos de instituciones financieras foráneas para convertirla a la moneda nacional y utilizar el producto de la transacción en proyectos de conservación. Esta transacción ha ayudado a que "Pro-Natura", organización particular dominicana, financie varios importantes proyectos de conservación.

PUBLICACIONES

Mientras más personas conozcan acerca del patrimonio nacional y cultural de Puerto Rico, más conciencia y entusiasmo tendrán para protegerlo. A estos efectos están dirigidos los programas educativos del Fideicomiso, quien publica y distribuye una variedad de libros y folletos que orientan sobre cómo proteger el ambiente.

1. Translate the text into English.
2. In class, discuss alternative translations of the following elements:
    i.   Cuidado con lo nuestro
    ii. marcando así el paso de su desarrollo futuro
    iii. patrimonio nacional
    iv. libros y folletos que orientan sobre cómo proteger el medio ambiente
3. Compare your translation of the following words with that of other members of the class: auspiciar, desarrollar, emprender, promover, proveer. Compile a phrasal glossary in this semantic area by citing the phrases in the text and your translations, in context, of these words. As a class, note down any other synonyms of these words you can think of in either language, then find an environmental context for them by searching the web and add them to your glossary.
4. Discuss the use of the subjunctive in the following sections of the text and compare your translations of these phrases with those of other members of the class. Decide whether the indicative would have been possible in any of these instances and, if so, how you might illustrate the resulting difference in meaning using translation into English.
    i.   El Fideicomiso aspira a promover grupos que auspicien y perpetúen la causa conservacionista.
    ii. han emprendido una innovadora estrategia para proveer alternativas técnicas y financieras que ayuden a los países del Caribe a desarrollar planes de protección ambiental.
    iii. Mientras más personas conozcan acerca del patrimonio nacional y cultural de Puerto Rico, más conciencia y entusiasmo tendrán para protegerlo.

IV. EJERCICIOS PRÁCTICOS INGLÉS > ESPAÑOL

Lea el siguiente texto y realice las actividades propuestas.

Environmental Management of Small and Medium-sized Cities in Latin America and the Caribbean

By Jaap de Vries, Paul Procee and Harry Mengers (extracto)[11]

With still growing numbers in urban population, the poor quality of the urban environment is a major concern to Latin America and the Caribbean. Problems with air pollution are becoming worse. The region faces degraded water quality, poor facilities for sewage treatment and solid waste disposal. Urban problems are made worse by inadequate housing and inefficient transportation systems.

In Latin America and the Caribbean, it is increasingly recognized that, in accordance with the subsidiarity principle, environmental issues with local externalities (in areas such as spatial planning, natural resource use, air and water pollution, solid waste management, sanitation and sewerage) are more effectively dealt with at the local level than at the national or provincial level. The subsidiarity principle states that the lowest level of government that can fully capture the costs and benefits should also provide the corresponding public goods and services.

While much attention has been devoted to these problems in large cities, much less is known about the large number of small and medium-sized cities. Most of the 13,000 local governments in Latin America and the Caribbean are small and medium-sized cities, although varying widely in size, geographical location and setting. In general, these cities are increasingly experiencing a whole set of environmental problems, be it due to urbanization, industrial development, land use change or other issues.

1. Haga un **vaciado terminológico** de este texto, es decir, identifique los términos referentes al área temática tratada en él: el medio ambiente.
2. Seleccione cinco de los términos del vaciado y llene la ficha terminológica como se muestra en el ejemplo. Estas fichas sirven para mantener un registro de los términos pertenecientes a un área temática determinada y serán de gran ayuda para futuras traducciones relacionadas con el tema. Esta clase de base de datos facilita el trabajo del traductor y le da **coherencia** a sus traducciones.

Entrada	solid waste disposal
Categoría gramatical	Frase nominal
Área temática y subárea.	Medio ambiente. Tratamiento de desechos.
Contexto y fuente	The region faces degraded water quality, poor facilities for sewage treatment and *solid waste disposal*. (Environmental Management of Small and Medium-sized Cities in Latin America and the Caribbean. By Jaap de Vries, Micaela Schuster and Paul Procee, Harry Mengers.)
Sinónimos y variantes	solid waste management (Administración de residuos sólidos)
Definición	Manejo y confinamiento de los diferentes tipos de residuos humanos e industriales.
Traducción	Eliminación de residuos sólidos; confinamiento de residuos sólidos; disposición de residuos sólidos.

3. Discuta cuáles fueron los elementos que tuvo en cuenta para seleccionar los términos.

ENGLISH

Acceptability The degree of usability of a term in a given text, both in the SL and the TL.

Acrolectal Related to the highest prestige form of unaffected speech of a given region, in this case the Caribbean.

Adaptation The modification of a ST so that it suits a different purpose, readership or region when translated into the TT. It is one of the four types of oblique translation established by Vinay and Darbelnet, according to whom it also involves accounting for a cultural reference that does not exist in the target culture. Many book and film titles are archetypal examples of this procedure.

Adequacy In translation this term is used to refer to the relevance of a choice of word, structure, form, meaning or purpose. It is determined by the text type, its communicative goal and its context. For instance, a word like "adequacy" would be translated in different ways into Spanish: in finance "capital adequacy" would correspond to *suficiencia monetaria* whereas "payment adequacy" in a legal text can correspond to *monto de integración adecuado*.

Amplification The addition of elements in the TT that were not present in the ST. The reasons for such an addition may include: the need to adjust to the function of the TT (for example, to add "colour" to a text); the lack of an exact word to translate a culture-bound element (an explanation of *aguadepanela*, for instance) or the urge to clarify ambiguities.

Argot The characteristic use of language (especially regarding vocabulary) of a group. It is sometimes used so that people outside the group cannot understand what is being said. (See Technolect.)

Borrowing One of Vinay and Darbelnet's procedures entailing taking an expression from a SL and reproducing it without modification in the TT.

Calque Reproducing the form of the expression in the ST but replacing the elements with equivalents in the TL (for example, basketball > *baloncesto*).

Communicative A communicative translation prioritizes the effects produced by a TT, which should as far as possible be equivalent to those of the ST. Thus, surface meaning and grammar are relegated to a lower priority. In extreme cases a communicative translation may result from a change of purpose from the ST to the TT (a report > an advertisement). It is sometimes contrasted with "semantic translation." Some of the characteristics of communicative translation are: it is reader-centred, pursues authorial intention, adapts and renders the thought and cultural content of the ST more accessible to the reader. It is also effect-oriented; the translator has to sacrifice the formal features of the ST. This is a very common procedure in the translation of jokes or puns, for instance.

Communicative paraphrase *See* Communicative *and* Paraphrase.

Compensation Accounting for a loss in one place in the ST at another place in the TT. The loss can be semantic or functional, as in the case of a metaphor, pun or sound effect.

Concision The ability to express as much as possible with few words. (see Information density)

Connotation The connotation of a word relates to the meanings it has other than the basic dictionary meaning.

Culture-bound A culture-bound term, word or text is one that carries specific meaning relevant to the source culture with no direct equivalent in the target culture. When a word refers to a process or item that is used exclusively by the source culture, the most common ways to treat it are: (1) to transfer it directly as a loan word (especially in the case of foreignizing or exoticizing translation); (2) to find a functional/communicative equivalent (a type of Adaptation); (3) to amplify (see Amplification) the meaning and connotations of the element, using brackets or a footnote depending of the text type.

Denotation The basic meaning of a word, as appears in a dictionary.

Dialect A regional variety of a language used by a specific group of people.

Domestication (domesticating translation) Adapting a text so that it is relevant and close to the target culture.

Equivalence the use of an expression that has a similar effect in the TT, without necessarily having any word-for-word correspondence

Explicitation Interpretation or clarification in the TT of the implicit (not overtly expressed) meaning of a word or phrase in the ST.

Foreignizing Translation The translation that keeps foreign elements as they appear in the ST so that the reader feels the text is a translation and comes from another culture or linguistic background.

Generalization A procedure used to make a TT element less specific than its ST counterpart, a common procedure for achieving greater economy of information.

Information density The ratio of information given to number of words used. Technical texts tend to have more Information Density than, for example, pedagogical ones.

Intertextuality The interrelationship between a text and other texts.

Literal Translation Translating word for word.

Mesolectal Pertaining to intermediate-prestige speech patterns and norms (as against low-prestige or "Basilectal" and high-prestige or "Acrolectal" forms).

Modulation A change made in the TT that alters the semantics and point of view of the message. It covers a range of procedures such as changing active to passive or vice versa, reversing cause and effect, or turning a negative expression into a positive one.

Omission A part of the ST is not reflected in the TT. This may be for various reasons, among them: including the part would lead to confusion; the meaning of the text being translated is not altered if a part is omitted; the part not rendered in translation is easily deducible or creates repetition and redundancy.

Paraphrase A change in the way an idea is expressed, finding other words and structures to convey the same or similar meanings.

Register The way language is used as determined by factors such as the geographical provenance, social status or age and gender of the speaker, or the degree of formality of the situation.

Skopos In translation theory the skopos of a translation is equivalent to its purpose.

Social register *See* Register *and* Sociolect

Sociolect The way people tend to use language in a different way (choice of vocabulary, grammatical structures, etc.) depending on their social status.

Sociolectal Pertaining or belonging to Sociolect.

Tautology The repetition in a sentence of the same sense using different words.

Technolect The language particular to a field used by a specialized group of people. For instance, doctors talk to each other in the specific technolect of medicine and lawyers in that of the law. (*See* Argot.)

Textual immersion A step taken prior to translation proper in which the translator examines and analyses texts (particularly in the TT) that have the same structure or purpose as the one they are going to translate.

Translation loss This occurs when a term or concept cannot be translated with all its connotations into the TT, thus eliminating some of the meaning or intention of the ST. This happens most commonly with Culture-bound terms and expressions, as well as with puns and jokes.

Transposition A change of grammatical category or word class from the ST to the TT, as in "after lunch" > *después de almorzar*. Such a change may be optional or "fixed" (obligatory).

Adaptación Estrategia que exige adecuar un texto a las condiciones y preferencias locales, a las necesidades del cliente o a las normas lingüísticas de la LM. En la Traducción Domesticada suelen adaptarse los modos de expresión a los de los cánones de la cultura meta; también podemos hablar de adaptación de los elementos culturales inexistentes en dicha cultura. En la teoría Skopos la adaptación se refiere a los cambios necesarios que hay que realizar en el TM para que cumplan la función que se busca.

Ampliación La ampliación es un procedimiento de traducción que consiste en añadir contenido, forma, palabras o frases para garantizar el entendimiento, desambiguar términos o frases, mejorar el estilo, darle naturalidad al texto o explicar un concepto que no queda claro en la traducción. Aunque en algunos ámbitos se critica este mecanismo (la subtitulación, por ejemplo), es esencial en otros.

Calco Es un procedimiento de traducción directa y se puede definir como la transferencia de una palabra o término de una lengua a otra mediante el análisis y la traducción de sus componentes. Por ejemplo: *volleyball* > balonvolea.

Coherencia Para que un texto se entienda es necesario tener en cuenta la consistencia conceptual del mismo, la coherencia garantiza esta consistencia.

Cohesión Los textos se conectan en su interior mediante mecanismos que nos ayudan a identificar qué parte de un texto se refiere a otra del mismo, o cómo está organizado estructuralmente.

Colocación La calidad de dos o más palabras de tener una alta Frecuencia de Coocurrencia, es decir que aparecen frecuentemente juntas en uno o varios contextos, y que pueden ser reconocidas como una combinación común por los hablantes. El caso más claro, y el más problemático para el aprendizaje de una segunda lengua, es tal vez el que se refiere a los complementos que por lo general acompañan a ciertos verbos, así como los adjetivos que pueden modificar a un sustantivo. En algunos casos hablamos de colocaciones fijas, es decir en las que una palabra no puede aparecer sin la otra.

Compensación Esta estrategia de traducción tiene como base la recuperación en una parte del texto, de palabras, significados, connotaciones, estilos, tonos y otros elementos que se habían omitido en otra parte del mismo.

Concisión La capacidad lingüística de expresar el mayor número de significados usando el menor número posible de palabras.

Connotación La connotación se refiere a los significados añadidos que puede tener una palabra o expresión y que no hacen parte de su significado primario. Las connotaciones se pueden presentar por motivos sociales (un cierto grupo de personas usa una palabra y ésta se asocia con dicho grupo, como el caso de los tecnolectos, o las jergas; *ver*: Sociolecto), históricos (palabras en desuso, o que remiten a una época particular), y otros.

Densidad informativa Es un término que en traducción se refiere a la cantidad de información que transmite un texto con respecto a su extensión (*ver*: Concisión). Los textos científicos especializados tienen una mayor densidad informativa que un texto turístico, por ejemplo.

Dialectal Perteneciente o relativo al Dialecto.

Dialecto El dialecto es una forma de habla distintiva de un grupo de personas determinada por la región a la cual pertenecen.

Equivalencia La equivalencia en traducción se puede dar en varios niveles. Se puede presentar equivalencia funcional cuando dos textos, uno en la LO y otro en la LT, cumplen la misma función. Hay también equivalencias formales, culturales, y otras.

Equívoco El significado de las palabras es generalmente equívoco, es decir que pueden tener más de un significado (como opuesto a unívoco), muchas veces dependiendo del contexto en el que se encuentren.

Estratolecto La variedad de habla dentro de una lengua regida por el estrato social al cual pertenecen sus hablantes. Algunas expresiones, palabras o términos son reconocidos como usados por una clase social específica. Lo mismo sucede con algunas construcciones sintácticas.

Explicitación *Ver*: Modulación.

Fidelidad Dependiendo de la aproximación que tengamos a un texto el concepto de fidelidad varía. En general se considera la fidelidad como la necesidad de no cambiar los significados ni las relaciones entre las partes del TO en el TM. Se puede ser fiel a la forma, por ejemplo en el caso de una traducción poética, o se puede ser fiel al contenido cambiando, sin embargo, el tipo de discurso (poesía por prosa).

Falsos amigos Este término se usa para referirse a aquellas palabras que en apariencia son iguales entre la LO y la LM pero que tienen significados diferentes. Algunas veces esto constituye un problema de traducción porque puede producir interferencia o una traducción errada. Los ejemplos más comunes son: *actual* en inglés / "actual" en español; *sympathy* / "simpatía"; *assist* / "asistir"; *apply* / "aplicar" (con el significado de solicitar), entre otros.

Fichas terminológicas Son una herramienta con la que debe contar el traductor que se piensa como una base de datos en la que se incluyen los términos que aparecen en el TO, su significado y ejemplo de uso dentro de una frase, así como sus equivalentes en la LM.

Frecuencia de coocurrencia La cantidad de veces que un grupo de palabras aparecen juntas en un texto, o en la lengua en general. *Ver*: Colocación.

Generolectal El estilo particular del habla de un grupo determinado por el género de sus miembros. Algunos autores no reconocen este término pues opinan que la diferencia entre la forma de expresarse de las mujeres y los hombres no es tan grande como para ser considerada relevante en los estudios de traducción.

Inmersión textual Es uno de los pasos que debería seguir un traductor antes de comenzar a trabajar en la traducción de un texto determinado. Se trata de leer y analizar textos similares (especialmente en la LM) al que se quiere traducir, para familiarizarse con ellos y así impregnarse de las fórmulas utilizadas en los mismos.

Intertextualidad Las conexiones que un texto, o parte de él establece con otros textos previos. La forma más común de intertextualidad son las citas. Sin embargo, hay formas más sutiles como la referencia o el calco de estilo.

Modulación La modulación es un cambio que el traductor considera necesario introducir en el mensaje. Para algunos autores estos cambios tienen lugar a nivel semántico. Se recurre a ella cuando la traducción literal, aunque gramaticalmente correcta, no produce el mismo efecto que el TO. Hay varias clases de modulación, las más comunes son:
- explicitación: algunas veces es necesario exponer en el TM lo que se da implícito en el TO.
- implicitación: es el caso opuesto a la explicitación, si el significado es obvio en el contexto no es necesario introducirlo en el TM.
- cambio de un término abstracto por uno concreto, o viceversa.
- inversión de polaridad de negativo a positivo, de positivo a negativo.
- cambio de singular a plural o viceversa.

Omisión Al contrario que la Ampliación esta estrategia consiste en no incluir en el TM palabras, frases, significados, connotaciones y otros elementos que aparecían en el TO. Se utiliza cuando los elementos se consideran innecesarios, repetitivos, redundantes o cuando el espacio físico para la traducción es limitado, como por ejemplo en la subtitulación.

Préstamo En ocasiones la LM toma elementos directamente de la LO sin modificarlos. Este fenómeno se viene dando cada vez más en el ámbito tecnológico de la página web. Esto puede deberse a varios factores entre los que se cuentan la falta de una palabra equivalente en la LM, la falta de un concepto en la LM que existe en la LO o el estatus de la LO. *Ver también*: Calco.

Registro El registro se refiere a la manera en que las personas varían el uso de la lengua dependiendo de su estatus social, la formalidad de la situación, a quien se dirigen y en qué contexto lo hacen, entre otros factores.

Skopos Algunas veces "escopos", es un término traductológico que se refiere a un acercamiento funcional a la traducción. Bajo esta perspectiva el elemento más importante a tener en cuenta cuando se realiza una traducción es su función tanto dentro de la cultura origen como de la terminal. En algunas ocasiones la función de un texto puede variar entre las culturas; el traductor debe encargarse de que el texto logre la función que se requiere, ampliando el sentido de Fidelidad, siendo libre de cambiar las formas y el contenido del texto. La Adaptación, por tanto, es parte esencial en este modo de concebir la traducción. *Ver*: Communicative, Adaptación.

Sociolecto Definimos sociolecto aquí como las características específicas que identifican a un grupo social en cuanto a su manera de usar el lenguaje. En esta definición se localiza a "sociolecto" como hiperónimo y, por lo tanto, incluye los Dialectos, Estratolectos, Generolectos, Tecnolectos, jergas, y todo elemento lingüístico que permita incluir a un hablante dentro de un grupo humano.

Tecnolecto El habla particular de un grupo humano determinada por su profesión. Esto incluye la terminología pero también la sintaxis y los modos estilísticos.

Tipo de texto (tipo textual) La lingüística ha intentado crear una clasificación en la que se puedan categorizar todos los textos que se pueden producir. Muchos intentos se han hecho para estandarizar dicha clasificación pero aún no se ha logrado consenso entre los teóricos de ésta y otras disciplinas afines. Los tipos textuales más aceptados son aquellos

 A TRANSLATION MANUAL FOR THE CARIBBEAN (ENGLISH–SPANISH)
UN MANUAL DE TRADUCCIÓN PARA EL CARIBE (INGLÉS–ESPAÑOL)

que se clasifican de acuerdo a la función comunicativa que enfatizan. Así, hay textos referenciales, expresivos, apelativos, contactivos, poéticos y metalingüísticos. Los estudios más recientes proponen la desaparición del concepto de tipo textual como mutuamente excluyente, ya que un mismo texto puede tener rasgos de más de un tipo textual.

Traducción diagonal Es la traducción que se realiza de una lengua a otra y de un medio a otro. Por ejemplo cuando un subtitulador debe realizar su traducción escrita a partir del TO hablado.

Traducción domesticada La traducción domesticada acerca el texto al lector: saca el texto de su contexto origen y lo sitúa en el nuevo contexto. En este tipo de traducción el texto se lee como si hubiera sido escrito en la LM. Esta filosofía de traducción lleva al traductor a reemplazar elementos cargados culturalmente de la LO por otros similares de la LM. El caso más citado es el de la traducción de la Biblia para los esquimales en la que supuestamente se reemplazó el "Jesús es el cordero de Dios" por "Jesús es la foca de Dios". Dado que los esquimales no tienen corderos, se intentó buscar un animal que fuera más común en su cultura. Esta traducción, si realmente se hizo, tiene el problema de que las Connotaciones de "cordero" en la cultura católica de occidente no se parecen a las que tienen los esquimales de las focas.

Traducción foránea (extranjerizante) La traducción foránea se opone a la domesticada en el sentido de que el énfasis del traductor está puesto en el autor y en la cultura origen. Este tipo de traducción tiene como objetivo acercar al lector a la cultura origen, muchas veces haciendo uso de Préstamos y Calcos. Este acercamiento hace que sea evidente que el lector se encuentra frente a una traducción.

Traducción horizontal Es la forma más común de traducción, la que se realiza de una lengua a otra en el mismo medio, por ejemplo de un texto escrito a un texto escrito. *Ver*: Traducción vertical.

Traducción interlingüística *Ver*: Traducción horizontal y Traducción vertical.

Traducción literal Es la traducción que se hace palabra por palabra.

Traducción vertical Este es un tipo especial de traducción que se realiza dentro de la misma lengua pero en medios diferentes. Por ejemplo, un texto hablado se puede traducir a un texto escrito, como es el caso de los subtítulos de la misma lengua del audio en una película.

Transferencia Nos referimos a la transferencia como la permanencia de un término, nombre o frase de la LO en el TM.

Transposición La transposición consiste en reemplazar una parte del discurso (por ejemplo, grupo verbal a grupo nominal, verbo impersonal a personal, o adjetivo simple a cláusula relativa) por otra, sin cambiar el significado del mensaje. A diferencia de la Modulación, la transposición surge de la necesidad de corregir una frase que de haberse traducido de forma literal no resultaría apropiada o bien gramaticalmente o bien estilísticamente.

Vaciado terminológico La extracción de los términos específicos de una materia que aparecen en determinado texto. Se utiliza en general para formar bases terminológicas que aseguren la consistencia en la nomenclatura en los textos que pertenecen a una misma disciplina.

Appendix A: Questionnaire "Encarnación Mendoza's Christmas Eve" / *Apéndice A: Cuestionario "La Nochebuena de Encarnación Mendoza"*

Name: _______________________

A: General Questions:
1. How would you characterize the quality of this short story?

2. How would you characterize the style of the story?
   (i.e. Is it realist, folkloric, etc.; what features of style do you notice most?)

3. How would you characterize the quality of the translation?
   (purely on the basis of its readability and internal coherence in English)

B: Readability:
1. Do you find the translator's footnote at the bottom of page 70 . . .? (please circle the letter of all answers with which you agree)
   a) Unavoidable
   b) Pedantic
   c) Interesting
   d) Disruptive/Distracting
   e) Irritating
   f) Useful
   g) Inconsistent
   Add any other comment you wish about the use of the footnote:

2. Are there any words or phrases in the story whose meaning is unclear to you? If so, please underline them in your copy and place a circled question mark next to them. Add any comment you feel is relevant.

3. Other than in the dialogue, are there any sentences or passages you find to be clumsily or jarringly expressed? If so, please circle them and place an asterisk next to them. Add any comment you feel is relevant.

4. A particular day of the year, "St. Johns's Day", is alluded to twice on page 73. What associations does this day have for you?

C: Dialogue:

    1. Overall, how convincing do you find the dialogue in the story? (please circle one)

        a) Very convincing
        b) Quite convincing
        c) Unconvincing
        d) Forced
        e) Too variable to generalize

    2. Do you think the dialogue is appropriate to each of the characters and situations portrayed? If not, indicate where it is incongruous.

    3. Are there any parts of the dialogue you find stilted or unnatural? If so, please indicate these in your copy by circling and placing a # sign next to them. Feel free to suggest alternatives the translator might have used.

    4. Do you find the dialogue to be recognizably Caribbean? Do you feel the translator should have made it more or less location-specific, and why?

Appendix B: Questionnaire "A World of Canes" /
Apéndice B: Cuestionario "Un mundo de cañas"

"A World of Canes" by Robert Antoni

Pre-translation survey

Dr Ian Craig and I are working on a project called *A Translation Manual for the Caribbean*. One of the chapters is about translating literary texts. We would appreciate if you could read the excerpt from Robert Antoni's "A World of Canes" and answer the following questions related to the language used in the story. The information given is intended to help in the translation of the story, so feel free to add any comments you think are relevant.

1. Do you recognize the grammar used in the passage as a specific variant of Caribbean English? Is it a specific dialect? If so, which?

2. Can the vocabulary used in the story be assigned to a specific country?

3. In general, if you had to ascribe the language used to a specific social status, what would it be? What elements from the text did you take into account to make your decision? Please give as many examples as possible.

4. What do the names evoke? Do they say anything about the person's age, character, etc.?
    Doudou
    Mistress Bethel
    Berry

5. How about these names for places? Do they evoke anything?
    Sherman
    Crossroads

6. Please define what these words mean to you in the context of the story:
    Bullying
    Meet up
    Pon
    Gallery
    Porch
    Ogle

7. Any other comments:

INTRODUCTION / INTRODUCCIÓN

1. Richard Allsopp, _Dictionary of Caribbean English Usage_ (1996; reprint, Kingston: University of the West Indies Press, 2003), 500.

2. Norman Girvan, "El Gran Caribe", http://www.kaleidoscope.caribseek.com/ Norman_Girvan/El_Gran_Caribe/

3. Richard S. Hillmann and Thomas J. D'Agostino, eds., _Understanding the Contemporary Caribbean_ (Kingston: Ian Randle, 2003), 10.

4. Thomas D. Boswell, "The Caribbean: A Geographic Preface", in Hillmann and D'Agostino, _Contemporary Caribbean_, 38.

5. http://www.uh.cu/infogral/estudiaruh/csoc/Ingles.pdf

6. The procedures in question were first set out in J.P. Vinay and J. Darbelnet, _Stylistique comparée du français et de l'anglais: Méthode de traduction_ (Paris: Didier, 1958). An extract describing these procedures in English can be found in "A Methodology for Translation", trans. Juan C. Sager and M.J. Hamel, in _The Translation Studies Reader_, ed. Lawrence Venuti, (London and New York: Routledge, 2000), 85–93.

1. TOURISM / EL TURISMO

1. This advertisement is published as a leaflet by Rumbos Cuba. For similar material in Spanish, see their web site: http://www.cubaonline.cu/rumbos/ (16 April 2003).

2. "Dominicana con todo" / "Dominican with everything", _Escape,_ 5, no. 42:6. This bilingual Venezuelan tourist publication has an associated (Spanish only) web site, http://www.escape.com.ve/.

3. _Guatemala: Nature_, leaflet issued by Inguat (Guatemala Tourist Board). See also http://www.nuestraguatemala.com/inguat.htm, the Tourist Board's web site with parallel texts in Spanish and English.

4. _Guatemala: Naturaleza_, separate leaflet issued by Inguat (Guatemala Tourist Board).

5. Este texto se encuentra en http://www.caribbean.co.uk/barbados/index.html .en-GB y su versión en español en http://www.doitcaribbean.com/barbados/ index.html.es. Para estudiar más textos similares ir a http://www.caribbean .co.uk y escoger un país. Encontrará el mismo texto en varios idiomas.

6. http://www.visitjamaica.com/planning_your_trip/features_general .aspx?guid=b8072dc3-4cfa-4ff7-8de2-8ee4e32dbf36

7. http://www.visitjamaica.com/planning_your_trip/features_general .aspx?guid=b8072dc3-4cfa-4ff7-8de2-8ee4e32dbf36

8. Merlene McDonald, *Teaching Tourism in the Caribbean: A Resource Manual for Teachers of Tourism at Secondary Level* (Barbados: Caribbean Tourism Human Resource Council, 2000), 66.

9. Merlene McDonald, *Enseñanza del turismo en el Caribe: Manual de referencia para profesores de turismo a nivel secundario en la región del Caribe*, trans. Martha Fernández (Barbados: Caribbean Tourism Human Resource Council, 2000), 67.

10. Otros ejemplos y una explicación más amplia se puede encontrar en http://culturitalia.uibk.ac.at/hispanoteca/Foro-preguntas/ARCHIVO-Foro/Plural%20sustantivos%20latinos.htm

11. http://www.ecotourismonline.com/circuits_esp.htm (26 May 2003).

12. http://www.bodasencancun.com/servicios.html

13. http://fy002.k12.sd.us/MainPages/feature.htm, Tropic Tours (24 de abril 2003).

2. COMMERCE / EL COMERCIO

1. http://www.acs-aec.org; http://www.iadb.org

2. http://www.sice.oas.org/trade/preftrade/pannics.asp.

3. http://www.sice.oas.org/Trade/preftrade/pannice.asp.

4. http://www.panamapacking.com/Aduanas-2.html. The term *congestionamiento de carga* appears in the last paragraph of the penultimate section headed "Visa provisional". English version at http://www.panamapacking.com/Customs-2.html.

5. http://www.edil.com/empresaasp.asp

6. http://www.edil.com/empresaasp.asp#english

7. http://www.conchaytoro.com/spanish/company/f_investor.html

8. http://www.conchaytoro.com/company/f_devoted.html

9. http://www.accuratecommunications.com/index.html

10. http://www.accuratecommunications.com/contact-us.html

11. http://www.accuratecommunications.com/quienes-somos.html

12. http://www.accuratecommunications.com/contactenos.html

13. http://www.acs-aec.org/trade.htm

14. http://www.acs-aec.org/comercio.htm

15. http://www.ftaa-alca.org/SPCOMM/ecomm5_e.asp

16. http://www.ftaa-alca.org/SPCOMM/ecomm5_s.asp

17. http://www.sice.oas.org/ctyindex/wto/tprs_cr5s.asp

18. http://www.sice.oas.org/ctyindex/wto/tprs_cr5.asp

19. http://www.venamcham.org/economia/unidad_comentario_semanal.htm. The English version is accessible from the same page.

20. http://www.accuratecommunications.com/business-writing.html

21. http://www.caribank.org/ Mission (19 de mayo 2003).

22. http://www.ielr.com/14a.htm (19 de mayo 2003).

3. JOURNALISM / EL PERIODISMO

1. http://tercera.copesa.cl/diario/2002/01/02/02.46.3a.ESP.BREVES.html
2. http://www.epasa.com/cartelera/peliculas/hacerse.html
3. http://www.thepanamanews.com/pn/v_08/issue_23/spanish_opinion_04.html
4. Translation by Dr Victor Simpson, University of the West Indies, Cave Hill.
5. *Jamaica Gleaner*, 5 de septiembre 2003, http://www.jamaica-gleaner.com/gleaner/20030905/business/business5.html
6. *Guyana Chronicle*, 10 de octubre 2003, http://www.guyanachronicle.com/ARCHIVES/archive20%2010-10-03.html
7. *Antigua Sun*, 23 de julio 2004, http://www.antiguasun.com/paper/?as=view&sun=473525106307252004&an=130959108707232004&ac=Regional
8. Traducción de Angélica Sáenz, Sede Bogotá, Universidad Nacional de Colombia.
9. http://www.miami.com/mld/elnuevo/news/editorial/letters/ (go to letters of 6 January 2004)
10. *Jamaica Gleaner*, 5 de septiembre 2003, http://www.jamaica-gleaner.com/gleaner/ 20030905/business/business5.html

4. THE CREATIVE ARTS I: LITERATURE / LA CREACIÓN ARTÍSTICA I: LA LITERATURA

1. Juan Bosch, *Cuentos escritos en el exilio* (Santo Domingo: Alfa y Omega, 1986), 63–76. First publication Santo Domingo: Colección Pensamiento Dominicano, 1962. Full text of "La Nochebuena de Encarnación Mendoza" at http://www.literatura.us/juanbosch/mendoza.html
2. Stewart Brown and John Wickham, eds., *The Oxford Book of Caribbean Short Stories* (Oxford: Oxford University Press, 1999), 70–79.
3. Ibid., 403–15.
4. Ver http://www.robertantoni.com en donde se halla información del autor y algunas de sus obras en versión inglesa y española.

5. THE CREATIVE ARTS II: FILM / LA CREACIÓN ARTÍSTICA II: EL CINE

1. *Guantanamera*, dir. Tomás Gutiérrez Alea, 105 min., New Yorker Films, 1995, DVD, Scene 2, "Take Me to Havana".
2. *La vida es silbar* (*Life Is to Whistle*), dir. Fernando Pérez, 106 min., New Yorker Films, 1999, DVD.
3. *Amores Perros* (*Love's a Bitch*), dir. Alejandro González Iñárritu, 153 min., Studio Home Entertainment, 2000, DVD.
4. Octavio Paz, *The Labyrinth of Solitude*, trans. Lysander Kemp (London: Allen Lane, Penguin Press, 1967), 67–68.
5. *The Perez Family*, dir. Mira Nair, 113 min., Orion Home Video, 1995, VHS.
6. *24* Temporada 1, creado por Joel Surnow y Robert Cochran, varios directores, 45 min. cada episodio, Twentieth Century Fox, 2001, DVD.
7. *Bolívar soy yo. (Bolivar Is Me / I Am Bolivar)*, dir. Jorge Alí Triana, 93 min., Venevisión Internacional, 2002, DVD.

6. LAW / EL DERECHO

1. http://www.oas.org/juridico/spanish/cybIV_CR.doc
2. http://www.oas.org/juridico/english/cybIV_CR.doc
3. http://www.oas.org/juridico/english/ministers_of_justice.htm Follow internal link to "Recommendations" section.
4. http://www.dtop.gov.pr/disco/Formas/Dtop-775.pdf
5. http://www.dtop.gov.pr/disco/Formas/dtop-775a.pdf
6. http://www.gobierno.pr/Familia/Agencias/ASUME
7. Translated by Melza Archibald, Barbados.
8. http://usembassy.state.gov/havana/wwwhact.html
9. http://www.cubaminrex.cu/Enfoques/lac_texto%20integro%20de%20la%20ley.htm
10. http://www.heroantigua.com/ccset_contract.doc
11. http://www.ecsupremecourts.org.lc/Judgments/2004_Judgments/Feb/11.02.04%20-%20The%20Queen%20v%20Eustace%20James.pdf
12. Traducción de Nieves Pueyo, Zaragoza, Spain.
13. Enrique Alcaraz Varó, *El inglés jurídico* (Barcelona: Ariel Derecho, 2002), 3.
14. Ibid., 86–87.
15. Para una lista completa de los gentilicios se puede visitar: http://europa.eu.int/comm/translation/bulletins/puntoycoma/87/pyc872_es.htm (8 February 2005)
16. Enrique Alcaraz Varó, *El español jurídico* (Barcelona, Ariel, 2002), 291.
17. http://www.cidh.org/Basicos/Basicos8.htm
18. http://www.cidh.org/Basicos/basic13.htm
19. Constitución de Barbados: http://www.oas.org/juridico/MLA/en/brb/en_brb-int-text-const.pdf
20. Constitución de las Bahamas: http://www.georgetown.edu/pdba/Constitutions/Bahamas/bah73.html

7. ENVIRONMENT / EL MEDIO AMBIENTE

1. http://www.tierramerica.org/2004/0119/ecobreves.shtml (STs 1 and 2, below).
2. http://tierramerica.net/english/2004/0119/iecobreves.shtml (TTs 1 and 2, below).
3. Jeanette Allsopp, *The Caribbean Multilingual Dictionary of Flora, Fauna and Foods* (Kingston: Arawak, 2003).
4. http://www.funredes.org/endacaribe/TramilInfo.html
5. http://www.funredes.org/endacaribe/traducciones/TramilInfo.html
6. Tomado de Dominica's First National Report to the Conference of Parties – Convention on Biological Diversity http://www.biodiv.org/world/map.asp?lg=0&ctr=dm
7. http://www.cep.unep.org/issues/mpamanual/Module%203.doc
8. http://www.cep.unep.org/issues/mpamanuales/Manual/Modulo%203.doc
9. http://www.ccanet.net/cgi-bin/csNews/csNews.cgi?command=viewnews&database=CREP.db
10. http://ponce.inter.edu/proyecto/fidei/fidei.html
11. http://www.iadb.org/sds/ENV/publication/publication_183_2069_e.htm

Select Bibliography / *Bibliografía Selecta*

Listed below are works on the Caribbean and on translation studies of fundamental use to translators in the region. / *Las siguientes obras sobre el Caribe y sobre los estudios de traducción son fundamentales para los traductores de la región.*

Allsopp, Jeanette. *The Caribbean Multilingual Dictionary of Flora, Fauna and Foods in English French, French Creole and Spanish.* Kingston: Arawak, 2003.

Allsopp, Richard. *Dictionary of Caribbean English Usage.* 1996. Reprint, Kingston: University of the West Indies Press, 2003.

Baker, Mona, ed. *Routledge Encyclopedia of Translation Studies.* 1998. Reprint, London and New York: Routledge, 2004.

Hillmann, Richard S., and Thomas J. D'Agostino, eds. *Understanding the Contemporary Caribbean.* Kingston: Ian Randle, 2003.

Malena, Anne, ed. *Les Antilles en Traduction / The Caribbean in Translation.* Special edition of *Traduction, Terminologie, Rédaction. Études sur les textes et ses transformations* 13, n° 2 (2nd semester, 2000).

Munday, Jeremy. *Introducing Translation Studies. Theories and Applications.* 2001. Reprint, London and New York: Routledge, 2004.

Newmark, Peter. *A Textbook of Translation.* 1988. Reprint, London: Pearson, 2003.

Venuti, Lawrence, ed. *The Translation Studies Reader.* 2000. Reprint, London and New York: Routledge, 2002.